The Transformation of Europe 1558–1648

The Transformation of Europe 1558-1648

CHARLES WILSON

WEIDENFELD AND NICOLSON
LONDON

© Charles Wilson 1976

ISBN 279 77015 2

George Weidenfeld and Nicolson Limited
11 St John's Hill, London SW11

Printed in England by
Cox & Wyman Ltd
London, Fakenham and Reading

CONTENTS

MAPS AND DIAGRAMS

AUTHOR'S PREFACE

A reader in the mid-1970s is in some ways better placed than his predecessors to appreciate the character of the century covered in this book. Like the past four decades it was a time of growing violence so continuous as to become a virtually unremarked fact of everyday life. Fighting war was intermittent but ubiquitous; cold war perpetual. Intolerance grew sharper, the cruelties of persecution more highly organized. Deference to dogma spread as dogmatic differences widened. Individuals everywhere were oppressed by governments and their agencies. Yet no government was itself safe from revolt. Price inflation was a powerful influence making for economic instability. Economic instability in turn made for a competitive society.

None of this will be unfamiliar to a modern reader. He will find it harder to comprehend other features of the age, especially its air of casualness, almost incomprehensible to minds accustomed to assume (despite much experience contradicting this) that men can predict the results that will flow from their conscious decisions and, to some extent, control events. Great military projects – like Spain's 'enterprise of England' of 1588, England's intervention in the Netherlands in 1585, Denmark's invasion of Germany in 1625, even Richelieu's entry into the Thirty Years War in 1635–6 – were launched in elementary ignorance of the risks they faced, or casually placed in the hands of commanders quite unfitted for office. The emergence of economic planning was equally insouciant: for example, James 1 of England's rash endorsement of Alderman Cokayne's project to reform a large proportion of English foreign trade, which ended in total disaster and a depression that lasted a decade. Few decisive results were achieved directly by war on sea or land. It sometimes seems as if natural catastrophes, accidents and deeds done in panic (like the Massacre of St Bartholomew) were more positive in their consequences. Politically, Europe sometimes seems to have been re-shaped as much by the forces of negation and exhaustion as by any deliberate decision. It was the failure of Philip II that enabled the Dutch and English to swing the centre of economic and political gravity from southern Europe to the north. Roland Mousnier has hung the course of French history in the seventeenth and eighteenth centuries on the assassination of Henry IV.

Not only was this an age of uncertainty: it was also an age of imprecision. In the early decades time itself was measured precisely by only a few people. Peasants and craftsmen knew how long they laboured only by general reference to daylight or darkness. If there is a leitmotif to the century it is a very slow but steady growth of concepts of precise measurement and computation. Space and location were equally uncharted. Even on land, few people knew the geographical pattern of the country more than a few miles from where they lived. Maps and navigational charts were an invention of the age itself. Most sailors kept close to land. One of the most important writers of the period on navigation significantly described his subject as the 'art' – not science – of 'haven-finding'. The facts of historical chronology were only vaguely known. In medicine, superstition was only very slowly modified as scientific experiment made men sceptical of ancient myth, the power of witchcraft, spells and potions. Even by the end of the period astrology remained almost as strongly entrenched as ever and the most advanced astronomy was still permeated with occultism.

Above all, men's constant preoccupation with religion presents obstacles to modern understanding: 'in the minds of most men of those times religion was the dominant concern, and we shall never make sense of their thoughts and doings if we try to analyse them only in political and economic terms'.[1] Other historians have argued that we shall not understand their ideas on religion unless we grasp how these were rooted in economic interests and contemporary social organization. Perhaps. But, as yet other historians have demonstrated, wherever its ultimate origins may lie, religious belief in violent, fanatic, destructive forms became an independent force. Religion, not race or class or even language, divided men: it was still a more powerful influence than patriotism.

A basic weakness that afflicted all the so-called 'New Monarchies' was that their ambitions constantly outran not only their financial but their administrative resources. The scope of their planning and scale of operations was modern; but the scientific and intellectual apparatus with which they had to operate was antique. Philip II's ambitions were on a Hitlerian scale; his mind was that of a medieval monk. The age is littered with the wreckage of plans devised by men who were of necessity Janus-faced. The only near-success story of the age was the rise of the Dutch Republic under William of Orange and Maurice of Nassau: because respectively they consciously developed and applied modern concepts of statecraft and technology to solve the problems of their state, economy and society. Around them lay a Europe that was still in varying degrees neo-feudal and predominantly agrarian. When states were at such different stages of social evolution the historian must be careful in his use of such concepts as a 'general crisis'.

Yet these dark monotones of the age were lightened and varied as time passed. By 1648 Europe was more varied in its economy, its political organization and its ideas than it had been a century earlier. A bourgeois republic and true exchange economy had won their place. The exact sciences were recognizable; and if toleration was still alien to most minds, it was at least becoming plain that the new aspects of society had to be lived with. Variety was an accepted fact of life.

Any author trying to cover a century of European history has to make drastic decisions of selection. I have chosen to try and write about the internal development and external relations of the European states. I have treated England as only one and not (in this period) necessarily the most important or interesting state in Europe. I have paid more attention to west than east and said little of the world overseas. I owe obvious debts to many scholars; the most immediate ones are acknowledged in the notes, the less immediate ones in the bibliography. Beyond that are the debts owed to authors read, half-remembered and perhaps forgotten over the years. I can only offer them general but grateful acknowledgment, and apologies for any mischief I may have committed in using their ideas.

I am greatly indebted to Dr N. G. Parker of the University of St Andrews for reading the manuscript, giving me the benefit of his advice and saving me from a number of errors. Also to Martha Bates, Hilary Lloyd Jones and Peter Labanyi for much skilled and patient help with the preparation of both text and illustrations.

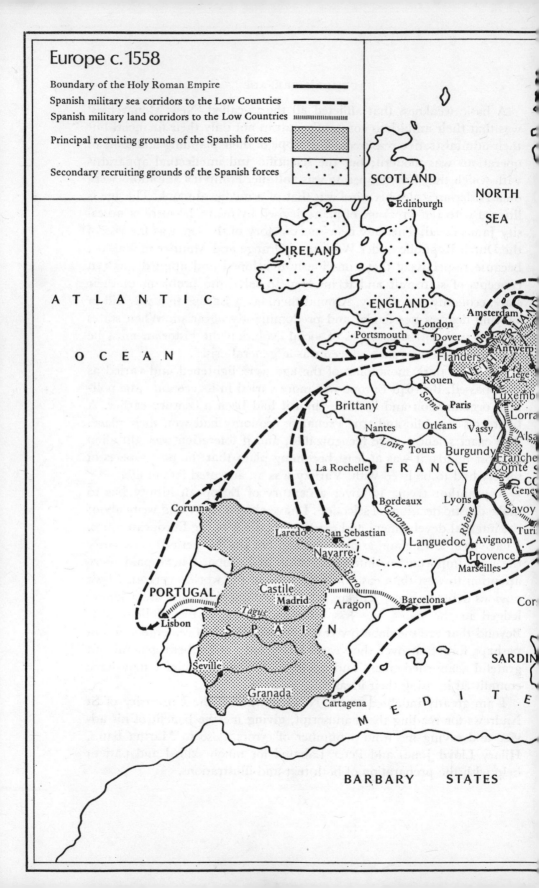

Europe c. 1558

Boundary of the Holy Roman Empire

Spanish military sea corridors to the Low Countries

Spanish military land corridors to the Low Countries

Principal recruiting grounds of the Spanish forces

Secondary recruiting grounds of the Spanish forces

SCOTLAND

Edinburgh

NORTH
SEA

IRELAND

ATLANTIC

OCEAN

ENGLAND

Amsterdam

London

Portsmouth

Dover

Flanders

NETHERLAND

Antwerp

Liège

Luxemb

Rouen

Brittany

Seine

Paris

Lorra

Nantes

Orléans

Vassy

Alsa

Loire

Tours

Burgundy

Franche

La Rochelle

FRANCE

Comté

CO

Gene

Corunna

Bordeaux

Lyons

Garonne

Savoy

Turi

Laredo

San Sebastian

Languedoc

Avignon

Navarre

Provence

Marseilles

Ebro

PORTUGAL

Castile

Madrid

Aragon

Barcelona

Cor

Tagus

S P A I N

Rhône

Lisbon

SARDIN

Seville

Granada

Cartagena

M E D I T E

BARBARY   STATES

SWEDEN

Finland

Stockholm

BALTIC

SEA

hagen

TEUTONIC
ORDER

Danzig

Prussia

andenburg

Berlin

g

Oder

Elbe

Silesia

Dresden
Bohemia

y

Prague

Moravia

E

avaria

ich

Austria   Vienna

Styria

AN

LIC

enice

a

PAL

ATES

e

NAPLES

Naples

SICILY

Malta

N

O

Vistula

Warsaw

P   O   L   A   N   D

H   U   N   G   A   R   Y

Belgrade

Bosnia

Serbia

O

T

T

O

Albania

Rumelia

Estonia

Livonia

LITHUANIA

RUSSIA

Novgorod

Moscow

Volga

Don

Ukraine

Dnieper

Crimea

Jedisan

Transylvania

Moldavia

Wallachia

Bucharest

Danube

Bulgaria

BLACK   SEA

Constantinople

AEGEAN

SEA

Morea

M   A   N

EMPIRE

E

A

N

Crete

SEA

Cyprus

THE PHYSICAL MATRIX

The belief that explanations of human behaviour and social phenomena were to be found in the nature of the physical world itself was
commonplace in the sixteenth and seventeenth centuries among
Renaissance writers and philosophers. A full exposition was provided by
Jean Bodin in his *De la République* in 1576, and was often repeated by
later writers. One of Bodin's themes anticipated Henry Thomas
Buckle's theory of the effect of environment on character.[2] There was a
contrast, he suggested, between the fair, strong but simple men found in
high latitudes and the dark, cunning men of the south. Hard winters
and rough soil bred good men. Rich soils led to sloth and softness (as
Herodotus had observed in the Persians). The best men, Bodin concluded, came from the best terrains and climates of which (naturally)
France was the most eminent. Somewhat similar notions were developed
by the English political arithmeticians of the seventeenth century.
Characteristically, the perception of the controlling force of natural
environment over the day-to-day lives of ordinary people came to be
formulated only when men became conscious of the possibility of controlling, to some extent at least, the forces of nature. In England, Bacon
shared with Bodin an approach to problems of scientific method which
is both pre-scientific and scientific. What later ages regarded as superstitions were constantly mingled with the explorations of the early
scientists. Yet inductive reasoning and the empirical examination of
natural phenomena were enough to develop the consciousness of man's
dependence on nature and stimulate enquiries as to how it might be
reduced. Thus much of the science of the early modern period was

essentially practical. Navigational instruments and the necessary computations to be made with their help, mathematics, agricultural improvements, drainage, microscopy – all had a practical relationship with efforts to limit and control the destructive powers of nature, although they often blended with other less practically directed preoccupations of the human mind and imagination with the nature of knowledge and the universe itself, as evidenced by the advances of the time in astronomy and optics.

Yet, with one notable exception, attempts to control the environment achieved only very limited success before the nineteenth and twentieth centuries. Not before then were the peasantry and peoples even of Western Europe freed from the age-old dread of famine in years of harvest failure and dearth. The proliferation of demographic studies of pre-industrial societies has emphasized how much men were at the mercy of the elements. 'One farmer's meat might be another's poison',[3] as a recent demographic historian has written. In eastern England, on the fairly closely grouped estates of one Cambridge College, it was regularly noted that a dry spring and hot summer would find the tenants of the college farms round Newmarket hard put to it to find their rents. Their lands were light and the heat quickly shrivelled the root of the barley. In the same kind of year, the farmers on the heavy clays of the Huntingdonshire college farms would be prosperous.

Temperature, as well as terrain, was vital. Slight variations of summer temperature might have only minor effects on the date and weight of the harvest in Central France; in Scandinavia similar variations might mean no crops at all, for the grain would never ripen. And crop failure brought heavy mortality to societies which had no obvious means of transport, trade or finance with which to make good their local shortages from overseas. In such areas, natural disasters were always holding back economic and demographic growth and their attendant cultural developments.

Buckle was perfectly correct to draw attention to the exceptional character of the Netherlands in early modern times. They certainly constituted the one incontrovertible example of an economy and society moving forward comparatively rapidly on all fronts – economic, social and demographic, religious, cultural, intellectual. The physical momentum came from the greater success with which the Dutch, in particular, managed to harness the elements to their own use. How exceptional the Netherlands were may be seen by placing them in the wider European setting.

So far as Europe as a whole was concerned, the facts of its physical geography in 1550 remained almost the same as they had been in 1250. Such changes as might have been revealed by an aerial photograph would have been economic and social. A village might grow here, another disappear there. Towns and cities would have been generally larger and more numerous. A new road might show up on occasion, but it would be counterbalanced by the submergence of an older one. Coastal erosion could alter the shape of an island: yet losses such as these were soon to be compensated by gains inland. In Holland the polders were increasing the area of farming land beyond the normal reach of flood-water. Dyking and impoldering had been going on busily since the twelfth century. They were to reach a new peak in the early seventeenth century. Drainage engineers, often from Brabant, were to lend their experience to the English projectors who planned to reclaim parts of South Yorkshire, the East Midland and East Anglian fenland. Other Netherlands experts were at work in Tuscany and farther south towards Ostia, in western France, and eastwards as far as Poland. Forests in Western Europe were generally shrinking. Kings and royal officials facing rising prices, rising costs and falling incomes were sloughing away capital assets in the shape of royal estates (of which the royal forests and hunting chases were a part) to help stave off bankruptcy or to bribe politically important subjects into acquiescence. In short waste lands of all kinds were diminishing as the pressure of bigger populations or smaller crown purses everywhere speeded their demise.

Other than that, the physical geography of Europe changed but little. Europe remained, as H. C. Darby has said, 'a peninsula of peninsulas'.[4] To the north of this 'great peninsula' lay the Baltic Sea, in reality a vast and relatively shallow lake. The Baltic received a vast input of river water and, being generally cold, lost little by evaporation. It was not therefore a very salty sea, its tidal movement was small, and its islands surfaced at frequent intervals. Ports were few and small, the northern ones being closed by ice from November to April. Copenhagen, with unusually good sea approaches accessible to large ships, had therefore emerged as an important centre of seaborne trade.

Athwart the entrance to the Baltic, through the narrow Sound, lay Denmark; beyond, to east and north, Sweden and Finland. In

Denmark and south Sweden were found the best soils, good pastures, dairy farms, cows and horses. Northwards these gave way to forests of conifers, punctuated by occasional mining villages, and farther north still to lakes and forests. Here, as among the mountains and fjords of Norway, the population was small and there was little economic development to encourage its growth except coastal fishing and the trade in timber where the forest met the sea.

South from the Gulf of Finland stretched a land of fishermen and trappers and the ancient prosperous city of Novgorod, partly subjected to Muscovy by Ivan III. In the mid-sixteenth century it was only a remnant of its former self. Plague and war had decimated this once-populous region. Since the end of the fifteenth century it was wide open to Muscovite aggression. So were the steppes to the south since the end of the Golden Horde of Tartars in 1395. Here, south of Moscow, were the most densely peopled (black earth) regions of Russia. Between Oka and Volga in riparian areas and forest clearings the Muscovites grew their rye, oats and barley. This was the base of their expansion north and west from the time of Ivan the Terrible onwards.

Along the north shelf of the great peninsula, from the plains of south and west Russia, through the immense Pripet marshes, across Poland, Germany and the Low Countries to the fertile lands of north and west France, ran the great plain of Europe. Britain formed a geological whole with this great region, bounded by the Atlantic, North Sea and Baltic to west and north, and by the Carpathians, Alps, Harz and Pyrénées to the south. Towards its eastern end, only a proportion of the great plain was cultivable. In Germany there were vast stretches of forest, heath and marsh which like the Pripet marshes defied the attempts of man to turn them into habitable lands.

In all these areas agriculture demanded reclamation; this could go forward only by the massive application of labour. Not steadily but at intervals from the first century AD until the time of Frederick the Great, armies of workers laboured to clear the forests and drain the swamps. By the sixteenth century the Elbe had come to form a rough line of division between the lands of manorial *Grundherrschaft* (to the west) and those of *Gutsherrschaft* (to the east). It was especially the lands of *Gutsherrschaft* which demonstrated the process of *Bauernlegen* by which the mainly Teuton lords (Junkers) subjugated and enslaved their peasantry. It was to be a common experience that wherever the land was poor, where it needed heavy doses of capital or labour before it could be made fertile, the peasantry almost inevitably lost ground to those with the enterprise and capital to undertake great schemes of development.

Farther west lay more tractable soils that were turned relatively easily to arable, pasture or viticulture, contrasting with the hard-won land of dykes and polders even farther to the west as much as with the sandy soils and marshes to their east. By 1550 France had largely recovered from the effects of warfare and plague which had laid the country to waste in the later Middle Ages. Terrain and climate had helped her recovery. Western France, like Britain, enjoyed the benefit of the stream of warm air brought from the Caribbean by the great oceanic, clockwise, circulatory system (loosely called the Gulf Stream). Eastwards, land mass and, southwards, higher altitudes brought greater contrasts of heat and cold. Not many vines were grown north of a line drawn from Nantes to Frankfurt.

The great northern plain was the granary of Europe. Much of its produce was consumed locally, either as part of the great peasant agrarian system of France, Germany and Britain, working still on a partially or wholly subsistence basis, or through sale in local markets. Other areas like the eastern parts of Germany and Poland sent their grain harvest down-river to Danzig or other south Baltic ports for shipment to Western Europe – even, in the late sixteenth century, as far as the eastern Mediterranean, where grain was short.

Within the cereal-growing area important variations of climate and soil influenced the farmers in choosing between cropping rye, oats, barley, wheat or buckwheat, and in balancing their precious investment of time and resources between stock-raising and arable farming. Rye, the hardiest of cereals, was grown more in the exacting climates of Eastern and Central Europe. Buckwheat, originally of Asian provenance, had become popular because it was suited to poor, badly tilled soils; it therefore grew in vast areas of Russia but as an easy crop it was also popular in areas of the west. Oats were needed when stock-raising was involved as well, but peasants in Scotland and other northern areas also lived on oat-cakes or forms of porridge made from oats. Barley was grown wherever domestic or commercial brewing created a demand, but sometimes also as animal feed. The finer varieties supplied the great breweries which were already a unique feature of London and a few Dutch and German cities. For beer was the drink of the north as wine was of the south. In England in the seventeenth century a plausible calculation suggested that no less than one-seventh of the national income was spent on beer. The consumption in Germany, the Netherlands, Denmark and Scandinavia was hardly likely to be lower.

The other comfort of the northerners was hard spirits, distilled from grain (potato distilling came later). The Dutch, Germans and Londoners drank gin – the name varied from country to country (gin, *genever*, *genièvre*), but all reflect the juniper flavour mixed in varying ways with the distilled spirits. It became popular round about 1600. Whisky (*usquebaugh*) had been distilled in one form or another in Ireland and Scotland for centuries. Farther north, in Scandinavia, Russia and Poland, akvavit or vodka were the traditional local spirits.

Stock-raising needed pasture lands, a moderate climate and suitable fodder – horses demanded hay and oats; sheep needed grass, rich or poor, according to their purpose. The basic requirements for animal farming were all supplied in England, France, Denmark and Germany. A traveller crossing England from (King's) Lynn to Bristol passed from areas which had for many centuries placed the emphasis on corn-growing and sheep-rearing to others which mixed a good deal more stock-raising into their economy. This was in large measure a consequence of geology and climate. The chalk and sand of the east gave way to Midland clay or limestone and then again to the rocky terrain of Wales and Cornwall as the traveller went west. There were perceptible differences of climate. Summer temperatures were significantly higher in the sheltered Thames Valley than elsewhere. Rainfall was heavy in Wales and western Scotland, and the west of England generally was moister than the rest. The east experienced more dry springs and summers. The results in farming terms – barley and sheep in the east; wheat and sheep in the Midlands; cattle in the north and west. For wheat the northern summer was too late for good crops; oats did better.

Such variations were found in Northern Europe also. Nowhere (except in parts of the Netherlands) had specialized farming emerged in its pure, clarified forms. They emerged largely as the result of sixteenth- and seventeenth-century experience. Differences in an age when much peasant subsistence-farming survived were largely a matter of emphasis, as peasants adapted themselves to their basic needs of food and necessities of life while bowing to the inescapable facts of terrain and climate. A pig could root anywhere, living on scraps or acorns. Other forms of stock called for greater care. Sheep did best on dryish ground. If they were to be bred for fine wool, they did best on less rich pasture. The finest wool in the world came from the merino sheep of Spain, itself a migrant from North Africa and a close relative to the goat. Its mutton was markedly inferior but its soft fine wool produced the finest of cloth. While the quality of merino wool emphasized the paradoxical merits of Spain's hot, sparse pastureland, the partial enclosure of Midland England for pasture in the sixteenth century seemed to prove that lusher grass meant better meat but coarser wool. The coming of new, cheaper cloths – the *Nieuwe Draperÿen* in the Netherlands, 'new draperies', worsteds, 'stuffs' in eastern England – was connected with the convenience and economy of using less fine wool from pastures that bred sheep to supply a growing population with food as well as textiles. In England, where sheep were bred almost everywhere, peasants and craftsmen wore woollen cloth. But this was exceptional: the peasantry of Continental Europe wore coarse linens made from flax, almost universally and easily grown by peasant farmers. Flax did not demand particularly good soil but it did call for much patient labour to weed and clean.

France, a great congeries of rural economies of widely different kinds according (once again) to conditions of climate and soil, linked the great northern flank of Europe to the Mediterranean flank. In north France the emphasis was on arable. But from the Massif Central with its variety of woods, forests and small mixed farms, the country descended gently down through the Rhine valley and one ecology gave way to another: of vineyards, olive groves, oranges, lemons and mulberries. 'A Valence le Midi commence', the French saying goes.

To the south of the 'great peninsula' lay the Mediterranean Sea, contrasting in every respect – climate, products, history, civilization. The Mediterranean was deep (2,538 fathoms at its maximum) where the Baltic was shallow, its coast, on the north side at least, irregular and deeply indented, rocky and mountainous where the Baltic was low and sandy. Its mild winters meant that most of its coasts were free of frost; deep roots enabled the olives, lemons, oranges and vines to withstand hot dry summers. Unlike the Baltic the Mediterranean was very salty, reasonably well supplied with a great variety of fish, while the general weakness of tides and currents made navigation – off the coasts at least – relatively easy and tempting. The mercantile republics of Italy expanded the trade routes of the Romans, linking up with the outside world via the Straits of Gibraltar to England and the north, eastwards via the Levant and overland to Persia and India, and northwards over the Alpine passes to Germany, Austria and Central Europe.

Around the Mediterranean lived a high proportion of the population of sixteenth-century Europe. Throughout the fifteenth and sixteenth centuries demographic expansion had been steady so that a figure of sixty to seventy million people by the second half of the sixteenth century (perhaps half or more of the total for Europe as a whole) is not an unreasonable estimate. The area was served by some 300,000 tons of shipping – again, probably about half the total of the merchant fleet serving Northern Europe and the Atlantic. Yet geography, geology and climate combined to belie the illusion of sunlit well-being that sometimes deceived travellers from the north. The Mediterranean was not all it seemed (and still may seem to the student until he examines carefully his map of contours and soil utilization).

In many places, the proportion of cultivated land was small; at best, it was very modest, ranging from 15 per cent for Greece to 40 per cent for Italy. Evergreen scrub covered vast areas and was cleared only at intervals, accidentally or deliberately, by the great fires which swept the countryside in the heat of summer. Large areas of upper hill and mountain were bare rock. The pastures were generally more suitable to goats and those hardy varieties of sheep which could survive on relatively poor grassland. Great migratory flocks walked from the summer pastures of north Spain to their homes in the south (for instance Andalusia) and back again. They provided the wool which was the staple of the great Spanish fairs like Medina del Campo. They gave rise to the rich and powerful association of sheep-rearers called the Mesta which played a vital role in the Spanish economy of the sixteenth century. Transhumant flocks were also a feature of Italy and southern France, though less dominant than in Spain.

The basic fact of Mediterranean life was simple: a sea ringed by mountains. From this all else flowed. The cultivable areas were those, mainly on the coast plains, where cities had grown – where the Po, Rhône or Ebro flowed down to the sea. Here the soil was cultivated intensely, planted with citrus fruits and the olive, which provided for Mediterranean peoples the edible oils or fats which dairy farmers provided for northern peoples. Yet cultivability was precariously suspended between mountain and sea. Separating the Mediterranean from the great northern plain were long ranges of mountains rising to 13,000 feet and stretching through southern France, northern Italy and the Tyrol. Transhumant flocks and dairy farms were characteristic of the agriculture of the mountain valleys. The Swiss Cantons (which by the early sixteenth century had achieved the form they were to retain until the French Revolution) early developed an export trade in cattle, cheese and butter to neighbouring areas of Europe. But the Alpine region stood at risk of paralyzing glacial movement, avalanches and spring floods. At the other end of the river system lay vast areas of marsh and bog – the Roman Campagna, the Pontine Marshes, the Tuscan *Maremma*. As the rain waters gushed down from the mountains, they slowed down on the plains to stand eventually in great stagnant pools filled with reeds and marshes. These not only made any form of agriculture impossible: they provided a breeding-ground for the mosquito, which injected the parasite into the blood of its victims which caused *malaria* (the word is itself Italian). Malaria was as deadly a disease as the bubonic plague and more continuous and permanent in its effects. *Acqua, ora vita, ora morte* said the proverb. And true, the cure was drainage, followed by irrigation works to bring fresh water. The history of these swampy areas since Roman times was one of cyclical progress and regression. The Arabs had brought sugar, rice, the mulberry and the cotton plant to Italy. The Moors had similarly diversified the agriculture of Spain, adding also works of drainage and irrigation along the Ebro and throughout Valencia. The cities and nobilities in both countries had provided the capital investment necessary to create large areas of green country around the cities. The sixteenth century was to see another cycle of activity, this time using the experience of Dutch engineers, especially in Tuscany. Yet here, as (in a different mode) in eastern England, the Netherlands and Eastern Europe, the developing entrepreneur with capital was indispensable to the costly works of drainage, reclamation, irrigation. The ultimate gain to total agricultural production was undoubted but long-term; inevitably, the dwellers of fen and marsh or semi-desert were the immediate losers. In the plain, it was said, the distance grows rapidly between rich and poor. 'The plains belonged to the rich,' for only they could afford to invest the resources needed to make them habitable, fertile and healthy.

North-east, across the Alps, lay the second and more northerly range of mountains – Carpathians, Tatra and the Harz – which enclosed the fertile lands of Bohemia and Hungary. Since the Magyar defeat at Mohács in 1526 all Hungary except a strip in the west was occupied by the Turks. Bohemia too had experienced invasion – but a peaceful one, by armies of German miners. Germany itself was a scene of mining, among the mountains and plateaux from the Rhineland and Westphalia to Silesia and Saxony. The Germans continued their exploratory push into the rich mineral areas of Bohemia, Slovakia, Carinthia and Tyrol.

These mineral deposits – especially of silver, gold, tin, copper – were of incalculable importance politically as well as economically. They not only provided the final opportunity for the great south German banker–entrepreneurs of Nuremberg and other cities – Fuggers, Welsers, Hochstetters – to set the seal on the success of their private businesses. They also provided kings and princes – the Austrian Habsburgs especially – with capital assets of enormous value. With the help of the Fuggers and their like, they could use these as collateral for loans to bridge the widening gap between imperial incomes and imperial expenditure.

Linking Europe internally, and with Asia, Africa and India, was a system of oceanic and river transport. Mediterranean galleys had come to Southampton and Antwerp in the Middle Ages. By the 1590s, Dutch and English shipping was to link Baltic grain producers with their Levantine markets and see a continuous flow of Baltic grain, timber and metals going south to be exchanged for Biscay salt. Less bulky cargoes – textiles especially, mail, travellers and their baggage – could go by road. But roads were generally bad, and in any case the transport of bulk goods (grain, coal, salt, wine, timber, naval stores) was prohibitively expensive. Ocean, river and, later, canal transport, was therefore the dynamic that made possible urban growth and economic development through the division of labour. The great centres of sixteenth- and seventeenth-century trade, government and civilization stood on or near sea or river. London, Marseilles, Paris, Copenhagen, Danzig, Prague, Venice, Florence, Genoa, Antwerp, Ghent and Amsterdam – all grew thanks to water transport. The amazing expansion of London from 1550–1650 would have been impossible had its people not been able to obtain food by the Thames, coal for domestic and industrial fuel, drinking water via Myddleton's 'New River' of 1609.

Nowhere was the dynamic character of water transport to be more vividly illustrated than in the Netherlands. Here (and in north Italy, the other most advanced economy of the fifteenth and sixteenth centuries) engineers had made fullest use of favourable geographical conditions to explore the problems and potentialities of canal construction. The Dutch, above all, were the outstanding example of a people who outwitted nature by re-creating their environment to an astonishing extent.

> How did they rivet, with gigantick piles,
> Thorough the center their new-catchèd miles.
> And to the stake a struggling country bound
> Where barking waves still bait the forcèd ground . . .[5]

Thus an envious seventeenth-century poet celebrated their achievement in satire. Holland was the creation of man, a land rescued from the sea, though occasionally the Dutch were reminded by disastrous inundations that their triumph over Nature was not complete:

> Yet still his claim the injur'd ocean laid,
> And oft at leap-frog ore their steeples plaid . . .
> The fish oft times the burger dispossest
> And sat, not as a meat, but as a guest.[6]

The engineers who created the polders, dykes, locks, windmills and watermills refused to accept as divinely ordained the static monotony and chronic scarcity of the regime to which the landsmen of Europe were subjected. Wind and water were to drive and carry, not merely to destroy or drown. Having created their land out of sand, they set to work to create an infrastructure of transport out of rivers and canals. Along them sailed barges loaded not only with peat, cheese and beer but with passengers travelling from town to town. By 1600 several hundred thousand people were using these weekly, daily or, in some cases, hourly services each year. Knowledge steadily replaced superstition, the innovational the habitual, in such things as medicine, navigation, astronomy, microscopy and cartography. But it was water transport which turned their country into an economy of water-linked towns. Of course their economy remained vulnerable to weather and water, drought and flood; it was also to be highly vulnerable to war. But so far as human intelligence, energy and will could influence the forces of Nature, the Dutch were to challenge, and with success, the destiny which too often submerged other areas of Europe. Here geography was servant as often as master.

Naturally the facts of geography had their most immediate impact on man in material regard. The harvest, good, bad or indifferent, was the dominant influence of the year, for the economy still lay very close to the soil. Not only man's food and drink depended on it but, directly or indirectly, almost everything he needed for his everyday life. The rigorous enquiries into the history of weather and climate in recent years have sprung from the renewed realization of their crucial importance.

Was there a 'Little Ice Age' between 1540 and 1600? It cannot be proved. But shorter and sharper disasters may well have had important consequences. The impact of the terrible harvests which afflicted France in 1630, 1635, 1637 and 1647–50 cannot easily be gauged. We only know that the economic distress was grievous. The resulting unrest certainly contributed to the internal strife which culminated in the Fronde.

Another major fact of life was the impact of the seasons. They necessitated the great migrations of transhumant flocks. They blocked the Baltic, Russian and Norwegian ports with ice in winter. Storms interrupted, and sometimes brought to a total halt, navigation in the North Sea between November and March. Even in the Mediterranean, merchant ships were laid off. The large galleys, especially vulnerable to wind and storm, did not venture out. On land or on sea, wars were abandoned or suspended. In the north especially, winter brought hardship, illnesses that sprang from malnutrition, privation, fuel shortages, unbearable cold. For luckier ones, winter was a time of peace, rest, comfortable domestic companionship and entertainment.

> Now winter nights enlarge
> The number of their hours;
> And clouds their storms discharge
> Upon the airy towers.
> Let now the chimneys blaze
> And cups o'erflow with wine,
> Let well-tuned words amaze
> With harmony divine.
> Now yellow waxen lights
> Shall wait on honey love;
> While youthful revels, masques and courtly sights
> Sleep's leaden spells remove.[7]

The poet who sang thus eloquently of the delights of winter was a Londoner whose talents won him entry to noble and court circles. For the mass of the rural European peoples 'sleep's leaden spell' lay over them through the winter. Only with the return of spring and summer could life be lived again to the full.

In other ways, too, geography and topography had a crucial influence on the political evolution of Europe. In earlier ages, the decentralized character of feudalism (and in places of manorialism too) had reflected the impact of distance upon the practical powers of government and the forces of law and order. Government and the dispensing of justice had been handed over to local magnates in return for grants of land and oaths of fealty. All this was a realistic recognition of the facts of geography: power was delegated. This, and the historic accumulation of accidents of heredity, conquest and defeat, had bequeathed a strange muddle of boundaries to the early modern age. When the aspiring rulers of the new, would-be centralized states set about the task of fixing the defensible limits of their dominions, they frequently found their heritage flying in the face of geography and (what seemed to them) reason. Invariably, in the disputes, wars and treaties which followed, geographical facts asserted their superiority over either historical or dynastic accident or language. After a long tussle Calais went back to France by the Treaty of Le Cateau-Cambrésis in 1559, and no amount of nostalgia on Elizabeth's part in the last decade of the century succeeded in getting it back – fortunately. The Danes fought a losing battle to retain their hold on the rich Scanian provinces of southern Sweden across the Sound. In the end they had to bow to the inevitable: Scania was reunited with the rest of the Swedish mainland in 1658. The object of French kings and statesmen in the seventeenth century, until Louis XIV at any rate, was to combine war and diplomacy with the facts of geography – in particular to use the Rhine in Alsace, the vital fortress of Breisach, long-disputed and long still to be disputed, which commanded a river crossing of crucial importance, together with the cities of Metz, Toul and Verdun, to strengthen French defences against the Austrian Habsburgs from the east. The facts of geography intruded into political and military history at every point, just as much as into economic history. At every point men's lives were under the influence of geography and climate. Yet beyond their apparent domination lay a world of choice and variety. The volume that follows is the story of the different ways in which different societies responded to the challenge of their environment.

ℬ 2 ℬ
ECONOMIES AND SOCIETIES: THE
FORCES OF MOMENTUM AND INERTIA

Of the relevance of economic to other kinds of historical evidence, a
great exponent has written:

> Of all varieties of history the economic is the most fundamental. Not the
> most important: foundations exist to carry better things. . . . Economic ad-
> vance is not the same thing as human progress. . . . But . . . its judicious
> structure and use have, in the course of ages, provided first for a privileged
> few and then for more, chances to practise high arts, organise great states,
> design splendid temples or think at leisure about the meaning of the world. . . .[8]

High arts, great states, temples and thinkers the near-century we are
studying could claim in unique abundance. Their occurrence at this
point in time is related, directly and indirectly, sometimes quite
obviously and sometimes obscurely, to the existence and exploitation
of material resources.

In recent years historians have tried to measure the impact of what
are supposed to have been the great international, even universal,
forces – demographic growth, price inflation, religious and ideological
systems – on the different nation states, their economies and societies.
Some have claimed to find identical or similar effects and responses.
This seems presumptuous and improbable. That such forces were
widely felt is certain. But different economies and societies responded
in different, even contrasting ways. The price inflation helped to ruin
Spain because her political and social system combined with the accident of monarchical inheritances to turn a declining producer into the
biggest spender and consumer of the age. Precisely the same forces

turned the unendowed, hard-pressed, politically fragmented northern Netherlands into the most vigorous productive economy of the world by 1600.

Each state, each culture had its own story because each had its own economic and social structure, reacting differently to the same problems. The historians who have drawn attention to what looked like a 'general crisis' of the seventeenth century have provided a valuable signpost for those trying to see European history as a whole. What became plain in the course of the discussion was that the intensity of the 'crisis' varied from very low (in the Nehterlands) to very high (in England and France); that in some places it was perpetual (Spain) and that yet other places (Poland, Russia, Sweden) were at too low a level of development to be able to experience any comparable 'crisis'. Economies tended to move from maximum development in the west and south (where water transport linked with urban growth to produce a variety of occupations and division of economic functions) to minimum development in north and east where land-mass, vast distances and climate combined to preserve a world of barter and barbarism. The reality of history is in the end a variety of response and experience, not a monotonous unanimity. To overlook the awkward mass of evidence – that the Protestant ethic was not always capitalist, that not all oligarchy was corrupt, not all autocracy stupid, not all peasantry oppressed – is to sacrifice variety to uniform abstractions sought often merely as a doctrinal exercise. Before examining this diversity however, let us first look at the general forces which in some measure affected every area, state, society and individual.

The World of Peasants and Craftsmen

Throughout Europe the great majority of the people depended directly on the land for their living. In the least 'industrialized' or urbanized societies (of France, Central and Eastern Europe, Scandinavia) the percentage might rise into the nineties. Where there were tradesmen, shopkeepers or weavers – say in parts of western England or the Netherlands – the proportion of the population that could be described as 'agrarian producers' might fall below 50 per cent. But this was exceptional: the norm was probably nearer 75–80 per cent. Moreover, those who were not land-owners, tenants or semi-independent peasant owners were still closely dependent upon the fortunes of agriculture. They affected the clothier and his growing dependent array of spinners, weavers, fullers, and dyers, who looked to the farm for their wool supply and who (being consumers not producers of food) were sharply affected by any shortage of food that sent up prices. A rise in the price of grain reduced the amount in everybody's pocket that was available for buying commodities *other* than basic foods. It therefore tended to affect adversely all other consumer manufacture. Not only the clothier but the brewer, the distiller, the shoemaker, the butcher, baker and candlestick-maker, would all feel the pinch. Unemployment would rise, the ever-present army of the 'poor' would increase.

Two circumstances of pre-industrial society may be noted. First, since 'industry' – even the word is a later usage replacing the older word 'manufactures' – normally employed little fixed capital in the form of plant or machinery, the merchant capitalist-organizer tended to move swiftly and easily in or out of business. When the market prospect was good, he would invest heavily in wool, flax or silk, recruiting his necessary labour *ad hoc*. Conversely, when the outlook was poor he would retreat, withdrawing his capital and his orders. Investment and employment tended therefore to expand and contract sharply and capriciously. Against these distressing fluctuations the labour force had one consolation lacking to their successors in early industrialized society: the man with no patch of land whatever was comparatively rare. Few men were irrevocably imprisoned in cities, without access to the countryside. Many a weaver or miner would make his way annually towards the harvest fields or offer himself for casual farm work. These meagre comforts did something to cushion him against the uncertainties of his lot, though the compensation was a small one.

But often, the countryside itself could not help him. The typical economy of the period was, as we have emphasized, anchored deeply in land and sea. This did not mean that it was thereby made stable. On the contrary, the vagaries of climate and the visitations of natural catastrophes left the pre-industrial economy under permanent threat of scarcity and famine. Ever since serious investigations of economic history began in the nineteenth century, evidence has accumulated of the central importance of the annual harvest. The harvest was the most vital single guide to the economic fortunes of any country from year to year, and no one was immune from its all-pervasive influence.

Above all it affected the small peasant producer. The general belief throughout Europe was that a bountiful harvest was an unquestionable blessing. Yet the blessing was shared unequally between producers. The lower prices that might (but were not bound to) follow a heavy crop did not necessarily harm the large producer, who sold on the market and had his costs well covered anyway. To the small producer, who usually lived on the brink of subsistence, it did not bring enough increase in yield to do more than relieve him of immediate anxiety about an adequacy of food for himself and his family, his stock and seed for the next harvest. Again, the big producer had resources to withstand a poor harvest. It might mean starvation for the small man.

The fate of producers of all kinds is important in this period, so crucial to recovery after the disasters of the fifteenth century, which had everywhere reduced the population well below the levels of the thirteenth century. A rough guide to the remarkable recovery of Europe between 1500 and 1650 has been provided by B. H. Slicher van Bath's study of crop yields. By comparing the quantity of seed sown and the quantity harvested we can obtain some idea of the condition of food production and the prosperity of agriculture. The increase in this yield ratio seems unquestionable during this century and a half. Thereafter there are falls of yield ranging from 8 per cent to 55 per cent in the first half of the eighteenth century. Plainly the period 1530–1650 was one of unusually high productivity per acre and per unit of seed.

Yield ratios also underline the different standards of technological expertise achieved in different areas of Europe. The Netherlands and England were well in the lead: from these rich western areas yields fell away as you went eastwards and south.

Average yield ratios of mixed cereal crops 1550–1649

	Netherlands England	France, Spain, Italy	Germany, Switzerland, Scandinavia	Russia, Poland, Bohemia, Hungary
1550–99	7·3	(6·5)*	4·4	4·3
1600–49	6·7	(6·3)*	4·5	4·0

* The figures in brackets are based on averages worked out from previous and later periods: no true figures exist for this century.

Not only were the Netherlands the most advanced area technically – rotation and variety of crops, selection of seed, manurial treatment of soil, the mixture of arable, vegetables, roots, poultry and animal farming

– but the area of cultivated land was increasing at rates hitherto unknown. Using the period 1715–39 as the base of the index (100), we find the following figures for our period:

New Polder Area (per annum) 1540–1664

1540–64	346·0
1565–89	75·3
1590–1614	339·9
1615–39	418·5
1640–64	273·0

The peak reached between 1615–39 (an annual average of 1,783 hectares) was not to be approached again until the mid-nineteenth century. Great fortunes were made by the developing entrepreneurs who provided capital and engineering skill to create the new polders, bonding in specialized agriculture to the exchange economy developing rapidly between 1590 and 1648. Here all men were legally free and many were prosperous.

With a larger emphasis on animal husbandry and the controversial policy of enclosures for pastures, England too made substantial agricultural progress. The inflation of wool prices (stimulated by the demand of the Continental clothiers supplied through the Antwerp market) brought about a substantial conversion of arable to pasture land in the Midlands. Thereafter English farming began to demonstate a propensity to adjust itself to market opportunity only a degree less remarkable than that operating among Netherlands agricultural producers. Nobility and gentry, graziers throughout the belt of land running from the south-west to the Lincolnshire coastal marshes, sheep-farmers in Yorkshire and East Anglia, freeholders and copyholders endowed with peasant cunning – all were seeking to enlarge and develop their holdings along the most profitable lines. The shifts in ownership were probably relatively small in relation to the total (so were enclosures), but the tendency to enlarge the farming unit wherever possible was certainly ever-present. And in England it was markedly assisted by the rule of primogeniture which existed over the majority of English shires.

The expansion of sheep-breeding fell away from about 1550 to 1580 with the collapse of the Antwerp market. But the demand for corn held up after its climax in the famine years of the 1590s, remaining on a level until about 1650. In northern France the peasant occupier continued to be the typical figure of the rural world. His holding was as a rule small – many were less than 2½ acres – animals few, surpluses precarious except in years of a really abundant harvest. Even more than his English neighbour, the French peasant depended for survival on the demand for labour in the forest or in the linen or woollen manufactures. Like his Spanish neighbour, he was exposed, as neither English nor Dutch peasant was, to poverty, famine, even death by starvation. Least of all was he able to face the added disasters of war, plague and the growing attentions of the tax-gatherer which fate was to impose on him. Such disasters turned poverty into desperation and mass violence.

Farther along the northern plain the number of smallholdings increased sharply in the sixteenth century. West of the Elbe, the German agricultural system resembled in a general sense that of north France and Midland England. This was open-field country cultivated by 'quit-rent' customary tenants. The *Erbzinsmann* paid his *Zins* just as his French neighbour, the *censier*, paid his *cens*, the English copyholder his fine. *Leibeigenschaft* – serfdom proper – was dwindling. The west German peasant suffered from onerous game laws and from natural disaster. His burdens, were, if anything, greater than those of the French peasant. But, in relation to his lord he was no slave. Conditions in East-Elbia were rapidly becoming entirely different. Here the German Junkers and their equivalents in Poland, Silesia, Hungary and (later) Bohemia were increasing their demesnes not only by reclamation but by encroaching on peasant holdings. The German peasant (an English traveller in north Germany in the early seventeenth century observed) might be low-rented by comparison with his English fellow, but he was 'tied to great slavery, to bring in his lord's corn and ... do him all the servile work that is to be done and his lord hath so much power over him as to take away all his estates, and his life'.[9] It had not always been so. The sixteenth century saw the steady and deliberate depression of the peasantry by the process of *Bauernlegen*. Between 1550 and 1618 the knightly class (*Ritter*) added some 50 per cent to the land under their control. Peasants, once free or semi-free, were bound to the soil and branded on their backs like cattle if they tried to run away. The districts where freedom survived were 'like small islands in a sea of noble power and peasant serfdom that engulfed most of Eastern Europe'.[10]

The motives behind the creation of these great Eastern European corn ranches are not altogether clear. One obvious explanation lay in the profits to be made out of the insistent demands by the Hanseatic merchants, then by the Dutch, for corn supplies which they in turn shipped to Western Europe and even to the Mediterranean markets. To this extent the peasantry of Eastern Europe was the victim of noble opportunism. Historians of Poland and other areas affected have interpreted the developments of the century as the creation of a kind of 'Baltic colonialism', where the peasantry were bled white by a combination of western merchant and eastern nobility exploiting the current shortage of grain in the west. There is a measure of truth in this. But it does not wholly explain the spread of the same system to areas of Poland, Silesia, Bohemia and Hungary which did not export grain. In reality the situation was more complex. The political rise of the nobility, the decline of the towns, the absence of a real bourgeoisie or of any alternative to agriculture as an opportunity for investment or as a source of income left the land itself as the prize in the struggle for power. The end of openings in the Church for younger sons, the visitations of plague and the growing incidence of war only sharpened the struggle.

The victim was always the peasant. In western areas, but more especially in East-Elbia, the fragmentation of holdings went on until the old customary tenantry disappeared and a mass of tiny cottage-holdings, often too small to support the tenant, came into being. The efforts of ruling powers like the Elector of Saxony (Augustus I, 1533–86) to compensate for this fragmentation by buying great estates and splitting them up into sizeable peasant holdings were not enough to reverse the trend.

A final consequence of the developments outlined above was the rise of the trade which Dutch observers were to describe as the 'mother' trade of Holland. This was the growing carriage of Baltic grain from Danzig and other Baltic ports through the Danish Sound. Between the mid-sixteenth and mid-seventeenth century 113,000 ships carried approximately six and a half million tons of Baltic grain through the Sound to the West. These supplies met emergency demands in, for example, England in bad years. A dearth in England, France, Spain, Italy, Portugal or other places was believed 'to enrich Holland seven years after'.

This was no new phenomenon in the 1620s, when it was much debated because of the drain on England's supplies of silver which it plainly involved. It had long been observed that 'in time of dearth of corn in

England there is . . . want of money. In time of plenty of corn in England there is no want.'[11] This did not simply refer to the need for peasants or others to spend their small surpluses on buying corn. That was only the microcosmic beginning of a process which ended (it was believed) by massive exports of cash to Holland or Danzig. The wheel had turned full circle. To those who pondered these things it seemed all too plain that the inadequacies of an unstable agrarian system had to be remedied as much, or more, from outside the system as from within. So long as any society found itself visited by famine recourse would be had to the dealers in Baltic supplies. They would demand payment in cash. Where would the cash come from? What would be the consequences of exporting it? These questions had already been posed by the European financial crisis of 1557–8. For that crisis, which helped to end the long war of France and the Empire, did not arise solely from the virtual bankruptcy of the Emperor and the King of France. It arose also because Europe was paralyzed by a scarcity of silver caused by the need to pay for exceptionally heavy imports of Baltic grain. These in turn were necessary because 1556 had seen a catastrophically bad harvest in Western Europe.

Along with the observation, empirical as it admittedly was, of such problems went a growing consciousness of another – the growth of population which we now see underlying many vital changes in sixteenth-century society.

Population: Thrust and Recoil

Half a century ago, few historians paid much attention to population movements as a major issue in European history before the steep increase in the late eighteenth century immortalized by Malthus in his *Essay* of 1798. Standard works written as late as the 1920s passed over price history almost as lightly. And when finally the sixteenth-century price revolution came to be taken seriously in the 1930s, it was for long seen exclusively as the result of *monetary* factors – first, currency debasement, and then the influx of silver from Central America and Spain. Only in recent years has the demographic expansion of the sixteenth century been recognized for the vitally important social and economic phenomenon that it was.

For reasons that remain obscure, a long upswing of Europe's population began just before the end of the fifteenth century. Throughout the next hundred or more years it left its mark on almost every country.

Food prices rose, real wages fell as the quantity of food obtained in exchange for a unit of industrial products declined. All this was evidence of mounting pressure of population on land. The increased agricultural yields were plainly not enough to offset rising prices. Figures suggest that demographic expansion was common to Germany, Spain, Italy, the Netherlands and England.

In western Germany, the population of the Principality of Osnabrück increased by over 80 per cent during the century. The rate was fairly typical of this area of Germany. In the south, an observer writing a decade after the Peasants' War noticed that although 100,000 peasants perished in the war, 'yet there is no lack of men: rather all villages are so full with people that no one is admitted. The whole of Germany is teeming with children.'[12] The rural population of the Kingdom of Naples, Sicily, Sardinia and the Canton of Zürich was said to have more or less doubled in the course of the century. Even in those areas and towns of Italy most devastated during the wars that followed the French invasion of 1494, recovery seems to have been complete by 1575, when two years of plague caused great losses in cities like Venice and Padua. But in 1600, despite all these catastrophes, the population of north Italy was probably higher than in 1500. In the Netherlands the wars of liberation caused enormous losses to the south. Many were killed, many died of disease, but many emigrated. And often the loss of the south became the gain of the north. If Antwerp declined by a half between 1568 and 1589 Leiden, Amsterdam, Rotterdam, Middleburg and other cities in the north doubled, even trebled, in size. The Province of Holland is a better guide to the rate of natural increase as distinct from increase by immigration (which accounts for much of the increase in urban populations): here the growth was of the order of 100 per cent in the course of the century. Poland, Scandinavia, the Balkans demonstrate similar trends.

In England and France the demographic evidence is still relatively scanty. But it seems likely that after the Black Death of 1348 the English population fell to a level below that of the thirteenth century. It was still below that level, but growing, in 1500. By 1570 it had probably regained its old level and by 1600 stood at between 4 and $4\frac{1}{2}$ millions. By the mid-seventeenth century it reached a figure between 5 and 6 millions, where it rested for nearly a century. In France the population was about the same in 1562 (when the Wars of Religion began) as it had been two and a half centuries earlier. Plague and other diseases added to losses in battle. Many a city was ruined and half-deserted by the time the civil wars ended in 1595. Yet still France remained the largest nation state of contemporary Europe.

Taken in isolation, almost every individual piece of evidence of population increase – registers of births and deaths, tax returns, mortality tables, casual expressions of opinion by observers such as ambassadors, travellers, and visitors – is open to doubt. But in aggregate they create an irresistible impression of general demographic advance. From 1500 to 1650 the battle for human survival was being won.

What caused the upswing? The answer must be given in two parts. The first is simple; the second infinitely complex. First, we may say, quite simply, that the size of Europe's population depended on the balance between the birth rate and the death rate. If a bath tap is running and the plughole open, the volume of water retained in the bath will depend on how much more is flowing in than escaping; so a population will grow as the number of births exceeds the number of deaths. The expectation of births in a pre-industrial society would be between 15 and 50 per 1000. (The first reasonably reliable figures in England are for the seventeenth century when the figure was 32–38 and rose steadily through the eighteenth century.) Death rates were much more variable, rising in bad periods to anywhere between 200 and 400 per 1000.

In practice, high death rates followed either bad harvests, war, or visitations of the plague, typhus and other diseases carried around by armies. Most important, because they struck at young mothers and the unborn children, were puerperal fevers. Infant mortality was particularly lethal to a society. The death of a young person removed a potential worker and potential parent. Which makes it necessary to introduce a complication into the bath analogy: for the *composition* of the content of the bath is also vital. An ageing population has less potential for production and reproduction than a younger one. It can, in fact, be observed that after a famine, when holdings and looms were vacant, a surge of marriages and births appears to make good the losses. 'Each baby-boom produced an echo after an elapse of roughly a quarter of a century as the babies began themselves to form families.'[13]

The second part of the problem is much harder to tackle: given that the balance of births and deaths governs the ebb and flow of population, how and why did the population grow in the sixteenth century and why did this momentum slacken by 1650? Was it that the forces increasing

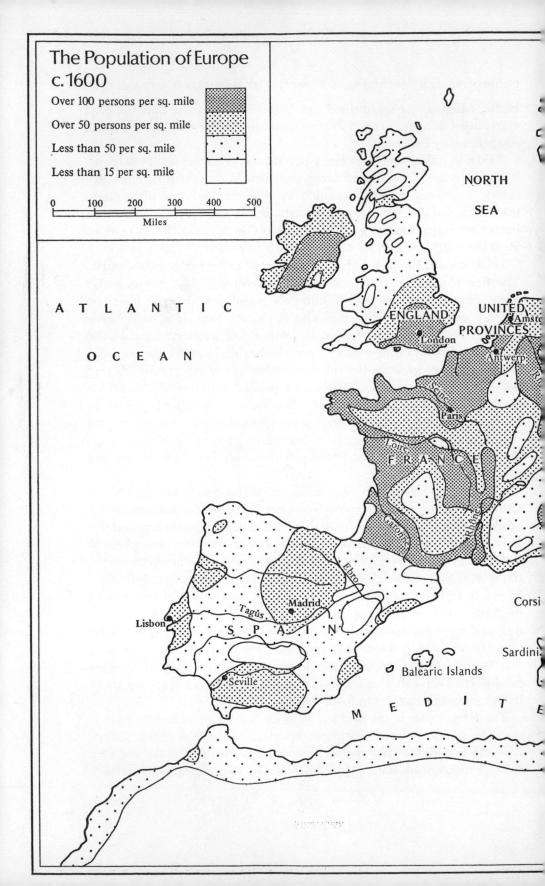

The Population of Europe
c.1600

Over 100 persons per sq. mile

Over 50 persons per sq. mile

Less than 50 per sq. mile

Less than 15 per sq. mile

0   100   200   300   400   500
Miles

ATLANTIC

OCEAN

NORTH

SEA

ENGLAND

UNITED
PROVINCES

London

Amste

Antwerp

Paris

Loire

FRANCE

Garonne

Rhône

Corsi

Ebro

Madrid

Tagus

Lisbon

S P A I N

Balearic Islands

Sardini

Seville

M E D I T E

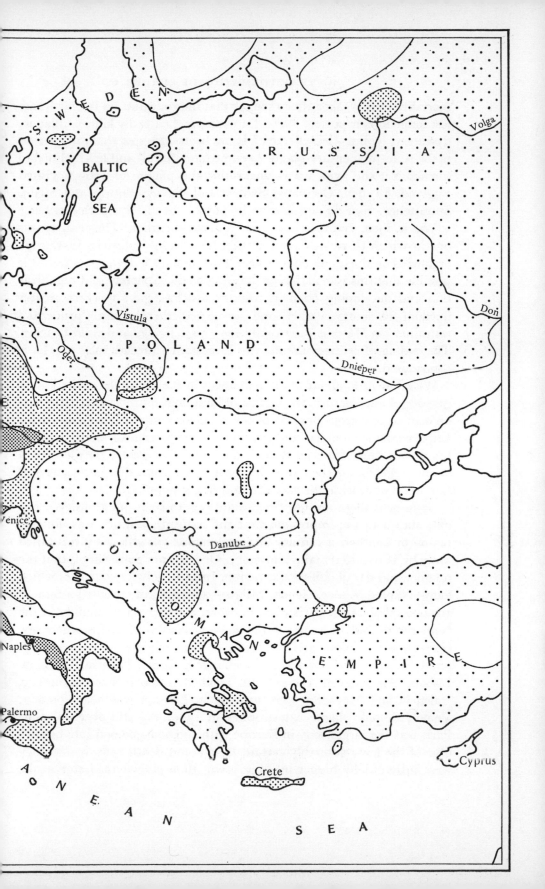

SWEDEN

BALTIC

SEA

RUSSIA

Volga

POLAND

Vistula

Oder

Don

Dnieper

Venice

OTTOMAN

Danube

Naples

EMPIRE

Palermo

Cyprus

IONIAN

Crete

SEA

mortality were weaker after 1500, or that the restraints on the birth rate lost some of their power? Were, for example the deadly killers – plague, dysentery, typhus – less effective? It has been suggested that for a period in the sixteenth century plague became more 'local' and less inclined to spread. Yet the evidence is uncertain: the plague of 1563–6 visited England, Sweden, Germany, Switzerland, Savoy, France and Spain. Subsistence crises do not seem to be notably less in this period either.

Was it, then, that men and women married earlier? The century was one in which there was a substantial increase of industries in Europe organized on the domestic (cottage, 'putting-out' or *Verlag*) system. It is possible that this system, looser than the medieval urban gild organization and developing often in country districts, gave workers greater freedom to marry earlier and weakened thereby the 'prudential restraints' (as Malthus was to call them) on marriage and child-bearing. The ending of celibacy among the Protestant churches may also have contributed.

We know little about possible changes in the virulence of the killing diseases or variations in the nature of human immunity. Did the development of new crops in some of the problem-areas of Europe make for better resistance – maize and rice in the Mediterranean, buckwheat on the poorer soils of the north and east? Did the greater possibilities of famine relief for stricken areas brought by sea from the Baltic stave off starvation or at least alleviate the suffering it imposed?

At present there are few precise answers to such questions. We can only stay with the impression that the sixteenth century was, for one reason or another, a century of demographic growth. Why this tailed away by 1650 also remains a mystery. One distinct possibility is that the number and size of cities was growing. In 1500 only five cities (of which four – Naples, Venice, Genoa, Milan – were Italian) reached a total of 100,000 inhabitants. Paris was the other. Another score, mainly in the Netherlands and Italy, was in the 30,000–50,000 range. Elsewhere few cities exceeded 20,000 and even cities of this size were not numerous. A hundred years later the scene has changed. Rome, Palermo, Messina, Lisbon, Amsterdam, Lyons had reached 100,000 and Hamburg, Valencia and Marseilles were nearing it. London was near 200,000; Venice, despite plague catastrophes in 1575, was still over 100,000; Paris was the largest city in Europe with 200,000–300,000 inhabitants. One of the few reasonably certain facts about death rates is that they were substantially higher in large towns than elsewhere. Later in the seventeenth century statisticians like William Petty and Gregory King concluded (quite correctly, as later figures proved) that the London death rate was so high that the city would probably have shrunk in size had it not been sustained by a continual flow of immigrants – not only from the Home Counties but from the Netherlands, Huguenot France and other areas where Protestants were persecuted. London was a veritable incubator for epidemics. Its houses of thatch and wood, its storehouses and granaries full of corn, the rotting heaps of human excrement and vegetable matter – all formed a perfect breeding-ground for rats and the fleas which carried the plague germ. Other diseases – especially typhus and syphilis, influenza and (after 1600) smallpox – also bred and spread in the city, helped by contemporary ignorance of the basis of hygiene or the nature of infection through human contacts. Deaths by violence were higher too: this was the age of the duel, the feud, the alehouse brawl. All were daily or nightly occurrences. So, whereas city life might seem designed to raise birth rates (and probably did), it almost certainly raised death rates proportionately more. Meanwhile, in the countryside, the rise in the yield of the farms that had helped to sustain the demographic increases of the sixteenth century was, for reasons which are also obscure, falling away. Was it that the early fertility of marginal lands newly broken up in periods of growth and demand had declined and been followed by lower yields? Or did the succession of economic crises, civil disturbances and disastrous wars reduce agrarian enterprise and labour? Again we do not know. We are left only with the certainty that by 1650 the great demographic expansion was coming to a close.

The Price Revolution
Detailed and systematic studies of price behaviour in many countries have shown that the general price level rose everywhere in the sixteenth century. In Spain the level of 1600 was $3\frac{1}{2}$ to 5 times the level of 1500; in Poland $2\frac{1}{2}$ to $3\frac{1}{2}$ times; in Italy (where the rise did not get under way until the 1530s) it was restricted to 2 or $2\frac{1}{2}$ times; in England, where the upturn began before 1500, 3–4 times. The problem of generalizing about prices with any hope of accuracy is bedevilled by differences of standards and habits of living in the European world. Yet, as with demographic increase so with prices; the figures, imperfect, inexact as they are, leave an unmistakeable impression of a great price upheaval which drastically affected the lives of all members of society who had to

buy or sell. Everywhere the sharpest rise came from the 1540s to the 1570s.

The price rise lasted into the seventeenth century. Then, at a time and a pace which varied from place to place, the turbulence subsided. In Germany, a decline was perceptible by the 1620s. By the middle of the seventeenth century the great inflation was at an end. It was followed by a long period of general price stability, punctuated here and there by temporary and local declines, until the second half of the eighteenth century.

When the early historians of the price upheaval tried to explain the phenomenon, they turned first to monetary causes. These varied from one country to another. In Spain, the enquiries of the American scholar, E. J. Hamilton, followed the flow of silver bullion from Central America to Seville, where a group of merchants seemed to be the claimants to some two-thirds of the influx (the rest belonging to the Spanish Crown). Working on an equation suggested by Irving Fisher, Hamilton concluded that (given certain assumptions, for example a steady velocity of circulation of money and no decline in output) if prices were four times as high in 1600 as in 1500 then the amount of money in circulation must also be four times that of 1500.

There were several difficulties about this. One was that Hamilton's evidence did not suggest that much of the American silver that reached Spain was exported before c. 1570. Yet elsewhere in Europe prices were also rising – in Germany and Poland, for example. This could be explained, possibly, by the rise in Continental silver production which added (like American silver) to the quantity of money available, reducing similarly the value of precious metals in relation to the volume of other commodities. Yet in fact we can see that Continental silver mining was itself explicable only in terms of the needs of an already expanding economy. The south German bankers saw new investments, new income and demand and higher prices in the silver (and copper) mines of Central Europe.

The scarcest and dearest goods in the sixteenth century were foodstuffs and the basic necessities of life; followed by goods which were desirable but less essential; and by the weapons, luxuries, ammunitions and supplies which were in increasing demand by governments everywhere. It was the needs of the government for such things which brought about the debasement of the English coinage especially between 1543 and 1551. This, with the war inflation, brought about a rise in prices in England. Measured against an index (1411–75 average = 100) they soared to 370 in 1556 and 409 in 1557. Similar war demands were to bring far bigger inflationary rises in 1598 and 1600. Ignoring the leaps and jerks in the inflationary process, the prices of 1600 were three to four times those of 1500; but food prices had risen much more than others.

The evidence suggests that mere reference to increased supplies of American silver – even to increased monetary supplies from other sources too – is not an adequate explanation of the price revolution. Before prices rose there were already higher demands for goods. Thus it may well have been these demands, coming from a growing population and more aggressive, centralized government, that stimulated the search for precious metals and made it possible for them to infiltrate the economy at an increased rate and exert a sustained inflationary influence. This would continue until the supply of food and other goods came into equilibrium with demand or until demand fell away.

All this is not to dismiss the importance of monetary supply as a factor in the sixteenth-century price revolution: very much the reverse. For we know that in addition to the debasement of coinages, to the increased output of European silver, and the bonus from the mines of Potosi and elsewhere, we should probably also reckon with a de-hoarding of existing but latent supplies of coin, plate and bullion already in private ownership in Europe. What part of Europe's total supply of precious metals – possibly some 40,000 tons of gold and silver compared with the 16,000 tons of (mainly) silver coming from America between 1500 and 1650 – was the result of de-hoarding we can only guess.

Like most of the basic economic problems of the day, the causes of the price revolution admit no precise analysis. All we can be sure of is that Europe as a whole needed more money in circulation as the century developed. The demand for food and for war supplies grew. Thus the search for and production of metals, precious and base, in America and in Europe was given greater urgency. So was the growth of corn behind the southern shores of the Baltic. All these demanded shipping; shipping demanded Baltic timber and naval stores. Spaniards, English and Dutch buyers scrambled for the means of payment – hard cash – and to obtain it they bartered European produce for American silver. For the Dutch especially bullion and coin represented international purchasing power in solid form. For them, little superstitious worth attached to gold or silver: only cash value. From the 1570s onwards, as Spain's increasing commitments in sea and land wars dictated, the silver that arrived at Seville was heavily earmarked to pay the bills for the supplies she could not produce herself. The silver no longer stayed at home. It went to Amsterdam or London or Genoa. Dutch merchants used it to pay for supplies they in turn bought overseas; Dutch traders on the Baltic bought corn and timber, and even the Dutch East India merchants used it to buy spices and textiles; Dutch Levant merchants paid with it for silks, spices, cotton. There was a steady flow of silver east, south and north. But in the course of its travels it (and to a lesser extent the gold supply) performed indispensable services, modifying the need for barter in remote areas, acting as backing for payments by means of bills of exchange and other forms of credit. In short it eased, loosened and expanded international trade.

Even if the increase of bullion supplies was not itself the 'cause' of the inflation, it is true that the price inflation could only *express itself* through the agency of more transactions at higher prices paid in the expanded supply of money which depended on larger supplies of silver and other metals. Of prices and precious metals in the nineteenth century Sir John Clapham once wrote:

the precious metals cannot of themselves produce prosperity. But they certainly promote activity. They fire the imagination; and even economic progress needs the fired imagination, not merely the grasping hand and the patient bowed back. . . . An age of rising prices is not necessarily an age of prosperity. But it is at least possible that the . . . stimulus which gold getting administers involves a real, and not merely an apparent, addition to the world's wealth. There might have been fewer useful activities and fewer useful things without it.[14]

Something very similar might be said of the silver-getting of the sixteenth century, with the proviso that some very wasteful and irrational things were done also; for at the root of the Spanish problem was the balance of payments deficit. Spain's overseas wars and domestic deficits were costing her dear. Prices went on rising long after the population of Castile began to fall, and did not stop until the last quarter of the seventeenth century; but from the late sixteenth century the inflation was in a debased copper currency – the so-called *vellon* inflation.

The price inflation can no longer be treated in simple monetary terms: it was the product of complex interaction between increased demands by government and by consumers of food, the expansion of monetary supply, destruction by war, shortages caused by plague and other diseases and the growth of demand by those classes which had either benefited by inflation, or had taken effective steps to see that they did not suffer by it.

There is no doubt that the inflation administered a shock to the status quo in every way. In the 1530s and 1540s in England it was assumed that rising prices were simply the work of profiteers. But none of the attempts to fix prices in England, Spain or France had much success. In 1563, Elizabeth's government ordered that wages should be assessed annually by the Justices of the Peace for the following year: the aim was not oppression, but national preservation of order. In 1576 another act allowed landlords to claim one-third of their rents in kind – grain or malt – valued at 1550 prices. Yet none of the measures had more than a marginal effect. The undertow of the current was too strong. The likely results may be sketched schematically as follows.

The important landowning class faced serious problems. In the western areas of Europe (England, Germany, France) the landlord had already become, to an extent we cannot know exactly, a *rentier*. A proportion of his rents, again unspecifiable and varying from one country to another, consisted of customary, often fixed, payments – the fine, the *cens*, the *Zins*. If such payments were fixed and hereditary, it was far from easy to raise them to follow prices up. The lord who failed, through indolence or inertia, to adjust would find himself sooner or later in difficulties unless he pulled in his belt. But his problems would be fewer (and might disappear or even be turned to positive advantage) if he possessed, or could create from recovered land, a demesne which he could himself exploit so as to take advantage of rising prices and not simply remain their victim. He could, additionally or alternatively, attempt to by-pass the customary laws that gave security of tenure and a stable rent to his tenantry. Of outright expropriation by force there is little evidence in England, nor much in France. But evidently a great deal of haggling went on and social pressure applied to alter the situation in the lords' favour and give them a share of the 'unearned increment' which the price inflation had bestowed on producers.

In France, much more than in England, the royal courts protected the customary tenants who occupied much of the land. By and large they survived to become virtual proprietors as the *cens* and other payments declined into insignificance. The French peasant's enemy was not so much his lord as the tax-gatherer. Sometimes, however, when the lord was also the money-lender (in Spain and France, possibly England too) the peasant borrower could be forced into surrendering his land. In other cases, lawyers revived ancient rights of lordship or raised points of law over waste land and pasture. Sometimes they found peasant cunning more than a match for them. Many a lord was thwarted. In other cases a full market price was paid by the lord who wanted to obtain control of a peasant's land. The picture is complex and untidy (it will be discussed in more detail below).

One thing is certain. At the head of the landowning class in each country stood the king. Increasingly the effective ruler, absolute or semi-absolute, much of the social destiny of state and society depended upon his decisions. As head of government he was the biggest spender. He was therefore the one who felt the price rise most severely, unless, like Elizabeth, he was that rare bird in early modern history, the parsimonious prince. Most were not. It was the cost of princely government, of dynasticism and its consequences, that terrified such bourgeois societies as that of the Netherlands and (to a degree) that of England.

In the lands of 'manorial', *rentier* lordship, customary tenures, *Grundherrschaft*, the peasant may have won only half a loaf: but except in times of famine or emergency he was not without bread or a measure of independence. It was otherwise, as we have seen, in Central and Eastern Europe, where the Junkers and other types of lord exercising *Gutsherrschaft* of some kind or other simply expunged the free peasant from the records of society, leaving no one between lord and serf.

Luck and management left the fortunes of the noble class, the really large landowners, very variable. Many choices were open to them and – in more cases than used sometimes to be thought – to those that had, more was given. The middling, less affluent gentry – the esquires and gentlemen of Western Europe – were much more vulnerable. Some of them raised their status and fortunes successfully during the dispersal and sale of church lands in England and Germany early in the Reformation. In England families like the Wriothesleys, Cecils, Sackvilles and Russells, gentry in early Tudor times, were peers of the realm by the seventeenth century. Others were those 'mere gentry' who sometimes turned, soured and penurious, to Calvinism and political dissent. In France they made up the large class of Huguenot gentry, some genuinely convinced believers, others political seekers, who fought the religious wars. Many of this class throughout Europe were undoubtedly hit by the inflation.

So were wage-earners everywhere: though we should refrain from supposing either that the wage-earner was normally entirely dependent on his wage or that he was the highly typical figure that he later became in an industrialized society. Often he received additional payments in kind – food, meals, part of the harvest. Often he had his own small plot of land, cabbages, beans or peas and a pig. Sometimes he worked on the land as well as in the woollen or other trades. Conditions therefore varied from region to region, trade to trade. In Spain, it has been remarked, wages kept up with rising prices better than elsewhere – in England and France, for example, where real wages seem to have fallen as population increase provided more labour. This differential response of wages to prices has indeed been made an explanation of the failure of Spain to develop industrially as early as England. Profits in England, it has been argued, were larger because the entrepreneur's wage-bill was lower: this is doubtful. Wages were also low in France, yet she enjoyed no early industrial expansion such as that which J. U. Nef has described in England's expanding coal, glass, soap, brewing and other industries.

In the Netherlands, the early inflationary years also saw the rise of Antwerp and the expansion of the 'new draperies' of west Flanders which more than absorbed any excess labour made available by demographic increase, leaving wages, salaries and incomes generally buoyant. This was exceptional – the Netherlands usually were. Generally, the increase of population tended to lower wages for unskilled work, to create or enlarge a menacing army of beggars and vagabonds. Skilled workers of any kind probably did better, as men prepared to swim against the tide usually do. In that casual, disorganized world, these were the people who formed the rank and file of the Calvinist congregations. And Calvinism gave point to the diligence and energy with which some of them pushed their way upwards in society.

Even more typical of the economy and society that emerged from this age of demographic and price increase were the mercantile classes of Europe – the great merchants of the overseas trading companies, the affluent masters of the city gilds and companies, the capitalist entrepreneurs who financed the expanding manufacturing industries in the suburbs and rural areas, the tradesmen and shopkeepers. These made up a sizeable proportion of the population of the cities now in an age of expansion, the centres to which migrants flocked in search of work and possibly fortune. The theme of enterprise rewarded is too popular in these times to be accidental. The age abounded in entrepreneurs for whom the changes and chances of the market were a constant source of opportunity. Venice, Antwerp, London and Amsterdam knew them well for they helped to create these great entrepôts of trade. Unlike the landowning class they were trammelled by little in the way of fixed capital. Their resources were mobile, easily liquidated and switched from one enterprise to another, from a poor commercial prospect to a better one. And just as they could migrate entrepreneurially, they could, if need be, migrate physically. Hundreds, probably thousands, left Antwerp, Ghent and the other crumbling cities of the southern Netherlands to go to the north Netherland or overseas, after 1567 and 1585. Unlike the great nobles of the south Netherlands they were not tied to their estates or titles. They were free to follow the market. In the future they might (like great London merchants such as Lionel Cranfield or William Cokayne) acquire noble status, become involved in high politics and marry their daughters into land and rank. But, in the sixteenth century, most were still mobile. And just as their fellows in Spain and Portugal were beginning to wilt beneath the oppressive weight of taxation and uncertainty imposed by the new age of crusades against Turk, Protestant, rebel and dynastic foes, the merchants of the north-western seaboard were casting off the shackles of medieval legal and collective institutional controls.

The signposts labelled 'inflation' or 'demographic change' rarely point in one direction only. We may say that logically or legally a member of this or that class or social or occupational group was, on balance, likely to benefit or lose in a particular set of economic conditions. We can never be sure that luck or ability will not falsify the general argument in the case of individuals or groups of key importance. Indeed it was the particular character of this upheaval of prices and population between 1500 and 1650 that it tended to destroy the very bases of law and logic. It added two further causes of uncertainty to the existing gambles provided by Nature. It weakened and in some cases destroyed institutions and unquestioned assumptions of medieval life. The Church, the hierarchy of saints, the fabric of belief, Pope, cardinals, priests, chantries, gilds, ancient customs, law, whole families, 'just' prices – in fact a whole way of life that seemed, in retrospect at least, stable and dating from time immemorial, had faded and gone. For the antiquaries of the seventeenth century like John Aubrey who laid some of the foundations of archaeology and history in England, history had broken off somewhere between the times of Henry VIII and Queen

Elizabeth. Before then were the 'olden times'; to some – but not all – they seemed full of good cheer, paternalistic care, unchallenged stability of ideas, comfort, peace and tranquillity. Others thought differently. For them a new and better day had dawned. Mansions had replaced castles built for fighting. The cultivated country gentleman and city merchant attentive to his business were replacing the belted knight. Libraries were replacing armouries. The hunt was to be more common than the battle. Yet to survive and prosper in the new society a man needed – more than ever – ingenuity and resource. The greater the capital or responsibility, the greater the need. Those who knew they were inadequately equipped with such talents required expert help – hence the growing tribe of lawyers, scriveners, bankers, and attorneys who people the plays of Elizabethan and Jacobean England and later of Molière. More than ever, social and economic life had become a game in which skill and chance were mixed. Shipwreck, bankruptcy and merchant cunning are the interwoven themes of many plays of the period. The merchant class had no monopoly of the skills needed to play the game: many a lord, country gentleman and village peasant also possessed or acquired them. But it was the merchants who represented the ethos of the age, its flexibility, sharpness and competitive, combative spirit. These were the outcome of the edge and urgency which the new economic and social factors had given to the struggle for survival. Nothing was more indicative of the altered conditions of the sources of power in the new Europe than the rise of the Dutch Republic, especially from the 1590s onwards. This small republic of merchant opportunists was not interested in self-sufficency. Certainly they did not produce enough to feed themselves or supply their own basic needs. They made a living by buying cheap and selling dear on international markets, not least to the Spaniards with whom they were to be locked in a desperate war. Recent research has convinced more than one historian that the same American silver whose consequences were so dire for Spain had 'a decisively favourable influence' on the Dutch economy 'thanks to the equilibrium established between productivity and the amount of money in circulation'.[15]

Economic Policies and the Concept of 'Mercantilism'
The preoccupation of the men of these centuries with precious metals has often seemed obsessive to later, more fortunate ages. Mistaken though it sometimes was in logic, it was in essence neither obsessive nor neurotic;

it was perfectly rational. Two major considerations stuck in the minds of thinking men. A coinage was necessary to keep the business of everyday life going; yet the coinage must consist basically either of silver or gold and England, for example, had natural resources of neither.

No great intelligence surely was needed to see that the size of the nation's stock of currency depended on the inflow and outflow of goods in trade. There appeared in 1549 *A Discourse of the Common Weal of the Realm of England*. It has usually been treated as the first sophisticated socio-economic analysis of the origins of inflation. In part this is true. It pinned responsibility for inflation firmly on the Crown, the deviser of debasement and therefore of inflation. The editor of a new edition in 1581 found a new villain. He blamed the influx of American silver. But the *Discourse* did more than this. It adumbrated, nearly three-quarters of a century before the formulation of Thomas Mun's reflections on the crisis of the 1620s, an embryonic balance of payments theory; in the words of the doctor, who conducts the 'dialogue' in which the argument is cast, England 'must alwaies take hede that we bie no more of strangers than we sell them ... (for so wee sholde empoverishe owe selves and enriche theme)'. A later editor added an extra note:

If we sent out more commodities in value than we bringe home, the over-pluis cometh in coyne; but if we bringe in more then the overpluis must nedes be paid for in moneye, and this is the measure of increasinge or diminishinge the coyne, except of that little which is found within the realme.

Such observations became a commonplace of empirical thinking on economic problems of the second half of the sixteenth and early seventeenth century in England. Loss of vital supplies of treasure was connected (correctly) with the need to finance recurrent imports of Baltic grain in times of dearth. By the 1620s the problem had changed – even reversed. The London Eastland Company, formed to promote exports of goods to the Baltic instead of exports of specie, found itself in difficulties because bountiful harvests in England from 1618 to 1620 made imports of Baltic grain unnecessary. As these had become the means by which Baltic buyers paid for their imports of English goods (mainly cloth), Anglo-Baltic trade languished. Something of the complexity of international trade began to dawn on the English. Concern for bullion *per se* began to take second place to those movements of trade which now seemed to have a stronger claim to be the prime mover of the flow of specie. This was the moment of truth for Thomas Mun, a merchant of European experience who sat as a member of the government commission to enquire into the deep and prolonged depression of English trade and industry from 1621 to 1623. His reflections were not published until 1664 (as part of the cold war against the Dutch then in progress) but his basic concepts were formulated by 1623. Like much economic theory of the time, they were the outcome of hard thinking under pressure of critical events. They can best be expressed in his own phrases: they occur in the chapter of the pamphlet *England's Treasure by Fforraign Trade* headed 'The Means to enrich this Kingdom and to increase our Treasure': 'The ordinary means to increase our wealth and treasuries by *Fforraign Trade* wherein we must ever observe this rule: to sell more to strangers yearly than we consume of theirs in value.' Thus, he explains, if England exports goods worth £2·2 millions and imports only goods worth £2 millions, England wins the difference in treasure. But if the import–export situation is reversed, England *loses* an equal amount of treasure.

But what of overseas trade (such as the East India trade) which demanded export of silver? Mun's answer was ready (he was not an East India merchant for nothing). It is true, he concedes, that for the India trade export of silver is needed. But, in the final calculation, the gains from the India trade earned by the re-sale of Indian goods in European and other markets meant that England recovered more treasure than it lost. India was evidently replacing the Baltic as the 'great drain' of European bullion. Trade – European and world-wide – had intruded on the parish of England as a problem, but also as a potential solution of the basic conundrums of everyday life. The economic crisis which made the Commission of 1621 necessary had originally arisen from Anglo-Dutch trade. An Eastland merchant of London, Sir William Cokayne, had observed that England exported (via the monopolistic 'Merchant Adventurers' Company) a cloth which was only half finished – as they said, 'in the white'. Cokayne's famous 'project' proposed to replace this traditional system by a new arrangement for exporting full-finished cloths, dyed and finished in England, not in Holland. This bold idea of wresting large sources of profit and employment from the ingenious Dutch and handing them to the English had great popular appeal. It promised more private and solid benefits to those (James I included) who backed Cokayne's ideas.

But the final result was total disaster. The Dutch took damaging reprisals. The English found that dyeing cloth was not as easy as it might seem. At least a decade of dislocation, unemployment and depression ensued. Yet Cokayne, sharper though he probably was, had pointed the way to a more spacious (though much-deferred) commercial and industrial future for England. More than that, he outlined a theory which, imperfect in logic, nevertheless contained a core of dynamic truth in the rudimentary conditions of the contemporary English economy. The 'balance of trade' might be achieved in four ways: by boosting exports of manufactures; by restricting imports of competing manufactures; by allowing and encouraging imports of necessary raw materials; and by controlling even prohibiting, exports of vital raw materials – notably wool, the basis of England's major industry – in order to hold down costs for English manufacturers. Little wonder that Mun's pithy masterpiece was to survive for a century and a half as the classic exposition of English economic nationalism and to be translated, studied, absorbed and applied by one aspiring European rival after another.

Part of its green-eyed inspiration lay in its keen observation of Dutch practice, which, though very different in its individualistic, atomized pursuit of pure profit, also embodied one feature common to the emergent economic thinking of the day: the perception that trade and industry offered an escape-route from the constrictions of agrarian economy and society. Mun was open to many criticisms and has been the target for many accurate marksmen; but his thinking, for all its nationalistic sentiment and faulty logic, reflected the consciousness of an expanding economic world of trade and industry. It was an attempt to provide a dynamic answer to the problems of stagnation, famine and poverty posed by an agrarian system bounded by static technology yet pounded by the forces of population growth and inflation.

The attraction of a more variegated and intensive economy was felt throughout Western Europe, though the vitality of controversy and the efficacy and persistence with which it was followed up varied widely from country to country. In southern Italy, an area poor and destined to be poor, a voice of protest came from the Papal prison at Naples. While a prisoner there Antonio Serra, a Calabrian, wrote his *Brief Discussion on a Possible Means of Causing Gold and Silver to abound in Kingdoms where there are no Mines* in 1613. His basic question was a natural one for someone from the *mezzogiorno*: why were the Neapolitan provinces so poor? Why were Venice and Genoa so rich? It was the same question the English were to ask about Amsterdam and the Scots about England down to the time of Adam Smith. It was a curious coincidence that from 1596 to 1607 Thomas Mun (whose arguments Serra's *Breve Trattato* closely resembled) was in Italy, where he seems to have gone bankrupt and fled back home. Both writers argued for the paramount importance of a favourable balance of payments as the objective which would do most to encourage manufactures and the right kind of export trade, cutting down costly imports by processes which a later age would call a mixture of import-substitution and industrial diversification.

Understandably, in a country more than normally agrarian even for the age, French economic thinking was behind that of the Netherlands and England. Nevertheless, in sixteenth-century sources (royal letters, edicts, *cahiers* discussed in the Estates-General and private writings) one detects a perceptible spreading of the notion that those trades or industries which *increased* the nation's stock of gold and silver were beneficial; those which decreased its stock were harmful. The function of money as a circulating medium was discussed in a *cahier* in 1484: 'Money is in the body politic what blood is in the human body.' After the middle of the century 'the value of a large supply of bullion was an almost axiomatic basis of argument in France'.[16] Perhaps because French habits in economic matters were authoritarian, the policies that emerged from such premises were aimed rather at preventing the leakage of bullion from France than at encouraging those who were able to build up the trades and industries that might be supposed to attract bullion. Yet there were exceptions. Permits were issued in 1557–62 to Venetians and Genoese to settle in France and develop manufacture of glass and textiles, to foreign mining experts (probably German) to look for and develop mines. A *cahier* of 1560 rehearsed the virtues of those merchants who exported French manufactures and thus won the precious metals of which France had no local supply. Edicts of 1572 prohibited the export of raw materials: it was better for France that they should be kept at home for domestic manufactures. The Assembly of Notables pleaded in 1583 for the free entry of foreign wool, flax, hemp, raw silk, copper, dyewoods. For the same reason, such ideas were the commonplaces of the writings of Jean Bodin. They became the leitmotif of propagandists for a national economic policy in the seventeenth century.

Barthelmy de Laffemas began his career as Henry IV's valet and ended it as Controller-General of Commerce. He was not the last

39

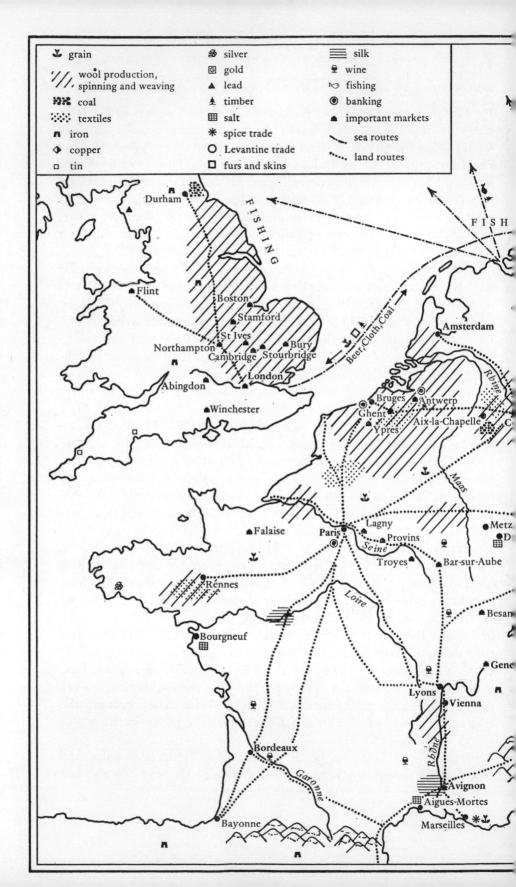

Legend:

⚓ grain

/// wool production, spinning and weaving

▨▨ coal

textiles

⋔ iron

◇ copper

□ tin

§ silver

▣ gold

▲ lead

♣ timber

▦ salt

✳ spice trade

○ Levantine trade

□ furs and skins

☰ silk

♀ wine

∽ fishing

◉ banking

▲ important markets

— · — sea routes

····· land routes

Durham

FISHING

Flint

Boston

Stamford

St Ives

Northampton

Cambridge   Bury

Stourbridge

London

Abingdon

Winchester

Amsterdam

Bruges   Antwerp

Ghent

Ypres   Aix-la-Chapelle   C

Maas

Rhine

Beer, Cloth, Coal

FISH

Falaise

Paris

Lagny

Provins

Seine

Troyes

Metz

D

Bar-sur-Aube

Rennes

Loire

Besan

Bourgneuf

Gene

Lyons

Vienna

Bordeaux

Garonne

Rhône

Avignon

Aigues-Mortes

Bayonne

Marseilles

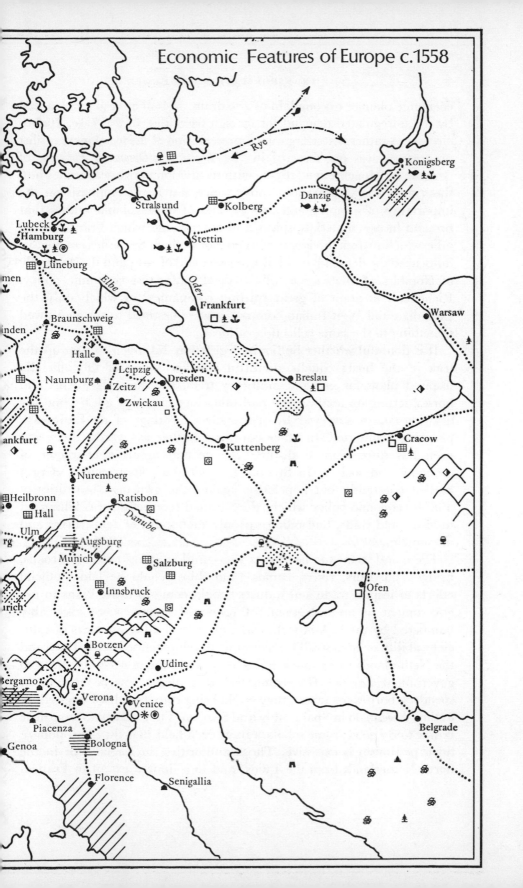

Economic Features of Europe c.1558

Rye

Konigsberg

Stralsund

Kolberg

Danzig

Lubeck

Hamburg

Luneburg

men

Elbe

Oder

Stettin

Frankfurt

Warsaw

Braunschweig

inden

Halle

Leipzig

Dresden

Breslau

Naumburg

Zeitz

Zwickau

ankfurt

Kuttenberg

Cracow

Nuremberg

Heilbronn

Hall

Ratisbon

Danube

Ulm

rg

Augsburg

Munich

Salzburg

Ofen

urich

Innsbruck

Botzen

Udine

Bergamo

Verona

Venice

Belgrade

Piacenza

Bologna

Genoa

Florence

Senigallia

economic planner to complain of the drain on bullion and coin caused by the unregulated demand for foreign frivolities, in this case, Italian circuses. A rather better-organized presentation of the usual mercantilist programme was put forward in the *Traité de l'Oeconomie Politique* of Antoine de Monchrétien (1615), with its division of overseas trades into those that won treasure and those which lost it; its emphasis on the importance of shipping and fishery, and of those colonial trades that brought in new materials, spices and other things which France would otherwise buy from foreigners with coin or bullion. Such ideas may have influenced the demands of the Estates-General of 1614 and the Assembly of Notables of 1626 for a fully fledged nationalist economic policy. Richelieu's creation of great trading companies (of which only the Canadian and West Indian companies were destined to survive) owed something to the same collection of ideas.

It is doubtful whether bullionist legislation did much to stop up the leak in the boat; equally doubtful whether many of the officially inspired plans for growing mulberry trees, breeding silk-worms and horses, setting up textile, glass and other factories, ever got beyond the drawing-boards surveyed by the endless meetings of de Laffemas's planning committee. In other countries farther eastwards, there was even less disposition to disturb the general agrarian character of economy and society. In Spain, the *arbitristas* (often secular clergy) battled constantly but hopelessly against the growing absurdities of official economic policy which, they argued (correctly), was killing off industry and trade, and piling up only mountains of debts, taxes and monopolies.

The moral seemed to be that as yet – until an infrastructure of roads, bridges, harbours, rivers, canals (and ships) could be laid – official efforts to inspire trade and industry could come to little. Plans to use government as an instrument of economic change were invariably hampered by the lack of technical experts and administrators of sufficient ability or honesty. The economic development of north Italy and the Netherlands owed much to location and human necessity; little to government *dirigisme*. Governments had immense powers for evil. As spenders, borrowers, taxers, they could bring ruin, or at least stagnation, as they were to do in Spain, Italy and Sweden. They seemed to have little power to do good; some scholars have even held that they had none.[17] Such pessimism is excessive. Those authorities (in England or in the north Netherlands from the 1560s, and to a limited extent in France) which gave permission to refugees with capital, enterprise, skill or simply the power of hand and muscle to find new homes and contribute to expanding wealth, discovered that they had made a remarkably profitable investment. For in this age most economic skills and innovations were carried in men's heads. All that government needed to do was to open the door to skill and enterprise. 'Here is Antwerp become Amsterdam', wrote an observer in the north Netherlands in the 1590s, surveying the formidable role newcomers from Flanders and Brabant were playing in the expanding economy of the new Republic. Such transference of industrial techniques made a contribution to English and Dutch economic progress which was undoubtedly vital, even if it is difficult to quantify.

Such influences should not be overlooked. But broadly the historian must try to balance the advantages and disadvantages conferred by the vast impersonal forces at work – especially those of population increase and price inflation – and the effects of increased rational attention to economic problems. The results were, inevitably, a patchwork of good and evil, success and failure. There was some stimulus to the production of necessities. Production of food and goods probably increased. Some groups of men benefited, especially commercial entrepreneurs and those landowners who burst through the barriers of law and custom to seize their share of the profits. Yet the constrictions on expansion and improvement in agriculture and industry remained tight. So while the growth of demand helped to break up the crust of habits which survived from the medieval economies, it also created new distress by sharpening the edge of natural disasters, plagues, bad harvests, famines, droughts, for the expropriated and rootless members of society. Vast armies of paupers, vagrants and unemployed flooded the roads and cities, creating problems of health and order beyond the resources of contemporary authority to control. Among the new exports of the age were the mercenaries (like the Irish, Scots and Swiss as well as the overflow of Spain's unemployed) who formed the underfed, often unpaid and mutinous armies of the day. Hence perhaps the violence and viciousness with which governments made desperate by their own impotence and bankruptcy persecuted minorities and dissidents like Protestants and Jews. Hence the need for the Poor Law of Queen Elizabeth in 1601 authorizing the raising of a poor rate to support the deserving needy, and the appointment of overseers to administer its outlay. Hence the extraordinary growth of charities, provided for mainly by the merchants of

English cities in the sixteenth and seventeenth centuries, to pay not only for bread and coal for the poor but also – and more fundamentally important – for their schooling and training in the socially useful arts through apprenticeship. Similar bourgeois philanthropy was characteristic of the Dutch cities and of Venice.

Whether analyzed by geographical area, or by class structure, economies under the pressures we have examined responded unevenly. An optimistic eulogy of Elizabethan society like William Harrison's *Description of England* (1587) must be read critically, although its encomia of the new buildings, replete with chimneys, windows of the new glass, growing inventories of linen and furniture are borne out by more objective evidence. Even Harrison's cheerful panegyric is interspersed with less edifying testimony to the nature of contemporary society – lists of 'the several disorders and degrees amongst our idle vagabonds' including 'priggers or prancers, swaddlers or pedlars, drunken tinkers, whipjacks, etc' (among the men) and 'morts, bawdry-baskets, doxis, kinching morts, walking morts, kinching coes, dells etc.', to quote only a few of the 'ungracious female rabble'. Yet even if we allow for Harrison's general optimism, it was something that the best journalist of the day *was* an optimist. The same might be said of the Dutch artists who were beginning to use their towns as backgrounds for group or individual portraits. These 'social' painters breathe growing confidence and optimism. Churches, houses, streets, flowers – whatever the subject may be – are light and cheerful. Sitters expected the artist to make the best of them and their world. The contrast between the treatment of poverty and the poor in Hieronymus Bosch's *Prodigal Son* (probably early sixteenth-century) and Jan de Bray's *Tending the Orphans* (1663) shows the transition through which the Republic had passed in the interval. Bosch's obscure but evidently pessimistic morality has given way to a gay and balanced treatment of the theme of poverty. Even the orphans are conspicuously cheerful and well-fed.

The evidence of social movement from literary or visual sources is notoriously unreliable and difficult to interpret. So are the so-called 'social statistics'. Yet there can be little doubt that the years 1550–1650 saw substantial economic and social progress in some areas of the west, especially along the Atlantic seaboard. It was patchy, subject to dreadful interruptions and exceptions (western and north-western France in the 1630s for example). If bouts of rural prosperity were partially counteracted by interludes of famine and dearth, urban growth was disfigured by frightful disease, poverty and mortality. Sometimes, and in some places, progress precarious, and almost imperceptible. But it was never wholly reversed, as it was farther east, beyond the Elbe, or in parts of Spain and southern Italy. To go east was to go from lands of modest hope, if hope often deferred and interrupted, to lands where hopelessness was not only endemic but deepening.

3

THE STRUCTURE OF POLITICS
IN THE MODERN STATE

THE POLICY-MAKERS

THE POLICY-MAKERS

The economic changes, linked with equally important changes in the nature of political institutions, add up to the transition from medieval to modern which historians have long seen as characteristic of the sixteenth and seventeenth centuries. These changes turned upon the nature of the state itself; upon the nature of the monarchical authority within the state; and upon consequential changes in the nature of those classes and groups within the state which were the repository of a degree of authority complementary to that of the monarch.

The relationship of politics to economic change was no more predictable than the course of economic change itself. Nor can it be argued that political or cultural change was a simple function of the latter. The 'new monarchy' and the 'modern state' meant different things in different places and arrived at different times. Just as the response of Spain and the Netherlands to the price rise was totally different, so was their attitude to monarchy itself. Though challenged by noble faction, monarchy in Spain survived, bankrupt but prestigious. In the Netherlands the nobility, the original leaders of opposition to the policies of Philip II, finally retreated into obedience to Spain, taking what was later Belgium with them. One of their number, William the Silent, continued the alliance with Calvinists and merchants to achieve independence for a loose federal republic of towns and provinces of the north Netherlands which contradicted every contemporary assumption regarding the need for a central authority.

In England monarchical authority was put on a firm basis by Henry

VII. The Tudor claim had been challenged by a combination of conservative interests during the Pilgrimage of Grace in 1536. It was to be challenged again in 1571 by the noble 'Rising of the North'. There was to be a rebellion by Essex in 1601. But such factions merely strengthened the common loyalty of the Protestant nobility, gentry, middle classes and common people to an authority whose general success had enabled it to be identified with the national interest. The contrast with Germany and the Empire was total. In England, Henry VIII and Elizabeth succeeded in harnessing the Reformation to their dynastic needs. In Germany, too, Luther had extrapolated an earlier revolt of lawyers, humanists, political thinkers and townsmen against the Pope and the rich prelates and ecclesiastical corporations who represented Papal interests in the country. Yet these linked protests against church corruption and for local independence ended, not by unifying Germany but by splitting it, destroying the already fading powers of the Emperor. The beneficiaries of the Reformation and the new economic ideas of the sixteenth century were the princes, especially the Electors of Bavaria, Saxony and later of Brandenburg. The princes needed income. They found it in the taxes they raised on goods passing in, out of or through their territory. So, while England was becoming economically more unified – even achieving a national economic policy enforced by government – Germany was each year becoming more divided by customs and toll barriers. Thus the great droves of thirty to forty thousand cattle which left Jutland each year to walk to Hamburg and onwards had to pay five separate lots of customs dues before they were through Schleswig. The same economic barriers which provided four hundred princes with money were also to keep Germany relatively poor and backward until the customs union of 1834.

Similarly, in Italy, albeit for quite different reasons, an area with an appearance of geographical unity (though as in Spain the obstructions of mountain ranges made the unity more apparent than real) was left divided by the events of the period following Charles VIII's invasion in 1494 into a collection of smaller states. More than anything, it was the devastation of the subsequent Franco-Spanish wars down to the Treaty of Le Cateau-Cambrésis in 1559 which damaged the high economy of north Italy. The sole surviving republic in any real sense was Venice, which remained the largest and richest of the north Italian states until the eighteenth century. Genoa, though remaining nominally a republic, was dominated from 1528 by the energetic admiral of ancient Genoese lineage, Andrea Doria, who put it under Imperial protection to save it from the French. Doria, still putting to sea to fight the Barbary corsairs at the age of ninety, was the kind of buccaneer who was thrown up by the *Calamitá d'Italia*. With equal but chillier ruthlessness the younger branch of the Medici extinguished the older line of their family by the murder of Duke Alessandro. With the approval of Charles v to his nomination the new ruler, Cosimo 1, swiftly marched against the noble families, led by the Strozzi, who opposed his rule. On 31 July 1537 he was completely victorious. So in yet another ancient republic was inaugurated a reign of strict repression, heavy taxation and aggressive campaigns against its neighbours. Siena and Lucca were eventually joined into the larger Grand Duchy of Tuscany. Thus Tuscany entered on the long reign of the Medici; a characteristic mélange of assassinations and poisonings, high culture and scientific exploration; of gross acts of tyranny and autocratic benevolence.

If it was true, as George Duby has said, that Italy had discovered an ethos different from that which governed the minds of rulers elsewhere in Europe – one in which trade did not demean but was seen as the source of wealth, and wealth as the source of power – then it is to Venice, Genoa, Florence and Milan that we must look for the evidence. Elsewhere, conditions were different. The Papal States, for example, certainly illustrate the theme of political centralization of the age. Throughout the sixteenth century the Papal frontiers were extended, Bologna, Ravenna, Rimini, Ancona, Ferrara successively annexed, while internally an emasculated Roman nobility were reduced to abject submission. Only a minority of dissidents ('banditry') tried to roll back the onward march of Papal aggression, grandiose town planning, luxurious and splendid buildings – and the burden of taxes they cost. St Peter's alone cost forty-four tons of silver to build – a whole year's Papal income as it was calculated in the 1590s. Yet the new state was a bureaucracy rather than a business. It lived on debts and taxes not on production. Much of its income had come from abroad. But this was less now than formerly, and income from Northern Europe was down to a fraction of its former volume. Hence the need for territorial expansion and bureaucratic efficiency.

Naples was, as ever, atypical. Under Spanish control from 1504, its history in this period was one of turbulence and riots, often provoked by famine. For an astonishing period it threatened to become a centre of Protestantism and attempts to introduce the Inquisition had provoked tumults in 1510 and 1547. Thereafter the monarchy and nobility patched up their differences by a kind of feudal contract recognizing their mutual rights and obligations. Possibly this was an indication of Neopolitan and Sicilian remoteness from the world of the new monarchy. Possibly it was a product of alarm at the recurrent outbreaks of popular resentment against unemployment, falling wages, rising prices, oligarchy and corruption. Unlike the revolts in France, Spain, Portugal, even England, the revolts of Naples owed little to noble leadership. The hunger riots of 1585, the revolt led by Campanella (the philosopher) in 1599 and by Masaniello (a fisherman) in 1647 owed nothing to noble discontent. Closer to the French outbreaks of the 1630s, there was also in them a genuine element of idealism, a search for justice against intolerable oppression and deprivation. The death of Masaniello has had an irresistible appeal for poets, operatic composers and radicals ever since.

The neo-feudal compact of Naples was not repeated elsewhere. The more usual trend was towards the consolidation of the state, the concentration of princely power and authority (contemporaries were beginning to doubt whether they ought to continue the medieval habit of distinguishing one from the other). The great sprawling empire of Charles v consisted of Castile, with Navarre and Granada, possessions in North Africa, the new colonies in America, Aragon, Valencia, Catalonia, Naples, Sicily and Sardinia, together with the Habsburg states in Germany and Central Europe, the Netherlands and Burgundy. Charles's empire brought vast liabilities but few assets, for the exploitation of the riches of America had scarcely begun and the military and financial resources of Germany could only be tapped through the cumbrous machinery of the Imperial Diet. The liabilities were only too evident: the Turk was advancing up the Danube and through the Mediterranean, while Lutheranism was dividing Germany state by state. Charles inherited the old quarrel with France, whose Francis i was also a candidate for the Empire. Against the Protestants Charles might have expected Papal help; against the French, help from the English. He received little from either but cold dislike.

The historian may be excused some hindsight if he discerns in the Imperial Declaration (1548) on the Netherlands and in the religious settlement of the Treaty of Augsburg (1555) a hint of what was to come later and form the nub of the treaties of 1648. The former effectively severed the Netherlands from the Empire and incorporated them in the Burgundian Circle; only a nominal feudal tie bound some provinces to the Empire. The Treaty of Augsburg, with its principle of *cujus regio, ejus religio*, had conceded to Lutheran princes not only the right to legalize Lutheran rites within their territories but to retain the church lands they had already taken. As a devout Catholic, even though betrayed by the Pope, Charles had shrunk from putting his own hand to the German religious settlement. In the 1520s in the Netherlands, when persuaded that his edicts against heresy were embarrassing foreign trade, he had agreed that they should not affect the foreign merchants at Antwerp and in other cities. That was as far as he would go. He was, after all, of the old dispensation, but not simply a bigot. His advisers were inclined to Erasmianism. His favourite confessor, Loaysa, believed in compromise. Some members of his court and chapel were later to be victims of the Inquisition. He might not stomach heresy among his own subjects; but the idea of co-existence with Protestants outside his dominions was not unthinkable. It was a dividing-line between the Middle Ages and the early modern world.

Charles's abdication on 25 October 1555 in the Hall of the Golden Fleece at Brussels was an admission of personal defeat. But it was also an admission that his ramshackle empire was out of date and impracticable. With him, his timidity and fundamental simplicity, some good went out of the world. His empire was divided into two: this was inevitable. Ferdinand took German and Central European lands of the Habsburgs. Philip took Spain and its Italian and colonial possessions, with – fatally – the Netherlands. Yet the real division now was more complicated. For if Germany and Bohemia were split into Catholic and Lutheran, the Netherlands was already dividing into Catholic and Calvinist. There was a curiously appropriate irony in the exit of the old Emperor, in tears, leaning on the arm of a favourite young prince of his court, William of Orange.

The impact of the Reformation on the political structure of France was equally dramatic, though totally different, in nature. Like Lutheranism in Germany, Calvinism in France spread with a rapidity that is astonishing in a world where literacy was still so restricted and communications so poor.

With all the confidence of a man who felt himself to be the authorized bearer of the truth, Calvin had already addressed protests to Francis I against the appalling corruption of the Church and appealed for royal leniency towards the growing body of Protestants. His writings suggest two conclusions: that the state of the Church in France resulting in part from the Concordat of 1516 between King and Pope was at least as deplorable as in Germany or England. The Concordat had given the King vast patronage in the Church. He nominated to bishoprics, abbeys and priories, and a flood of secular and scandalous appointments had resulted. Typical of the pluralism and corruption was the Cardinal of Lorraine who was Archbishop of Rheims, Bishop of Metz and Verdun and prior of eleven abbeys, commanding a known income of three hundred thousand livres a year. Under the wing of such leading ecclesiastics, the lower holy orders had become a refuge for the idle, ungodly and illiterate. That, at any rate, was Calvin's view, and it was widely held. As a second consequence, Calvin inherited – indeed he was himself a part of – an already large and receptive audience which eagerly awaited doctrines designed to reform the French Church.

Calvin's careful system of church organization, designed to purify not only the Church and the priesthood but the morals of the laity too, had an extraordinary appeal which went far beyond that of Luther's theology. It was most potent when addressed, as it was in the earliest stages, to the professional classes (in France especially to the lawyers), to merchants, to university graduates, including the worthier members of the lower clergy and friars. By the 1550s the enthusiasm for reform was spreading to the gentry and the nobility – to the whole mass of those, in fact, who were discontented, anti-clerical, looking for promotion and resentful for not being given it. Its strongholds were around Lyons, throughout Provence, Languedoc and Navarre, around Orleans, in parts of Normandy, and Brittany, and around Bordeaux. By 1560 it had more than two thousand churches.

Before 1550 there were already signs that in France, as in other countries, this was to be the age of a new monarchy. Francis I had evinced many of the qualities needed for a national hero: he was handsome, chivalrous, warlike. The Concordat with the Papacy promised to speed him on the road to absolute authority: he never arrived. On the contrary, under Francis and his successor, Henry II, France slid even more deeply into bankruptcy caused by the incessant and as yet unprovoked wars against Charles V and even England. Francis, disciple of Machiavelli and would-be 'Caesar' (as his mother Louise of Savoy proudly called him), sat willingly at the feet of the Roman jurists like Duprat and Payet, the prophets of centralized government, autocracy, bureaucracy, anti-feudalism and anti-nobility. Their work was in one sense supererogatory. The basis of true feudalism, the mutual contract between king and nobility, was already disappearing under external pressures more powerful than those of individuals. The course of events was, however, to be diverted or postponed in the case of France by a disastrous series of accidents.

The first was the death of Henry II in circumstances of characteristic triviality during the festivities to celebrate the signing of the peace treaties of 1558 between France, the Empire, Spain and England and the marriage arrangements that followed. The king was wounded in the head by his opponent's lance in a tilting match with the Count of Montgomery and died soon after. His death was little mourned. Henry had few brains and less charm. His cold fanaticism had only embittered the discontents of all France. But his death had one consequence which was to cost France forty years of misery, slaughter and destruction. Innately stable as the post-feudal institutions of France were – the customary privileges and duties, the strong sense of legalism – they were not strong enough to fill the gaping hole which now yawned in the French polity with the accession of a minor, Francis II, feeble in mind as in body and still strongly influenced by his mother, Catherine de Medici. She was typical of the prolific and successful Tuscan family from which she came, Florentine merchants who had risen via trading and finance to vast wealth and political power, the ancestors of royalty in England as well as France. Three Medici Popes ruled the Church between 1500 and 1560, including Clement VII. Catherine, by default the key figure in French politics for nearly thirty years, came out of the shadows only gradually, for as Henry II's wife she had been eclipsed by his mistress, Diane de Poitiers. Now she girded herself to steer, successively, her four sons through the political jungle which her husband had bequeathed. The sister of Alessandro de Medici, she had all the dramatic instinct, the ambition, the sharp sense of intrigue and the ruthlessness of the Medici. She was often compared with her contemporary, Elizabeth of England: the comparison is not a good one. She was self-indulgent and loved luxury (witness her designs for her Palace of the Tuileries) where Elizabeth was economical, even mean. She had none of the sense of *rapport* with the people over whom she ruled or their traditions which sustained Elizabeth through successive crises. She was not French. She had none of the confidence that came from belonging to a genuinely successful and popular dynasty. She inherited no entourage of tried and trusted servants of state. She was lonely, suspicious, unconfident and she had none of the political ability or prudence which enabled Elizabeth (in domestic affairs at least to distinguish between a short-term expedient and a long-term policy. Worst of all, the problems she had to face were incomparably more complex. For now, bursting the restraints placed on them by a combination of bribes, punishments and military diversions of half a century, the nobility of France posed a serious threat to monarchy. Of the great nobles the chief were the Bourbons, next in line for the throne to the Valois; the Guises, powerful in Church as well as state; and their great rivals, the Montmorencys. Between them, these three great clans shared a substantial proportion of the territory of France – the Guises in the east, the Montmorencys in the middle, the Bourbons in west and south. Religion in these areas tended to follow their patronage. The Guises, led by the Duke of Guise, brilliant soldier and captor of Calais, and Charles, Cardinal of Lorraine, were unshakeably Catholic. Anne de Montmorency, Constable of France, was likewise a staunch Catholic but his three nephews were Huguenots, and of these Gaspard de Coligny, the eldest, was Admiral of France. Of the Bourbons, Louis of Condé and Antony of Navarre were already converts to Calvinism by 1559. The accession of Francis II in that year saw the opening of a struggle for power between these three great noble houses. It was to divide the country for the best part of a century until the realization of its futility finally brought France face to face with her absolutist destiny in the person of Louis XIV.

Elizabeth of England's problems were serious but much less daunting when she succeeded her sister Mary in November 1558. Mary's marriage to Philip of Spain and her bloody persecution of English Protestants had made her unpopular and her death had been the signal for indecent rejoicings. Elizabeth had learned prudence the hard way. She had never been legitimized after her mother, Anne Boleyn, was divorced. She had narrowly escaped an involvement with malcontents and she was imprisoned in the Tower of London by Mary in 1554.

Elizabeth came to the throne with great assets and serious liabilities. The assets were her lineage and the success of her father and his ministers – Thomas Cromwell in particular – in developing Parliament as a partner in the work of government; its functions included those of mobilizing the support of the 'political nation' behind Tudor decisions, especially over royal marriages and divorces, the consequential succession arrangements, the settlement of the Anglican Church after the breach with Rome, and the provision of funds for the maintenance of the monarchy and its politics, domestic and foreign. All these institutions and policies were continued and developed by Elizabeth, in so far as she was able to do so within the limits imposed by her sex. The anti-clericalism and chauvinism which underlay the English Reformation had already downed some of those great feudal magnates (especially in the remote and backward regions north of the Trent) whose wings had not been sufficiently clipped by Henry VII and his ministers. The Pilgrimage of Grace (1536) had been an ill-organized rising of confused conservatives in religion and much else, a rabble that numbered in its doomed and straggling ranks great lords, gentry, priests and peasants. Several hundred of them were executed. Opposition to Tudor rule was thereafter muted, if not wholly extinguished. The spoils of the Reformation – lands of abbeys and monasteries – found their way into the hands of enterprising men. The great beneficiaries were the gentry.

It was these 'middle sort of people' – some now risen to the nobility – with whom the queen surrounded herself. The House of Commons contained many of the knights and esquires who had prospered; the House of Lords not a few who had prospered even more bounteously. More important still, they were the men who occupied offices in her palaces, her household and, above all, in the Privy Council. This was where the executive business of the realm was done. Everything, from trivial matters affecting individuals to the great issues of diplomacy, peace, war, government income and expenditure, was discussed and decided in the Council. The business was in the hands of men of talent. They might also be men of birth and breeding, but essentially the Tudor Council was a meritocracy. Paulet, Bacon, the Cecils, Walsingham, Mildmay, Sackville – held office not by right but by ability. Mostly they were country gentry, often with some sort of legal training at the Inns of Court. But they survived because they had stamina and judgment. Not a few of her admirers – Walsingham (the 'pale puritan' whom Elizabeth did not like but found indispensable), Thomas Wilson, Daniel Rogers, Thomas Bodley – were puritans who had gone into Genevan exile in Queen Mary's time. As servants or members of the Council they were in the curious position of helping to 'manage' their fellow puritans in Parliament – to keep an eye on their Protestant patriotism, to see that it did not lead Parliament and England into expensive anti-Catholic foreign policies of which the Queen disapproved. For, despite the wide powers of the Council in government, the Queen always had the last word.

Elizabeth faced, with equanimity, two challenges to her commanding authority. From 1568–71 the old religion represented by the Duke of Norfolk and the northern Earls – the Percys and Nevilles especially – and in 1601 Robert Devereux, Earl of Essex, her favourite but a man of rash and ungovernable temper, set themselves up against her. Both represented the dying gasp of a feudal nobility which saw itself as having a feudal *claim* to participate in the government of England. They realized, on the block, that they had lived too long and learnt too little. In the new scheme of things devised by the Tudors and the professional servants whom they had bound to them, there was no place for such pretensions. Government was now a pyramid of power. On the top sat the monarch. Her power rested on a base broader than that of the old hereditary nobility. For the nobles there was still room, but they were increasingly to be creations of the crown, mostly of gentry origin, not Howards, Percys, Nevilles or Dacres. They survived on sufferance of good behaviour; they had no charter to disturb the national peace from their backwoods redoubt in the north or elsewhere.

So the realm was slowly knit together. It is too soon to speak of 'national policies' except in fairly broad terms, meaning a degree of unification and a sense that within the boundaries of England and Wales men could expect to be treated alike, to be subject to the same laws. Yet there were intimations already of a measure, small and imperfect, of economic nationalism. Customs might be still thought of principally as a source of revenue rather than as an instrument of economic policy designed to protect, say, English manufactures. It would be a little time before the Lord Treasurer (Burghley or his successor Thomas Sackville, Earl of Dorset) thought of his office as carrying much responsibility beyond that of maintaining the revenues of the royal 'Manor of England' and ensuring a measure of social and economic stability. Yet spasmodically the Lord Treasurer would intervene in other matters. To guard the realm's currency and bullion was among his duties. To see that coinage, weights and measures were uniform and to conserve England's output of wool, so that English clothiers might command adequate materials to maintain fullest employment and maximum exports, also came within his purview. From such sparse but significant beginnings the larger concepts of economic nationalism which developed later were to flow. Everywhere the English state was taking over the regulation of industry and economic life from the gilds and town governments. The laws made by Parliament might still have a medieval flavour. The maintenance of the 'just price', the condemnation of speculators and all middlemen who profited by scarcity and the common misery, the suspicions of usury – all lived on for the moment. But increasingly the intention was to embody them in national laws made by a national legislature and uniformly enforced by a national judiciary. Intention often ran a long way ahead of performance, but the change of climate was unmistakable.

Embryonic all this might be; and easily exaggerated by hindsight. But it already went beyond contemporary developments in, say, Spain. Outwardly, the Spanish mode of government had something in common with that of England. Philip II, from the moment he became king, bent himself towards policies of unification and centralization. On the face of it, the Spanish administrative system bore some resemblance to that of Elizabeth. There was a Royal Council, served by a succession of diligent secretaries. Of these Mateo Vasquez stood out as the principal for nearly two decades after his appointment in 1573 as royal secretary. He was Seville-born, of humble origin, carefully trained in the exigent school of cathedral management at Seville and the even more exigent service of the Inquisition, where he became secretary to Diego de Espinosa, regent of Navarre, president of the Casa de Contrataçion (which handled the American silver supply), Inquisitor-General from 1564 and President of the Royal Council from 1565. He was made cardinal in 1568. His training and assiduity gave Vasquez an unassailable pre-eminence in the administrative history of Philip's reign. His finger was in every pie.

At the centre of the growing labyrinth of government – supervising in detail the Inquisitorial witch-hunts, the detailed and misguided fiscal exactions, the daily torrent of diplomatic memoranda on the state of France, England, the Netherlands, the Turks and the Indies, his ear cocked to catch the verbal hints, libels, innuendoes on Spain's ambassadors and generals overseas too secret even to be committed to paper, and busy with a thousand personal trivia – sat the king himself. His psychology is so oddly fascinating that it is not surprising that it came to form the basis of the 'Black Legend' elaborated by historians like Motley, for whom Philip became the embodiment of evil. The truth seems to be that his was a case of a son dominated by a powerful father. His early years as King of Spain demonstrated repeatedly his timidity, indecision and hesitations. He mistrusted himself as much as those around him and his insecurity was not lessened by the personal misfortunes which befell him – the loss of his three wives and the madness of his son, Don Carlos. As he grew older his youthful nervousness was overlaid but not dispersed by an increasingly bigoted obstinacy. This also grew not from strength but from feebleness of character. The retreat to the Escorial, the ceaseless pursuit of work for its own sake, the incessant, laborious minuting and composition of papers on every conceivable topic important or trivial, the endless manipulation of an elaborate system of personal espionage and informing – all point in the same direction. They were not the means of coping with reality but of escaping from it: not a policy but an anodyne. The decisions that were to reduce Spain to ruin and poverty for centuries were not the mysterious working-out of some destiny hatched in the mines of Potosi; they were the product of a mind in the Escorial that grew each year more remote from reality.

Though the period saw Spain steadily decline from pre-eminence and wealth to defeat and poverty in Europe, Spanish domestic government, in its grim repression and its rigorous economic *dirigisme* approached dictatorship more nearly than any contemporary major power.

In Sweden, it had appeared that Gustavus Vasa, that 'greedy and ruthless tyrant' who also ran Sweden 'with the assurance and authority of an improving landlord',[18] might erect a new centralizing, hereditary monarchy with the support of the *riksdag* and its four estates playing a role somewhat like that of the Tudor Parliament. Yet it was not easy to 'improve' this backward land of poor soil (the good soil in the south belonged to Denmark, the hated enemy), forests and lakes. Sixteenth-century Sweden had no towns, no squirearchy, no middle class. Its trade was often still conducted through barter, and its industries, such as they were, by gilds. The only natural allies of the prince were the peasants who divided Sweden with their noble masters. So Gustavus's ambitions were abortive. After his death in 1560 there was a reversion – the first in the cycle – to an aristocratic constitution when the Swedish nobility took to reading revolutionary neo-Calvinist literature like the *Vindiciae Contra Tyrannos* and the Council of Nobles resumed its role in politics.

This phase ended with the murder of Erik Sparre, the spokesman for the aristocratic party, in 1600. Sweden reverted once more to monarchical but not absolute rule. When Gustavus Adolphus succeeded in 1611 it seemed only too likely that he might move further towards absolutism, educated as he had been to regard the years of aristocratic rule as a victory for treachery. Yet in practice he honoured his pledge to respect the powers of the Council of Nobles and more than two decades of harmony followed – not least perhaps because the king was so often away on military business. With his death in 1634 the *riksdag* itself began to press for more of a say in government. Slowly the social structure of Sweden was changing. Towns and ports had grown, the nucleus of a gentry and merchant class was emerging to contest the claim of the great magnates to their monopoly of office and their exemption from tax. By 1650 'a whole new middle class was angrily knocking at the gate of power'.[19] The old dualism of power was under challenge. Sweden was to be the only country in Europe where the medieval estates managed to transform themselves into a parliament and one of the few havens of constitutionalism in the age of seventeenth- and eighteenth-century absolutism. There was indeed throughout the struggle for power a redeeming degree of respect for law and personal liberty that placed Sweden nearer to England than to Spain or Germany in matters of government.

Monarchy, in one form or another, was increasingly becoming the symbol of the new territorial groupings which were partially consolidating themselves into nation states. The orders of society were arranged in a way which contemporaries thought of as a set of concentric rings. The imagery was extended further. Was the prince not the sun, around which the planets moved in orbit, ranging from the greatest to the smallest? Did not

> The heavens themselves, the planets, and this centre
> Observe degree, priority and place. . . .[20]

But how, in a world which had no police and only temporary and unreliable armed forces, was 'order' or 'degree' to be observed, except by universal and dutiful recognition of the chaos which would surely follow if the hierarchical principle was broken or rejected.

There were nevertheless three states in sixteenth-century Europe which were not monarchies. One, the confederation of Swiss Cantons, had thrown off its allegiance to the Empire to achieve independence under government of patricians and great landowners who had long since acquired an ascendancy over the peasantry, finally confirmed in the last war against them in 1652–3. Apart from the evolution of Calvinism Swiss affairs were largely parochial. Very different and of lasting fascination was the second and most ancient of the exceptions to princely rule, the Venetian Republic, and the third and newest exception, the

Dutch Republic. The former was still in 1550 full of vigour (*pace* these pessimist historians who used to mark Venetian decline from the Portuguese discovery of the Cape route to the Indies), still the largest and most resilient of the north Italian states. By the 1580s Amsterdam was preparing to assume the role formerly fulfilled by Antwerp as the greatest entrepôt of north-west Europe and combine with it the industrial role formerly played by Ghent and Bruges, now being drawn back under Spanish obedience. H. R. Trevor-Roper has epitomized the European role and relationship of these areas a little before our period begins:

By 1500 all the techniques of industrial capitalism were concentrated in a few cities strung along the old Rhineland route from Flanders to Italy. At one end was Antwerp, heir to Bruges, and Ghent, commanding the old Flemish cloth industry and financing the extractive industry of Liège; at the other end were the Italian cities, the commercial and financial cities of Venice and Genoa, the industrial cities of Milan and Florence. To these had recently been added two new centres: Augsburg, whose cloth industry raised the huge financial superstructure of the Fugger and other families and enabled them to rival even Antwerp, concentrating in their hands the extractive industry of Central Europe; and Lisbon, the capital of a new world-wide commercial empire, with possibilities of long-distance trade undreamed of before. These were the centres of European capitalism in 1500. In some way or other, between 1550 and 1620, most of these centres were convulsed, and the secret techniques of capitalism were carried away to other cities, to be applied in new lands.[21]

Of all the great cities of north Italy, Venice took the most unconscionable time to die. Its galleys, descended from the triremes of the ancients, with their galleries of oarsmen, were becoming outmoded, vulnerable to artillery in war and to piracy in peace. Like the other Mediterranean powers, Venice lagged behind the English, Dutch and Portuguese. Like them, Venice was powerless to retain her outposts in Greece and the islands of the eastern Mediterranean before the grinding pressure of the Turks, backed by seemingly inexhaustible resources of manpower and the heavy artillery which they borrowed from Western expertise. Euboea was lost in 1470, Cyprus in 1571, Crete survived until 1645. Yet in 1550 Venice probably still commanded larger fertile territories than any other Italian state. (The Papal States were larger but more mountainous). The *terra firma* stretched more than two hundred kilometres westwards, past Verona, beyond Bergamo and almost to Milan; northwards another hundred or more kilometres to the Alps and the boundaries of Tyrol and Corinthia; then eastwards around the north coast of the Adriatic and southwards past Istria. And as she felt the strains of war and competition in trade growing, her great merchants turned their capital and enterprise increasingly to land and industry.

How was Venice governed? Of the Italian city states in the fifteenth century Ranke wrote: 'They were neither nations nor races; neither cities nor kingdoms; they were the first *states* in the world.' Contemporary writers in the fifteenth and sixteenth centuries debated the nature of their government *qua* states, and later historians have often adopted their terminology, defining some as 'republics', some as 'despotisms'. Venice was a republic. Yet just as the so-called 'despotisms' showed a regard for law and order, legitimacy and hereditary privileges, so the 'republics' were usually careful to avoid anything like popular democracy. Venice was more oligarchic than Florence, where the struggles between old families and *arrivistes* had let in a measure of democracy through the gilds and there was some popular participation in the vigorous, if corrupt, political life of the city.

More than any other Italian state, the Venetian Republic had become recognized as politically stable. Since freeing itself from the Byzantine Empire it had been ruled by the elected Doge, the chief republican magistrate, assisted by *procuratores* (proctors); its governing elite consisted of some two thousand or more adult male patricians. In the city of Venice itself, the patriciate was by now a closed caste; similarly in the other cities of the republic like Brescia, Padua or Verona, where governors appointed by Venice itself for short periods of office conducted a sort of colonial surveillance. The Great Council had come to consist of a thousand members as Venice had been faced with the task of absorbing into her government all those newly rich who had risen on the tide of her prosperity. Below them were the shopkeepers and craftsmen, a second-class citizenry but nevertheless a citizenry, who could still influence the life of the city through their gilds and corporations. The rulers could therefore still talk of liberty as a virtue of the republic. The Venetian ruling class remained strongly associated with trade; they did not (like some of the dependent-city rulers) become *rentiers* or mere officials, and they still wore the long gowns with wide sleeves which proclaimed their civil, rather than military, origin. They were generally a prudent, even puritanical caste, economical and utilitarian. There was little vulgar ostentation in their way of life; the Venetian poor were carefully provided for; the less fortunate young trained in useful arts. But oligarchy, like despotism, needed its public safety committee, its spies and informers, its apparatus of control over sedition: '– for its people there was perhaps, little to choose between the corporate authoritarianism of a dominant city and the personal absolutism of a monarchic ruler – save that the first was more enduring'.[22]

Yet was this the whole truth? Was Venice merely another closed oligarchy, another elitist, pseudo-libertarian clique? There are both circumstances and individuals to suggest a different view. In accumulaing a mercantile empire, the Venetian Republic had also accumulated responsibilities, material and political, and developed a broader vision of the world and of her place in it. The *relative* decline of her power by the late sixteenth century speeded the process of accommodation by reducing the number of problems Venice could solve simply by force of arms. Her policies became more devious, more subtle, more diplomatic and less military. Their commercial involvements alone – apart from their innate humanism – made the oligarchs unwilling to join in Papal or Spanish confrontations with the Turks or Protestants. This breadth of view was to be represented by the philosophers, scientists, poets and artists who provided the ethos of the Venetian Indian summer – above all by the humanist Paolo Sarpi, the historians Tiepolo and Niccolò Contarini, the geometrician da Ponte.

When our period opens, the northern terminus of the nexus of trade routes by land and sea which ended in the north Italian quadrilateral of Venice, Milan, Genoa and Florence was the Netherlands. Still formally a part of the Empire, they had come into it through the incorporation of the Netherland territories of the Duke of Burgundy, who in the course of the fifteenth century had acquired Flanders, Brabant, then Holland, Zeeland, Luxembourg, Hainault and other Walloon (French-speaking) provinces. After 1477, the Netherlands had passed to the Habsburgs. But the association with the Empire had been weakened, as we have noted, in 1548. And within the Netherlandish conglomeration of cities, the centralizing urge was, and was to remain, weak. The Dukes of Burgundy and the Habsburgs had done something to create a common consciousness among the feudal magnates and city governments who composed these *Lagelanden* of Europe. The Walloon nobles of the south – Hainault especially – had been enriched by Habsburg grants of estates, Habsburg endowments from taxation and high office. The most exclusive international noble club – the Order of the Golden Fleece – had been created for their benefit. They had been appointed to the 'stadholderships' of the different provinces.

The other repository of wealth and power besides the (largely) Walloon nobility were the cities, numerous, sizeable, rich and peopled by an independent race of craftsmen and tradesmen who pursued their ancient rights with an indomitable obstinacy that did not waver before the Emperor himself. As often as not Ghent – 'energetic, opulent, powerful, passionate, unruly Ghent'[23] – second city of the Netherlands after Antwerp, was found at the centre of opposition to the tax and religious policics of its overlords. And Ghent, with the other cities, the great and growing complex called Antwerp especially, was part of Charles's empire which by a natural but tragic mischance was handed over to Philip of Spain. The problem needed no elaboration except perhaps to Philip and those of his advisers who knew only Spain: he came to the Netherlands not as a king, but as duke, or less, in each of his provinces. And in each he faced formidable 'liberties' and privileges, supposedly ancient, claimed by custom or grant by both the nobility and the cities.

Of the cities, in 1550, Antwerp was by far the largest. The first half of the century saw its rapid development from a leading centre of trade and industry into a world entrepôt at the crossroads of Europe, standing athwart the east–west trade routes between Britain and the Continent and the north–south routes for the Baltic and the Mediterranean. For Guicciardini, that wily and observant Florentine, Antwerp was 'the truly leading city in almost all things, but in commerce it heads all the cities in the world'. The volume of its trade dwarfed even that of Venice. The Venetians themselves admitted it. 'I was astounded and wondered much when I beheld Antwerp, for I saw Venice outdone', wrote a Venetian envoy. From 1500 to 1576 (when it was sacked by the Spaniards) Antwerp was 'the harbour of the Renaissance', headquarters of the northern business of the great Fugger family, centre of the Portuguese spice trade, and staple for the rapidly rising import of English cloth through the Merchant Adventurers' Company. In 1550 their trade reached a record level of 132,000 pieces exported from England, and the majority of this passed through the Antwerp market.

The international character of Antwerp had communicated itself to its governors and thinkers in somewhat the same way that Venice's character had passed into the thought and policies of her political and cultural elite. The Habsburgs had been forced to grant far-reaching privileges to Antwerp especially, reinforcing the Cortenburg charter by which the towns of Brabant kept in check the Emperor or powers of the imperial representative through a council of nobles, commons and clergy. Taxes were negotiated between the representative (the Duke of Brabant) and the City of Antwerp. As imperial margrave the Duke exercised his criminal and civil jurisdiction through the judicial officers but these had to be Brabanters and *poorters* (freemen) of the city. Two burgomasters and eighteen aldermen were the real rulers, with advice from a larger council representing the burghers, nobles and gilds.

Down to the outbreak of the revolt and for a quarter of a century after, the provinces south of the line of the great rivers were much richer than those of the north, with their smaller towns, fishing ports and little in the way of an aristocracy save in Utrecht or Gelderland, where a modest gentry was to be found. It is only possible to understand the rapid rise and transformation of the north into the most advanced economy and civilization of Europe by 1620 if we grasp how much of the wealth, knowledge and culture of the southern Netherlands transferred itself bodily to the north, especially after the arrival of the Duke of Alba and his Spanish troops in 1567. Along with many of the merchants of the cities and the skilled artisans of their many industries went, in abundance, the habits of questioning and independence in political and religious affairs. It was no accident that among the early advisers and closest intimates of William the Silent was the Antwerp dignitary, banker and merchant Jacob van Wesembeeck, a man whose broad economic, political and religious vision was to make itself apparent in many of William's ideas and policies. Notions of political and religious radicalism spread north and west with the exodus of men of more liberal views as well as the dedicated Calvinists and other Protestants who were numerous in Antwerp, Ghent and the industrial areas of west Flanders.

Such was the flood of political and economic experience from the south which went into the melting-pot of northern rebellion. After the 1580s when the south withdrew from the revolt, this experience continued and was reflected through the political arrangements of the seven northern provinces alone. The dominance of the northern towns and their middle-class, mercantile character was mirrored in an immediate diminution of aristocratic influence and representation in the States-General, the traditional assembly of the Netherlands. Only one member represented the nobility as compared with eighteen representing the towns. And indeed it was the town governments, the 'magistrates', who were in future to be the real rulers of the Republic. This class was – as Johan Huizinga, the great Dutch historian, affirmed – formed gradually from the upper strata of the merchant class and was never entirely detached from trade.

The fundamental character and ultimate influence of the class has been the subject of long debate among Dutch historians. For some, like Geyi or Huizinga, it formed a relatively liberal, humane oasis in a contemporary sea of mindless dynastic irrationality, cruelty and religious bigotry; for others, like Robert Fruin, its distinguishing marks were arrogance, selfishness and dishonesty. Whichever view may be right, there can be no doubt that in this class resided such sovereignty as existed in the politically fragmented, atomized society of the Netherlands. This was the source of officers for service in the federal and provincial councils, the army and navy and the voluntary organizations which preserved law and order in the towns and are immortalized in the great collective portraits of their gilds and clubs by Hals and Rembrandt.

Even under Habsburg rule, the towns had secured a considerable measure of freedom of action, but the ruler, his representative or representative Council of State, and the local stadholders, had preserved a rudimentary structure of central government. With the Revolt this now virtually disappeared. Theoretically, the local stadholder, as the surviving remnant of central government, still had a say in the election of local magistrates; but even this fell into disuse. Only in emergencies did the stadholder intervene in local affairs. In practice, sovereignty rested with the towns.

There were to be infinite complications in the relationship of the town magistracies with the House of Orange, as with the House of Habsburg. The quarrel with Spain had broken out because agreement was out of the question between, on one side, the interests of a commercial and industrial society operating an international exchange economy and entrusted to a group of men of flexible, empirical outlook, and on the other, a ruler like Philip II to whom politics was essentially the art of the impossible. Policy – foreign and religious especially – had to be adaptable to the basic interests of the Netherlands. From the time that William the Silent emerged as leader of the revolt, prudent and responsive in the exercise of his vague and limited powers, many members of the Holland town governments dealt, even with him, with reserve and even suspicion. To anticipate the motto of the later bible of Republican policy, the so-called *Maxims of Johan de Witt* (1662), they were already actuated by its fundamental rule – *Ab furore monarchorum, libera nos Domine* ('From the Rage of Monarchs, good Lord deliver us'). More even than among the Venetian oligarchs, distrust of dynasticism, its corruption, extravagance, irrationality and irrelevance to the needs of the governed, was the hallmark of the policies of the oligarchs of the Dutch Republic. And because the Church itself was inextricably a part of the dynasticism of its hereditary rulers, the oligarchs were as determinedly anti-theocratic as they were anti-dynastic. Rid of the tutelage of Rome, they were not prepared to allow the Roman mantle to fall on the shoulders of Geneva. As a class they were therefore rigidly opposed to any claim by the Calvinist pastors to control such elements of local government as education, welfare or religious enforcement. As in the Venetian Republic, an intensive and efficient system of poor relief was directed, not at redistributing wealth, much less at improving social mobility, but at eliminating the beggar and upgrading the children of the poor to respectability and employment. As in England, these were the objects of the private benefactors as well. That such paternalism is out of fashion should not necessarily prevent us from admiring, with Huizinga, the achievement of a ruling caste 'that governed a country for so long, with so little coercion, and generally with so much benevolence'.

4

KINGS AND NOBLES: PARTNERS
OR RIVALS?

The use of the term 'Modern History' in this volume implies no dramatic breach with the past. The business of government everywhere still had a greater or lesser measure of continuity with earlier times. Sixteenth-century governments inherited the duty to preserve law and order: much of the preoccupation with 'economic' problems, when it was not purely fiscal was *au fond* political. For a perpetual threat to the stability of thrones and dynasties came from idle mobs of unemployed driven desperate by starvation and poverty. If the problem had been alleviated in some degree and some places by the growth of trade and industry, it had been made worse in others by the growth of population and the failure to adjust naturally static economies to growing demand, for food especially. The whole problem of government was rendered more acute by the rising cost of wars and of financing the increasingly inflated courts with their growing trains of office-holders, real or sinecure, each with his own establishment of followers, to say nothing of the executants of the programmes of amusement, higher and lower, necessary to ward off *ennui*. And in one important sense, princes shared their problem with the nobles and land-owning gentry who surrounded them. For they too usually suffered by a tradition which left them dependent on incomes that were not easy to expand, derived from capital assets that were not easy to convert into liquid resources – land in particular. The tradition that a king must 'live of his own' and appeal for help only in cases of emergency was no longer helpful in an age when inflation and war seemed to be virtually continuous. In such conditions, only one solution offered itself: more and higher taxes, direct or indirect. The latter were easier and cheaper to collect. Hence the proliferation of imposts of all kinds – even in a society like the Dutch Republic. For if the Republic suffered nothing comparable to the extravagance of royal courts, they did have problems of defence, naval security and war – almost continuously. The Netherlands rebelled not least over taxation. Yet the growing *accijns* (excise duties) vied with those of France by the seventeenth century. The English protested over the Stuart levy of ship-money, but it was the Parliamentary Commonwealth which copied excise from the Dutch; and the governments of the Restoration were to inherit from the Interregnum habits of taxing Englishmen more heavily than Queen Elizabeth would ever have dreamt.

These economic factors worsened a relationship between crown and nobility which had always been complex and had from time to time (as in fifteenth-century England and elsewhere) degenerated into civil war between the monarchy and its 'over-mighty subjects'. Yet basically the feudal compact had lasted because it gave advantages to both contracting parties, lords and vassals. Now the old casual arrangements of the Middle Ages gave place to new, more exigent fashions in taxation; laxity to observance; authority to power; tolerance – in its general 'Erasmian' sense – to intolerance; princely prestige to doctrinal divine right. Everywhere institutional blunt edges were sharpened; dogma replaced informal understanding. Reformation and Counter-Reformation, Calvin and Loyola, were all part of this process. And the end, inevitably, was confrontation and conflict.

One symbol of change was the geographical concentration of royal power. The old peripatetic habits of medieval kings gave way to fixed royal residences. Charles v as Emperor had lived up to his universal office by his incessant travels. No monarch until Napoleon, it has been said, was so widely seen in Europe and Africa.

Yet in this, as in so many respects, Charles represented the end of an era. By the 1560s the universal Empire had faded: Philip ii's Spanish Empire was anchored in the Kingdom of Castile, in the Escorial, that remarkable collection of buildings of which the principal feature was, significantly, the vast church. The palace proper accounted for less than a quarter of the whole; inside it the smallest room was the cell where Philip died and from which he could see the celebration of the Mass during his illnesses. The building of the Escorial took thirty years, from 1563 to 1593. The setting was the dry, gloomy, windswept wilderness some thirty miles north-west of Madrid. To this Philip retreated, with an army of bureaucrats and nobles. It was not only Flemings and Dutch who found this a sinister development. Aragonese and Catalan nobles also saw in the move a portent of a narrower world, no longer universal or even Spanish, but Castilian, parochial in outlook and ideas. The decline of Toledo's industries and population was commonly ascribed to the brilliant counter-attractions offered to its moneyed classes by Madrid which quadrupled in size (100,000 by 1600) after Philip designated it *única corte* in 1561.

Yet Philip's move was not unique. Everywhere the growth of great cities went hand in hand with that of great courts and palaces. Giovanni Botero, the Jesuit political philosopher and administrator of the Papal estates, had clear theories based on his Roman experience about the meaning of this partnership. The residency of a prince magnified cities and attracted people, he wrote,

For where the prince is resident, there also the parliaments are held and the supreme place of justice is then kept. All matters of importance have recourse to that place, all princes and all persons of account, ambassadors of princes and of commonwealths, and all agents of cities . . . all such as aspire and thirst after offices and honours rush thither amain with emulation and disdain for others. Thither are the revenues brought that pertain to the state and there are they desposed of again.[24]

Rome, a city of pilgrims and prostitutes, of piety and conspicuous consumption, had room for half a million visitors by 1600. The Capitol was building, to Michelangelo's plans, from 1564; Sixtus v, pontiff from 1585–90, was the greatest town-planner of his age, developing impressive perspectives and noble vistas. Thus, starting from Italy, the Baroque city became:

a huge theatrical setting for the display of the court, the princes of the church, the nobility and other powerful persons. It was the visual aspect of the political and social change from the city state, with its free citizens, to the capital of the absolute monarch, with its court and its subject inhabitants.[25]

This last was a point of great practical importance. London produced through its customs-house a very large proportion of the indirect taxation due to the Crown before 1640; Stockholm and Antwerp likewise. Such valuable yields were best collected at their source, before the till could be robbed. To the north of Copenhagen, the Danish capital since the mid-fifteenth century, Christian iv built his great castle of Frederiksborg in the early seventeenth century on the site of an earlier building. To Frederiksborg was carried the produce of the toll at Elsinore, on the Danish Sound, the largest single toll in the world. There the king in person could see the solid coin brought in, counted and then slid down a chute to his treasury in the vaults below.

Paris, like London, had long been a political capital. From Paris came the legal customs that spread to the rest of France. But from the time of Francis I Paris also began to be the centre of royal life and ceremonial. The Massacre of St Bartholemew (1572) took place in Paris because it was here that the nobility were assembled for the marriage of Catherine de Medici's daughter, Marguerite de Valois, to the King of Navarre. The civil wars postponed the overhaul of Paris, still dirty and unplanned. Not until Henry IV had restored peace could he and his ministers set about making Paris a fit architectural context for royalty.

The Tudors were slower to follow the fashion. Elizabeth, economical as ever, might be found with her court and officials in one of the royal palaces in the country outside London – Windsor, Greenwich, Oatlands or Nonesuch. Only one – Whitehall – was in London itself. It was still, like the others, a modest affair. The Queen was as likely to be found ensconced with her royal train in a great noble house in the country as in one of her own palaces.

So while in the old commercial cities of the Continent, politically so important in the late Middle Ages, the ruling patricians were seeing their influence whittled away – at Lübeck, Nuremberg, Strasbourg, Augsburg, Cracow, Novgorod – it was the *political* capitals which grew and prospered. Venice held on grimly. Amsterdam and the Dutch towns grew, as did London. But in general there was a strong contrast between the spontaneous growth of commercial seaports, especially along the Atlantic seaboard and the decline of the inland cities where the prince was all-conquering.

Within the political capitals, and the courts they contained, another confrontation was developing between monarchy and nobility. In each court the nobles who surrounded the throne in search of jobs and influence to offset their rising costs and diminishing real incomes became grouped inevitably into factions. Every court in Europe was the scene of festering jealousies and vendettas. Some were of long standing, between ancient enemies. Others were between old nobility and new upstarts from the ennobled bureaucrats. One such feud, in the Netherlands, helped to bring down monarchy and transform political institutions for ever.

The dilemma of court politics was not new, and it was to survive for as long as the institution of monarchy itself: for in a profound sense the fate and fortunes of monarchy were intermingled with those of the nobility and gentry. Kings could not rule without the co-operation of the nobles: yet it was sometimes even harder to rule with it. Many of the European nobility had ancient rights and privileges which made it difficult for them to avoid head-on collision with an aggrandizing prince. Others were great office-holders under the throne and pledged by oath to support political systems which acted as positive curbs on noble ambitions. Throughout Western Europe 'the function of the aristocracy was inherently self-contradictory'.[26] Nor was the danger of conflict purely a domestic matter. The aristocracy shared another characteristic with the royal dynasties. They were essentially international. When the King of Poland, Sigismund Augustus, died in 1572, some forty thousand voters took part in the election of a successor. Henry of Valois, brother of Charles IX, King of France, was duly elected. But his concerns were much less in Poland than in France, where he was busily engaged in securing his rights to succeed to the throne. He immediately ran into difficulties with those Polish nobles to whom he rashly granted generous concessions in order to win their votes. His problems in France were no less complicated, for here he faced the efforts of the Protestant Polish nobles to get concessions for their French co-religionists.

His next successor but one in Poland, Sigismund III Vasa, was the son of John III of Sweden. He had been on the throne for only two years when the Habsburgs began intriguing to gain the Polish throne for themselves with the inside help of an 'Austrian' party of Polish nobles. The object was to persuade Sigismund that he should relinquish his Polish kingdom and turn all his attentions to Sweden. This resulted in a split among the nobility. The leading noble, John Zamoyski was a Catholic, but he shared in the tolerance towards Protestants, even to Moslems and Jews, which temporarily marked religious sentiment in Poland. Zamoyski's influence, and the widespread (and natural) xenophobia among the nobility, helped him to overcome the differences which might have separated him from the Radziwills (who were Calvinist). Nobles of both faiths therefore agreed to support the 'Peace of Warsaw' of 1573 which maintained a rare, if precarious, religious toleration in Poland until 1631.

Though clearly exemplifying the dilemma of government in the early modern state, Poland not only succeeded temporarily in avoiding its worst evils but positively benefited from its balance of forces. Sweden managed likewise to avoid a head-on civil war. So, until 1642, did England. But, sheltered though her isle might be, if Elizabeth ever ran any risk of supposing that her throne was protected from the tempests of international conflict, there was always the situation in Scotland to remind her. There, in dangerous proximity to the most dubiously loyal fringes of England, Mary, Queen of Scots, herself descended from the Guises on the side of her mother, Mary of Lorraine, was a permanent magnet for disaffected English Catholics, Guise supporters in France and agents of Philip II in Spain.

Though less spectacular, the other side of the problem also illustrates the complexity of the international scene – in this case Protestant. For if, quite outside the fanatic pro-Catholic party, there were Privy Councillors who favoured an accommodation with Spain – and they included the great Lord Burghley and the Earl of Sussex – there were others who were equally convinced opponents of any such policy. Men like Walsingham, Thomas Wilson, William Davison, Daniel Rogers and Philip Sidney saw their campaign to win the Queen's help on behalf of the Netherlands as a search for a necessary successor to England's old ally, Burgundy, against both Spain and France.

Such policy disagreements in the English Council pale beside the melodramas that were being played out in Spain. Here, at the accession of Philip, the Spanish nobility, ecclesiastical and secular, worked off their revenge on the Walloon nobles (like Chièvres) who had long dominated the old Emperor. While Philip scribbled minutes on state papers, prayed and pryed, the noble factions in his council and juntas grouped themselves for or against particular policies by a simple process of family connections. If the faction led by the Duke of Alba, a great soldier with a distinguished record under Charles v, but arrogant, greedy and unpopular, attached itself to a policy, the counter-factions would inevitably oppose it. In the early years of Philip's reign, his sense of inferiority drove him to look for allies against dominating personalities like Alba. It drew him towards Ruy Gomez de Silva, a lighter, suaver, perhaps marginally more liberal-minded politician whom he ennobled and promoted to be Prince of Eboli. At Eboli's side was Eraso, an inveterate intriguer, corrupt and underhand but useful, especially in affairs concerning the Netherlands, where he had contacts with the leading nobles. Against the Eboli faction were ranged Cardinal Granvelle, a formidable politician, and Antonio Perez, a smooth and ingratiating diplomat, had access, through a vast network of spies and informers to intelligence about everything and everybody. Although technically only a royal official, he was soon in a position to influence the warring noble factions and take increasing liberties with his master's confidence.

The distinction between official and noble was one that was not easy to preserve in sixteenth-century governing circles. The nobles, as Richelieu was to assert repeatedly in the next century, were a main artery of power in the state. Much as they might detest them, sensible kings had to confess that they were indispensable. Noble influence inevitably meant faction, and Philip, like Elizabeth, knew that he could not ignore its force. He could only try to channel it to his own ends. So for the time being the Eboli faction had its way. Alba had to wait, intriguing patiently until his time should come. By 1566 it did come, with the spread of trouble in the Netherlands. Alba became commander-in-chief of the army sent to put down the riots. But no sooner was he out of the way than the Eboli faction began to gain ground. And so the intrigues were to continue until Philip's death and after.

Any 'constitutional' implications were unimportant. For Philip, as for most contemporary princes, the executive arm of government assumed whatever form seemed most convenient – usually a diffuse and informal series of committees or juntas in which (with the help of his officials) he would try to play off one noble faction against another. The officials, however, tended to rise to the top in the power struggle. After Eboli's death, Perez joined his ambitious widow in a clash of power and was duly imprisoned. He escaped to become the leader of the revolt of the Aragonese nobles in 1591. His end was an exile, wandering through the courts of Europe. Lesser men were less lucky. Juan de Escobedo, one of Perez's confidants, seconded to Don John of Austria as secretary on his mission to the Netherlands, learnt too many secrets about his master. After three attempts to poison him had failed, Perez had him knifed in a Madrid street. Eraso and his friends in the Eboli faction in 1566 were conveniently dispensed with as the faction found itself slipping on Alba's return to favour. Several were condemned by the Inquisition and publicly burnt at Valladolid.[27]

While in England the worst of the problems of the post-feudal age were over by 1550, in France they were still to come. Nowhere in Europe was the failure of a royal line to produce a king of regal authority felt with such catastrophic force as in France after the death of Henry II. This was due to her unique socio-political structure. A French lawyer writing early in the seventeenth century, Charles Loyseau, saw France stratified into 'Orders' (or ranks or 'Estates') hierarchically arranged. At the top, in theory at least, were the high clergy – 'the ministers of God take the first place of honour'. After them came the nobility of ancient family and immemorial honour, and joined to them the nobles who owed their rank to office or lordship. After this came the Third Estate, which comprised all the rest of society which was of any consequence by reason of wealth or professional status. Each 'Estate' was sub-divided, ranging from cardinals to minor orders, princes of the blood to small squires, academic doctors and lawyers to merchants and traders, workers and craftsmen down to beggars.

Each sub-order had its social symbols of dress, coats of arms, titles, styles of address, order of procedure on ceremonial occasions, privileges, exemptions from taxes (like the *taille*) or billeting of soldiers. Each had its set of penalties for crime. In outward appearance it was all neat, tidy, geometrical and legalistic. In reality much less so. For example, though the secular noble order was legally second to the higher clergy, it was socially superior to them. And the most serious social and political conflict was that which split the nobility between the ancient hereditary families and the *noblesse de la robe*. It was this which was in the end to bring about the failure of any kind of constitutionalism in France and render her resort to absolutism almost a foregone conclusion.

Already the social attributes of status were more important than mere wealth. For anyone not a gentleman by blood it was extremely difficult to enter the gentry or nobility. And already, since the mid-sixteenth century, the official hierarchical arrangements Loyseau described had been increasingly supplemented and overlaid by the so-called *fidélités*: men of all ranks had taken sworn oaths of allegiance to their patrons. Thus a kind of gang-structure, mafia protection-system had emerged. Its essence was not class but local *solidarity*. A lord would protect his villagers and their cattle against tax collectors, distraining bailiffs and billeting officers. Undoubtedly there were elements of repression and brutality in this emerging system, but in many respects it resembled a neo-feudal organization of rural life based on an exchange of mutual service. And it sprang from the same basic cause as its medieval original: the weakness of the monarchy and the absence of effective central government.

It had long been characteristic of the French system of government that it was a network of customary rights, duties and privileges over which presided a king of authority, exceedingly strong yet never arbitary nor absolute in any modern sense. The prestige of monarchy stemmed from its image and function as the 'fount of justice'. From the judicial character of kingship, personified in a king who must be male, French, Catholic, legitimate, all governmental and political institutions in France derived. The Estates-General had emerged from meetings of the great barons about the royal court. Yet whereas in England similar meetings had developed along the lines of legislative and representative assemblies, the French emphasis was on their *legal* character. Especially important were the *parlements*, the groups of local legal advisers who retained their authority long after the representative assemblies had relapsed into silence. As in England and Spain, there remained throughout the royal council, from which both the foregoing institutions had been, as it were, subtracted, without diminishing its executive authority. By the second half of the sixteenth century it was dominated by the nobles, some of ancient lineage, some ennobled by virtue of the usefulness of their services.

Members of all three estates (including the third) enjoyed some degree of exemption from taxation; yet this did not prevent constant quarrels breaking out and the darkness which descended on them from 1614 only registered a general impotence which had long been a fact. France was 'a federation, given unity and coherence by the Crown, but composed of distinct, if sometimes overlapping groups, whose members saw no reason to cede their rights or privileges and thus lose their separate identity'.[28]

Once the unifying power of the monarchy was withdrawn or nullified, as it was from 1559 to 1594, France was left to the brutal play of tribal warfare between the *fidélités*. Each squire hastened to attach himself to his local protector and a new but distorted feudal pyramid was formed. At the top were the three great clans of Guise, Bourbon, and Montmorency. Though their enemies were always ready to castigate them as foreigners (being a cadet branch of the House of Lorraine), the Guises claimed precedence over the Bourbons. The second duke, who succeeded in 1550, inherited his father's martial skill and a gracious manner that contrasted with the brutishness of Anne de Montmorency, the Constable of France. By 1557 he was Governor of Dauphiné, Grand Chamberlain, Prince of Joinville and hereditary Seneschal of Champagne. In the closing phases of the war against the Empire, Guise added to his already distinguished reputation as a general. When Francis II succeeded in 1559, he and his brother, the Cardinal of Lorraine, found themselves *de facto* rulers of a large part of France. Only Catherine de Medici stood in their way, quick to seize on the distrust which the Guises – the cruel and rapacious cardinal especially – roused among the lesser nobles and gentry.

The Bourbons, originally based in the central provinces of France (now the department of Allier), had a record to equal that of the Guises, numbering among their distinguished members Charles Duke of Bourbon, Constable of France. By marriage with Jeanne d'Albret, heiress of Navarre, Antoine of Bourbon became King of Navarre in 1554 and joined its kingdom to the ancient Bourbon territories. Their son was to become King of France as Henry IV.

The Montmorencys were perhaps the most illustrious, ancient and martial of the noble dynasties. The name derived from the small town which was for long the main family seat, about nine miles north-west of Paris. Between their appearance in the tenth century and the French Revolution, the Montmorency family provided six constables and twelve marshals of France, several admirals and cardinals, grand officers of the Crown and grand masters of the knightly orders. Even Henry IV admitted that, after his own family, the Montmorencys were the first house in Europe. Branches of the family were found outside France, in Brabant, Hainault and Luxembourg. Like the Guises and Bourbons their ramifications were wide and deep. The influence of these three noble tribes permeated the whole of France, through their dependants and sub-dependants. Between 1560 and the triumph of Henry IV in 1593 they were to rule France.

Across the border, in the southern provinces of the Spanish Netherlands, and especially in Hainault and Brabant, a class of nobles had developed into the dominant political and social force, strongly reflected by Burgundian and Habsburg land grants. Some – like the Montmorencys – were related to the great French house. All were French-speaking and most were to be suspended between loyalty to Spain and susceptibility to French influence. High-living, martial and with few constructive political gifts, they clung tenaciously to their ancient privileges (or what they construed to be their ancient privileges) and shared in some degree the prevalent easy-going disregard of doctrinal precision in matters of religion. The nobility everywhere were susceptible to this casualness; in the Netherlands, the tendency was reinforced by material interest. With substantial properties in the great urban centres of commerce and industry, the Netherlands nobility were constantly reminded of their stake in the economic welfare of the country. Like the Venetians, they too were conscious that Catholic orthodoxy no longer ruled a world which had to accommodate Protestant and Muslim within its commercial arrangements. As a class the great Netherlands clans – Croys, Lannoys, Lalaings, Montmorencys, Lignes, Glymes, Hennins, Berlaymonts – were more than usually bewildered by problems of conflicting loyalties. The Eighty Years' War was in large part the story of their doubts, their half-hearted apostasy from orthodoxy and their final return to it.

If in France the civil wars of the century 1530–1650 were the last lurch towards an aristocratic state before the final onset of absolutism; if in England, the age of Elizabeth saw the slow submersion of noble political influence – the old nobility of Russia, the Boyars, found themselves faced with the most brutal and absolute tyranny of the age. Ivan IV – rightly called the Terrible – and his *dvoriane*, a military caste of ennobled warriors, had achieved a gigantic expansion – westwards into Lithuania, the Baltic States, northwards over the vast basins of Oka and Volga, south and south-east past Kursk and Kazan to Astrakhan and the Caspian Sea, south-west to the Sea of Azov. Their valour had to be rewarded by grants of land and of serfs to work it. The *oprichnina* of 1565 marked the victory of this military caste – some six thousand of them – endowed with lands confiscated from the boyars. The coup, executed with unexampled ferocity, turned thousands adrift, leaving Muscovy the most perfect model of absolutism in the world. It was built on the foundations of the loyal *dvoriane*, the serf state and the all-pervading doctrine of obedience to authority preached by Ivan. By this doctrine of hierarchy that encompassed the whole of society from the family up to the Tsar's immediate followers, Ivan took his revenge on the boyars who had made miserable his childhood. It was the concept of 'degree', common enough in Western society, inflated and distorted into a justification of tyranny and enforced with a brutality unknown elsewhere in Europe even in that brutal age.

Two factors explain the peculiar ferocity and totality of Russian absolutism. The causes were not economic but military: first, the rapid expansion of the Muscovite state and the demand for military service; second, the sanctions with which this Russian 'imperialism' was endowed by the Russian Orthodox Church. Its fifteenth-century prophets saw Moscow as the last *civitas dei*, the rightful successor to Rome and Byzantium. The mythology was carried into ludicrous detail but its logic was inescapable: the tsar was the universal head of Christianity and his ruthless campaigns against his neighbours, Christian or Muslim, must accordingly be crusades for Christ and his Church.

Ivan's successes left behind an inflammable legacy of hatreds which ignited after his death: while he lived they were snuffed out without mercy. Like Napoleon, Hitler and Stalin, Ivan owed everything in his successful period to his central location in a land-based war of expansion. He did not, like Philip II, face the hazards of long lines of communication at sea and the risks of sea battles. Muscovy spread like a forest fire. And despite the 'time of troubles' which was to follow, Ivan's rule of terror set the pattern that Russian history was to follow for centuries. Russia was finally stamped as imperialist and absolutist, a land of serfdom, xenophobia and terror from which all organs of government except those of the state itself were eliminated.

Estates, Bureaucrats and Bankers

Officially, the voice of the people, arranged usually in three parts – lords, clergy and commoners – was the 'Estates' or 'Orders'. Often the system was itself a dual one; there were local Estates and a general or national Estate. In some countries, as in France or the Netherlands, the Estates-General was composed of members who were little more than mandated delegates of the local Estates. Their powers were limited to doing what their local Estates told them to do, and to recommending (but not ordering) the local Estates to do whatever they might have agreed with the king. The main business of the Estates was to air local or widespread grievances, especially financial ones, and to discuss other problems of general concern. Religion figured increasingly on the list of pressing matters, for example, in France in the Estates-General of 1561: it was usefully linked with finance in the discussions of the First Estate where the clergy were induced to make large grants of money to the Crown after hearing alarming versions of the spread of the Protestant heresy. (The Third Estate had stoutly refused to pay anything.)

It is still the custom among historians to make respectful obeisances to these supposedly representative assemblies, while usually acknowledging

77

regretfully that they did not achieve the constitutional glories of the English Parliament, the more delayed and less glorious distinction of the French Assemblies of 1789, or the supposedly patriotic and constructive role of the Netherlands Estates between 1557 and 1579. It seems doubtful whether, in themselves, these widely varying institutions deserve the reputation which has been accorded them, largely in the reflected glory of later events in England and the Netherlands. That it was customary for the monarch to meet 'representatives' of his subjects is not in question; nor that they met, rank by rank, to talk about taxation and other questions which affected governors and governed. Nor that here and there one may detect the seeds of later changes in the political system. But these are far from adding up to a logical chain of constitutional development from feudalism, via absolutism, to constitutional government. Only in one case can this be claimed: the English House of Commons, which differed so much from Continental assemblies as to make it a case apart. Nowhere else is there any genuine continuity between these medievally-rooted assemblies and later 'parliaments'. Even in the Netherlands – and in England too – the phenomenon of a general upheaval leading, in the one case, to a permanent Republic and, in the other, to constitutional monarchy resulted from many other factors, interwoven with accidents of personal genius. That powerful forces, interests and emotions were churning among the classes 'represented' in the Estates is not in doubt. What seems today more than doubtful is whether the assemblies themselves were in any sense ever an effective forum where such forces were forged into a weapon against prevailing absolutism.

In the first place, they did not represent in any effective way the material interests of the governed or 'exploited', and such logic as can be discerned in their development was influenced by many other factors – the force of religious differences and individual and class jealousies and ambitions. The First and, to some extent, the Second Estates, though not the Third, were drawn from those classes with a strong natural propensity to support monarchy against any signs of opposition from the lower orders. Accidental happenings – the blunders of the Valois kings after Henry II, of Philip II in the Netherlands or of Charles I in England – could help to split the natural loyalty of the upper strata and even join part of them to the social groups below. But there were also inherent weaknesses in the nature of the assemblies. They were essentially *consultative* bodies, often too large and never possessed of precisely defined powers even to discharge their supposed functions, let alone assume the executive functions that belong to monarchy.

Always, in the background, was the fundamental problem of *ultimate* power; what the English were to identify as the practical problem of sovereignty. Essential to this were the residual powers of the executive: the prerogative. The need for prerogative was not removed by the existence of an assembly or parliament. On the contrary, even in England, where the legislative powers of Parliament had been raised to unique status by the early Tudors, the Crown still retained the power to intervene, legislatively and judicially, in ways which remained generally acceptable until Stuart times. Laws could be suspended for a period or dispensed with in this case or that. Certain cases could be referred to the Prerogative Courts. Reasons of diplomacy or the safety of the realm might be adduced to justify special taxation. But while in England such intervention was regarded as exceptional, in France it had become normal. Theorists like Chasseneuz argued that extraordinary conditions justified the Crown in imposing extraordinary taxation. But who decided when conditions were 'extraordinary'? Only the king could decide. When the same question was asked in Bates's case in England in 1606, he and his lawyers – and many other people, John Selden among them – saw clearly what the issue was. It was stated again and again, down to the great question of Ship-Money in the 1630s. In the end royal prerogative went; but it took a civil war to dispose of the issue. In France resistance to the royal claim to have the last word simply crumbled away; with it went any fundamental need to assemble the Estates-General. Its meetings had long been only very occasional. That of 1614 was the last before 1789.

Estates could be killed by neglect, as in France, or by royal manipulation and pressure as in Castile: here the Cortes had been reduced to a single chamber of thirty-six members representing eighteen towns after the nobility had refused Charles v's demands for a tax. The Castilian nobility were henceforth allowed to contract out of their tax liabilities in return for yielding up any claim to political power against the Crown. In the other kingdoms of Spain – Aragon, Valencia and Catalonia – there was more blood in the Estates system. But even in Aragon Philip only found it necessary to summon the general Cortes twice (1563 and 1585). At other times, the meagre yield of Aragon taxes was obtained by persuasion. In Piedmont, the Duke of Savoy took tougher measures. One meeting of the Estates in 1560 gave him revenue enough to establish a large standing army and thereafter levy taxes at will. The only ducal concession necessary was to give the nobles a free hand to deal with their peasantry. Similarly, in Germany, the Duke of Bavaria finally crushed the Lutheran party in 1564 by bribing the leading nobles and destroying the opposition. Henceforth Bavaria became an orthodox Counter-Reformation state ruled by an absolute prince – the perfect model to be followed later in Bohemia after the much more serious conspiracy of 1618. It need hardly be added that in the Russia of Ivan the Terrible, neither the *duma* of the now politically impotent boyars nor the *zemsky sobor* which was supposed to represent the subservient service nobility after 1565, gave their patron the slightest trouble. Only in England did Elizabeth find it important to keep a managing hand on the Commons. For though few would have agreed with the wiseacre who said early in her reign that Crown and Commons constituted a Parliament, it was noticeable that the wealth represented by the members of the Commons was overtaking that of the Lords. By 1593 Francis Bacon would be arguing, prematurely but ominously, that the grant of taxation was exclusively the concern of the *elected* members of Parliament. The Elizabethan Parliament was beginning to show signs that it understood the need to redress some of the fatal weaknesses which beset the Continental Estates – not all of them, for sessions were still too short, precarious and infrequent. Eleven years of purely personal rule by a king were still possible, as the reign of Charles I was to show. But England was relatively small. So was its population, especially the gentry and professional classes. In the absence of any competing provincial assemblies, Parliament was already beginning to assume something of its later and often-remarked character of a club. Members were beginning to know each other, especially if they travelled to London from neighbouring regions or had common interests which brought them together in Westminster. One such interest was the concern for the peculiar English form of Protestantism which came to be called 'Puritan'. The group which took most 'managing' in Elizabeth's Commons House was the 'Puritan choir', a vocal, dissident group whose Protestant patriotism often outran that of the Queen. Members were also becoming more literate, more articulate. A handful of Marian exiles had their own specific and influential view of world politics. Others had been on a Grand Tour and knew the Netherlands and Italy at first hand. The House also contained its nucleus of lawyers, skilled in debate and draftsmanship.

Although the Netherlands Revolt had its reluctant beginnings in the States-General during the phase of aristocratic opposition to Philip (sometimes called 'the revolt of medievalism') it owed little to the institution of the general 'states'. By 1566 the spearhead of opposition was Calvinist, middle-class, artisan, urban or suburban, and a wide rift opened between these and the old noble opposition. It took the brutality of Alba and the excesses of the imperial soldiery to piece the broken fragments of the opposition movement together in 1576. But in 1579 it fell apart again, this time for good. In the end, Alba's prediction was in a sense proved right. 'States-General' or 'Cortes' – it was the same thing. Appeals to old loyalty, a little persuasion, some force if necessary, and the opposition would fall apart.

The persistence of revolution in the northern provinces derived from different causes – from a new and changed economy, the rise of an independent urban patriciate linked closely, town by town, by a spontaneous combustion of feeling in defence of principles of government outraged by the arrogance and ignorance of Spaniards whose very tread 'killed the grass beneath their boots'. The rebels were helped by geography and terrain and the political genius of William the Silent. The States-General was dispensable. The nobility faded and disappeared from the scene, to be replaced by what Renier picturesquely called 'the dictatorship of the middle class' that was seventeenth-century Holland. Only here and in England did the changing character of the representative, oligarchic assembly reflect a change in the socio-political structure. Elsewhere, assemblies existed to be manipulated, managed, bribed, ignored or simply rubbed out.

The prince was usually the symbol of the age in government. How were the increasing costs of his task to be covered? To some extent, by ignoring or overriding any resistance to tax increases by the assemblies. Thus the French king could impose a tax on wine in 1561 although the deputies withheld their consent. Indirect taxation was enormously increased: it was less susceptible to control and far easier to collect than direct taxes, which either had to be exacted from the victims in cash, or in kind, which in turn involved re-sale of goods and all the expenses attaching to it. Yet, squeeze their subjects as they might, sixteenth- and seventeenth-century governments could not cover their rising costs from taxes alone. France and Spain were bankrupt by 1557 and Elizabeth inherited at her accession a large debt and a debased currency. Governments were therefore on the look-out for other means of raising cash: if taxes were not enough, what capital assets could be mustered for sale or used as collateral for loans?

Most convenient were physical assets: the crown lands in particular. Even Queen Elizabeth, prudent economist though she was, was forced back on the ancient expedient, abandoned by her father and grandfather, of selling them off. Contemporary French governments were much more reckless. With revenues often covering only half their expenditure, they sold off crown and church lands in much larger quantities.

Another source of revenue was the prerogative power of the Crown – to regulate trade, for example. Out of this grew abuses such as the monopolies which made Elizabeth's Parliament of 1597 the most noisy and fractious of the reign. Sir Walter Raleigh, for example, had been given by Elizabeth the right to sell licences for taverns for thirty years. Other monopolies conferred the sole rights over import or export of specified commodities, and the suspicion was widespread that the purpose (and result) was that the favoured operators put up their prices. Such plain abuses were indefensible. The chartered or joint stock companies were more debatable. It could be argued that in the conditions in which foreign trade had to be conducted it was necessary for the good of the realm to channel it through companies of men who could bargain for privileges with foreign governments and raise the large amounts of capital necessary, for example, to build the great ships and forts needed by the East India Company or later the African Companies. The Queen found it convenient to have at Antwerp a Company (the Merchant Adventurers) dependent on her favour and commanding the proceeds – vast in contemporary terms – of the sale of the greater part of England's exports of cloth. In time of need they could serve, as it were, as royal bankers. Yet Elizabeth's stratagems of this kind were trifles compared to the manipulations of governments in France and Spain. In France the Crown simply sold to anybody who could pay *lettres de maîtrise* which gave them the right to set themselves up as masters of gilds. In Spain, the Mesta (the corporation of sheep-breeders) had bought from the Crown the tolls levied on the flocks of its members for a lump sum. They enjoyed small benefit, for the Crown then proceeded to sell similar privileges to non-members of the Mesta. This was followed by new taxes on sheep.

Such shifts and devices and the pressure behind them helped to bring about a revolution in the management of public finance. Faced with vast and rising costs and little in the way of an effective bureaucracy to

1   In the European economy of the sixteenth and seventeenth centuries the harvest was still the pivot on which the whole economy turned; a detail from Breughel's *Landscape with the Fall of Icarus* (1588).

2 & 3 The revival and growth of Leiden's textile industries was largely due to the work of refugees from the Southern Netherlands. Two paintings by Jacob van Swanenburgh from a series depicting the different aspects of the industry; (*above*) shearing and combing; (*below*) spinning, warping and weaving.

4   The continuing demand for precious and base metals was characteristic of the inflationary, expansionist phase of the sixteenth century; a detail from Lucas Gassel's painting of sixteenth-century mining operations in Germany.

5   *right* Much early industrial expansion was achieved with little or no attention to technological innovation. Particular exceptions were the textile industries of North Italy and the Northern Netherlands. An Italian water-driven spinning frame from an early seventeenth-century engraving.

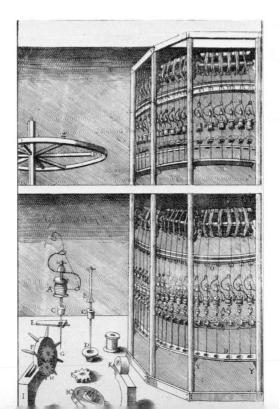

6 & 7 Law and order in the major European states were continually threatened by the contrasts of wealth and poverty. The nobility maintained a lavish way of life; (*above*) a detail from *Spring: Elegant Company on a Picnic* (1587) by Lucas van Valkenborch, a Fleming who fled from Antwerp and Alba's persecution to settle in Germany. At the other extreme were the armies of beggars roaming the countryside in search of food and shelter; (*left*) a seventeenth-century engraving from a book of French proverbs.

Il a bien chaud qui tout ses habits porte
et neanimoins contre ces francs Narquois
du moindre hyver tant que eur est trop forte
n'ayant aulx pieds que la paillie le bois

A Jeuneffe, oyfiue vieilleffe penible

pour ringst par vice.

Espoir des gueux

Il n'ont pas besoin de fort hyuer

lque part qu'il aille il se promene
jours dans ses bois

8 *above Queen Elizabeth I Confounding Juno, Minerva and Venus* (1569) by Hans
Eworth; such courtly allegories served to perpetuate the mythical image of the
Queen which gave her a unique hold on the imagination of the English.

9 *below* The assembly of the Estates-General at Orleans in 1561.

10 *Fishing for Souls* (*c.* 1614) by Adriaen van der Veen, an allegorical painting symbolizing the bitter religious conflict that engulfed Europe in the sixteenth century. The Dutch Protestants and their allies (on the left) confront the Catholic forces, led by Philip III of Spain (on the right), while in the river between, rival parties attempt to capture recruits to their respective causes.

11 *far left* The massacre at Vassy in March 1562 inaugurated years of bloody civil strife in France; a contemporary engraving.

12 *left* John Calvin; a contemporary portrait by an unknown artist.

13 *above* An anonymous sixteenth-century painting of the Huguenots of Lyons at worship.

14 *below* The massacre of St Bartholomew, a seventeenth-century Dutch engraving.

help them, governments had everywhere to fall back on help from private enterprise. Armies had to be paid, weapons purchased, ships built; yet the inflow of cash tended to be, at best, uneven. Governments therefore bargained with individuals or groups of merchants who had enough capital to buy up the crown rights to tax or to mine gold, silver, copper, alum, etc., and the technical resources to exploit them. Sometimes the Crown merely handed over to the financier the right to his taxes in return for a fixed capital sum. Various other arrangements were tried, all to some extent anticipating and easing the flow of revenue to the Crown. When Philip II came to the Spanish throne in July 1556 he found that all his revenues had been 'assigned' for the next five years to pay off loans to the government. Revenues could also be 'farmed' by private entrepreneurs who made themselves responsible for the collection and advanced capital to the state, subtracting their cut for trouble, labour – and risk. Such devices were natural resorts of governments hard-up for cash and reliable administrators, but they bore heavily on subjects – at least many thought so.

Yet even these short-term expedients were no solution. It was not a long step therefore to the most important innovation of all in public finance which augmented, in theory at least, the cash resources of governments by a multiple which varied between about 8 and 20, according to the state of credit. It consisted in selling to investors the right to an annual payment of interest on a capital sum which they handed over to the government – sometimes in perpetuity: such 'annuities' – *renten* in the Low Countries and Germany, *monti* in Italy, *censos* in Spain, *rentes* in France – had been sold by urban governments in Europe for a long time. The system now spread to the nation states. Both France and Spain had sold millions of livres and ducats worth of *rentes* and *juros* by the 1550s. In 1557 Philip converted another seven million ducats of short-term debt into these *juros*. This began a process of borrowing which by 1598 brought the total debt of Spain up to eighty-five million ducats, the annual interest to 4·6 million – and this was already deeply in arrears. The course of events in France was similar. Like their Spanish enemies, no French king ever succeeded in paying off his capital debt or even honouring the interest payments. A great part had to be liquidated by simple repudiation by Henry IV in 1599. French governments of the early seventeenth century inherited conditions of anarchy in the public finances which continued through the century. If the prudent and skilful Dutch were in difficulties with their funded debt (as they were from

1572 to 1586) it was not surprising that imprudent dynasts, who cared much for glory and little for solvency, should plunge up to their ears in bankruptcy. Only the Venetians and Genoans girded up enough capital and skill to come through relatively unscathed with the Banco del Giro and the Casa di San Giorgio. The new system itself was in principle sound, but dangerous in the wrong hands. It increased – disastrously, in some of the cases examined above – the purchasing power of governments, but it was essentially the system which Holland and England were to operate with conspicuous success later in the seventeenth century. The danger was that the earmarking of specific revenues as a source of interest for loans was wide open to abuse in an age of corrupt and irresponsible government. The sufferers – even in the Dutch Republic – were the consumers, who saw higher and higher taxes imposed on the necessities of life. In many countries investors also suffered. Interest payments never reached them, disappearing into the pockets of the manipulators and parasites, who refreshed themselves freely and without risk from the public purse. If there was a 'seventeenth-century crisis' this was certainly one source of it.

The Nature of Nobility

The decline of nobility has often been antedated by historians who believed that the 'new monarchs' rose in an alliance with the middle classes directed against the feudality. In fact, with the exception of the Low Countries and Switzerland, the sixteenth and seventeenth centuries witnessed the actual decline of many cities. On the whole the nobles kept their privileges intact, except in the Dutch Republic. True, in England, the old nobility lost ground. In a famous controversy on the period 1561–1640, R. H. Tawney saw the Crown and the entire aristocracy losing ground to the rising gentry; out of two and a half thousand manors examined, the share of the Crown declined from 242 to 53; that of the peerage from 335 to 157; while the 'gentry' share rose from 1,709 to 2,051. H. R. Trevor-Roper, in a trenchant criticism, showed, however, that this rise included 'manors' which accrued to gentry *ennobled* in this period. If these were credited to the peerage, their share actually rose (from 335 to 343) while the increase in gentry manors was much less (from 1,709 to 1,865). Ignoring for the present the difficulty that a 'manor' was not a constant unit of measurement, the only conclusion seemed to be that the indubitable loser was the Crown, which alienated a large number of manors. But from general evidence we know that

while the old nobility (for instance of the border lands between Wales
and Scotland and England) were in difficulties, new men were being
raised to the peerage and to a considerable degree the future of England
was to lie in their hands.

The concept and law of 'nobility' fluctuated widely from one country
to another. In Biscaya, all native-born men were *hidalgos*. In the Grison
Cantons of Switzerland there was no nobility at all. In Castile, Poland
and Hungary, the proportion of nobility to the whole population was
relatively high – 5–10 per cent. England had slightly fewer; France,
Italy, Scandinavia and Bohemia much less. In Italy and Spain, nobles
tended to be an urban class; in France and England, Germany and
Poland, they lived in the country. Nor were they by any means invariably rich, though they tended to share the pride, if not the wealth,
of nobility. Except in England, it was the privilege of most nobles to be
exempt from some if not all the burdens of direct taxation. English
nobles had only one special legal privilege: the right to be tried by their
peers. But this descended, like their estates, only to the eldest male heir.
On the Continent, nobles were often less severely treated at law, more
lightly burdened with billeted soldiers, exempt from flogging and hang-
ing, and allowed to wear swords. On the other hand, in Germany, the
Spanish Netherlands and particularly in France, the nobility were not
allowed, under pain of *dérogation* (loss of noble status) to engage in
occupations regarded as servile or degrading, such as manual work or
shopkeeping. And while Germany and England paid due respect to
academic distinction as a qualification for noble status, the French
nobility would have no truck with any such notion. Loyseau described
even the minor gentry of France as 'insolent', 'birds of prey whose only
occupation . . . is to live off others and persecute each other'.[29]

In the sixteenth century, except in England, the nobility were closing
their ranks, emphasizing their status and privileges against the rest of
the society, becoming a more closed caste with greater stress on the
heroic virtues of fighting and duelling, and the distinction of ignorance.
Successive economic reformers were to fight against *dérogation* in France
in the interests of economic progress – in vain.

Significantly, Castiglione's *Il Cortegiano*, written in 1528, was translated by Thomas Hoby into English in 1561. It was prefaced by a little
sonnet by Thomas Sackville, later Lord Buckhurst, later 1st Earl of
Dorset and Burghley's successor as Lord Treasurer of England. Although
a cousin of the Queen, he came from gentry stock. Yet his entire life was

ruled by the precepts and examples of this curious, didactic, yet entertaining dialogue on the character and etiquette of gentlemanliness. Despite the Tudor adage that 'the Englishman Italianate was a devil incarnate', it was the Italian influence which was the only identifiable and calculated attempt to soften the crudity of social manners. England was enjoying a century and a half of freedom from war. Men were able to reflect on the arts of civility. Fynes Moryson, travelling in Europe in the 1590s, was struck by the open use of force in France and South Italy, the quarrelling and brawling in the Netherlands, the number of murders in Bohemia, the way German and Polish lords treated their serfs like animals. Spaniards and French had to endure almost continuous war, civil and international, between the end of the fifteenth century and 1660. Its brutalizing effects and the poverty and disease in its wake are still difficult to imagine. But one result was to widen the gap between the class of military leaders, whose habits and ideals derived from their martial preoccupations, and the rest of society.

The more peaceable development of English society in the Tudor age had another important result. It created the climate – literary, artistic, musical, chivalrous, if often artificially so – in which kingship itself developed its own myth. It enabled Elizabeth to turn herself into a legend, reflected in the dream-like quality of Spenser's *Faerie Queene*, in part an allegory woven around the supposed history of the Tudors.

The Elizabethan legend became a central feature of the mythology by which the queen established a unique hold on the imagination of the English. To the court poets she was Gloriana, Belphoebe, Cynthia, Diana, 'England's Astraea, Albion's shining sun'. To the makers of ballads and broadsides she was Bessy, the simple, virtuous handmaiden of the land, the people's heroine. Even from her opponents she managed to extract the same personal devotion as she won from the simple crowds of artisans and peasants who cheered the progress through the cities and countries of England which marked each summer of the first twenty years of her reign. Her speeches – composed with a superb feeling for the prose rhythms of English – delighted the ears of the crowd as the water-pageants, tiltings and processions delighted their eyes. For the portraitists she was not so much a person as a queenly effigy, rich with jewels, impersonal: an icon rather than a portrait. Poets revived the medieval allegory of love with its complex sexual imagery, to portray the affair between queen and people: the nation played Lancelot to the Queen's Guinevere. The political cosmos pivoted around the regal sun.

Yet all this could scarcely have been achieved without social changes in the nature of nobility and gentry which were unique in Europe. It was not decay itself that was unique; for in France and the Netherlands, to say nothing of Scotland, similar symptoms were visible. Lawrence Stone has tabulated the abundant evidence of the strains which a whole way of life, especially elaborate building and spending, put upon fortunes that were not easily expanded. Income from landed estates contained a large proportion of customary tenures not easily replaced by contractual forms of leasehold. Other misfortunes were the result of pig-headed obstinacy, like the Earl of Oxford's campaign against his wife and his father-in-law, the great William Cecil, Lord Burghley, or the wanton extravagance of the Earl of Essex.

Down to about 1570, the shift of power was not spectacular. The Queen continued to govern in collaboration with the nobility, balancing a group of reliable administrators in her Council against the noble legatees of the feudal tradition. Burghley and Sussex were played off against the Earls of Leicester and Warwick; Burghley, Buckhurst and Nottingham against Essex, even in the 1590s. Lord Cobham, conservative in all his preferences, would be balanced against the puritan gentleman, Walsingham, in the elaborate mission despatched to the Netherlands to try and find a way out of the impasse there between Protestants and Catholics in 1578. Elizabeth showed infinite patience in this process of taming the old nobility and easing them out of their positions of power. Talbots and Stanhopes were allowed to break the peace of Nottinghamshire for years without serious punishment. After all, the Crown could punish in Star Chamber if it was really necessary; but on the whole the Queen was a believer in *solvitur ambulando*. If it was not a good policy in foreign relations, it seemed to work at home. Slowly the Tudors taught the lesson that 'there was a higher authority whose will could in the last resort override even the greatest magnates of the realm'.[30]

The changed situation was reflected in Parliament. The House of Commons membership grew from some three hundred to around five hundred and the numbers of the gentry sitting in it from some 50 per cent up to 75 per cent, even though the newly created seats were for borough representation. But Elizabeth was frugal in creating peerages and even knighthoods. Under her grandfather the number of peers had actually fallen (from 57 to 44). By 1530 the numbers were back to 50–60, and there they remained until James I's time. Elizabeth usually demanded exceptional talents (as in her 'spirit', Burghley) or blood relationship to herself (as in the case of Thomas Sackville) before she would look kindly on the creation of titles. Although her caution was not necessarily the reason for the flood of new creations under James, these did something to restore the balance between the Houses which Elizabeth's creation of borough seats had upset.

And now the nobility launched into the fever of building and high living which has been seen by some historians as the source of the financial problems which left them embittered, penurious and jealous for their remaining political power. In 1550 most of them were housed – much as they had been in the Middle Ages – in draughty, barely habitable castles or rambling ranges of domestic buildings. From the 1570s they seem to have felt free to make a change. One after another the great palaces of Elizabethan England begin to rise – Burghley House, Stamford, Theobalds Park, Hardwick Hall 'more glass than wall', Wollaton, Knole – all lavishly furnished. The 'building of country houses between 1570 and 1620, must have been the largest capital undertaking of the period'.[31]

This was indeed an age of conspicuous expenditure in England; and it arose while in France and Germany nobles and gentlemen found themselves pressed too hard by the wars of religion to compete in such things. In Italy, the greatest age of urban building was over in Florence and Tuscany; but around Rome the great cardinals were still building their villas. And in the *terra firma* of Venice, a hundred rural villas like Palladio's jewels, the Villa Barbaro at Maser and the Villa Rotunda at Vicenza, crowned the glories of Late Renaissance architectural display. But, for the moment, the scale of Italian private architecture seemed small to the English nobility as they set about designing their rural palaces. The Venetian Ambassador in 1554 was astonished by the habits of the gentry in rural England 'where they keep up very grand establishments both with regard to the great abundance of estates consumed by them, as also by reason of their numerous attendants, in which they exceed all other nations'.

Were the nobility of England hopelessly impoverished by their domestic extravagances? Some certainly were. But the case of Lord Mountjoy in the 1560s, who was said to have mortgaged all but £5 a year of his income, was untypical. True, in the 1580s and 1590s the Earl of Leicester, the Earl of Shrewsbury, Francis Bacon, Lord Grey of Wilton, the Lord Treasurer Winchester were all in debt. Professor

Stone has seen the last two decades of Elizabeth's reign as a time of rising noble debt, high interest rates, widespread mortgage of landed estates. But whether this describes the bankruptcy of a whole class is much more doubtful. The gradual development of a credit market had made it easier to borrow money. No doubt some borrowers fell into the trap and overreached themselves. But equally, many recovered their equilibrium in succeeding decades. And there were always the others who prudently saved, ingeniously and profitably married off their children and actually improved their fortunes. There is no answer to the question, was this the long train a-laying which finally blew up with the Civil War? The fashionable habit of using long-term economic evidence to explain problems of political decision can never yield more than a balancing of probabilities. Thomas Wilson, writing towards the end of Elizabeth's reign, remarked of the nobility: 'Some daily decay; some increase according to the course of the world.' There was, and still is, not much more to be said.

꧁ 5 ꧂

THE STRUGGLE FOR EUROPE

The End of an Era

When Charles v, Holy Roman Emperor, met the Imperial Diet at Augsburg on 1 September 1547 he seemed to be about to realize not only his dream of a universal empire (an inheritance from his grandfather Maximilian) but also his ideal of a purified and unified Church (an inheritance from his grandmother Isabella of Castile). Francis i had died in March and fear of a renewed French attack in Italy was removed – at least for the moment. The League of Schmalkalde formed, sixteen years earlier to protect the interests of the Protestant princes against the Emperor, was in disarray, and John Frederick of Saxony, Charles's most formidable opponent, had just been utterly routed at the Battle of Mühlberg and forced to resign his electoral dignity. Most of his territories were forfeit, those in Bohemia going to Charles's brother Ferdinand. In short, the Emperor's enemies were either defeated or forced to come to terms. Armed with the support of the German princes, Charles was able to call on Pope Paul iii to recall the General Council of the Church from Bologna to Trent.

Five years later, his dreams were shattered. The new Pope was even less prepared than his predecessor to accept Charles's views on the responsibilities of the Papacy. The new French king, Henry ii, felt secure enough by the summer of 1557 to interfere once more in Italy. The German princes had recovered their spirits and one, Maurice of Saxony, had managed to form a threatening alliance with the French, securing at the same time the neutrality of Ferdinand of Austria, who was always jealous of his brother. Tortured by gout and asthma, Charles alternated between moods of intense irritability and deep lassitude. In

90

May 1552 he was caught with his troops on the Ehrenberg, at the castle commanding the pass to Innsbruck. After a humiliating attempt to escape north to the Netherlands, he fled in a litter across the Brenner to Villach. Sick and exhausted, he hung on with his customary obstinacy for another six years while the fighting, more pointless, more hopeless than before, ravaged Italy from Siena to Naples. The Italians found it hard to know whether the Emperor, the French or the Turks brought them the worst misery. Yet in reality the strength of the combatants was ebbing away. For all his ceaseless strivings and journeyings, Charles's control over events and policies had never been more precarious. Gattinara, his Piedmontese counsellor, had taught him to see the imperial title as a thing ordained by God himself; to see himself as the leader of Christendom against the Muslims and Lutherans. Yet the world knew that Charles's vast empire was simply the residuum of a series of accidents of heredity, his claim to the title the fruit of the largest hand-out in bribes to the Imperial Electors ever known, backed by an unprecedented loan of half a million florins by the House of Fugger, to whom an equivalent proportion of Charles's revenues was accordingly pledged. The Spaniards were unimpressed by an Emperor who was burdened with the insoluble problems of a Germany always divided by princely ambitions, and now by religious strife as well. The direct control of the Habsburg lands in Germany and Austria had been turned over to Ferdinand, Charles's brother. The ties with Hungary and Bohemia were strengthened by Ferdinand's marriage to Anne of Hungary and the marriage of his sister Mary, later Regent of the Nether-lands, to the King of Hungary and Bohemia. A few years later the best part of Hungary surrendered to the Turks after their victory at Mohács (1526). Meanwhile the Spanish inheritance brought with it the compulsion to face the Turks in North Africa and the Mediterranean, while the Aragonese claim to the Kingdom of Naples added another reason for extending the war against France on Italian soil.

Doggedly, Charles had done his best to face his problems, or at least fend them off. A quarter of a century earlier, he had persuaded the Imperial Electors to recognize his brother as prospective heir to the imperial title. But now Charles's eldest legitimate son, Philip, must needs inherit Spain and the Netherlands; yet Ferdinand would not budge from his claim to the Empire. A bitter family quarrel ended in the division of the vast, ramshackle Empire, which not even the mumbo-jumbo of dynasticism could now hold together.

Having summoned the Diet to Augsburg in February 1555, Charles left it to Ferdinand to thrash out a settlement between Lutherans and Catholics, harassed and hampered by a rapid succession of Popes. In the end a compromise was reached. Each secular prince and imperial city was to decide which of the two religions – for no concessions were made to Calvinists or Zwinglians – should be adopted in his jurisdiction. Non-conformists would be allowed to leave with their property. All church property secularized before 1552 was to remain so, but no more was to be secularized. Any Catholic dignitary who became Lutheran hereafter was to relinquish his office, with all its revenues and patronage. This was only accepted by the Lutherans under protest, but for half a century, the Augsburg settlement gave peace to at least one part of the *Christianitas afflicta*.

The cost was high. Charles was forced to abandon his ideal of a universal empire ruled by a single faith. His loss was the gain of the princes, but of the princes only. The Augsburg negotiators had no time for toleration. On the contrary, the principle *cujus regio ejus religio* represented the harnessing of Lutheranism to a political, and essentially intolerant, purpose. The only freedom contemplated was the freedom to depart. The spirit of Lutheranism was debased in proportion as its political edge was sharpened. During the next half century the missionary zeal of Protestantism was to be manifested in the more precise, equally intolerant and pitiless doctrine of the Calvinists. Against them were to be ranged the agents of a Roman Church purged of its grosser abuses – a more efficient, learned and less nepotic Papacy and hierarchy, the dedicated Order of the Jesuits and, above all, the implacable Supreme Tribunal of the Inquisition under six universal Inquisitors with power to punish, imprison, censor, confiscate and kill. Confrontation was to be total.

In matters of religious belief, Charles was merely conservative or indolent, as in many other things; no philosopher, and certainly no theologian, he failed almost entirely to understand what dogma meant, and his blundering and spasmodic attempts to enforce religious orthodoxy merely brought him into head-on collision with a succession of Popes whom he shrewdly assessed as being no better than they ought to be. This was now to be changed. Neither Ferdinand nor his son, the Emperor Maximilian II, nor his grandson, the Emperor Rudolf II, inherited the religious bigotry of Charles. That passed, in fullest measure, to his son Philip. In Philip, his father's aim of reuniting the

Church lived on. For a time it was to be restrained by fears of the power of the Guises inside France and outside – especially in Scotland and England. Once these apprehensions were eventually removed, the union of Habsburg and Guise in the Catholic League gave the Counter-Reformation in Europe the strongest and most effective military and political backing it had ever enjoyed. It therefore provided the major link between the civil and religious wars in France and the Netherlands and in turn with Catholic intrigues in England and Scotland.

By the time the treaties of peace were signed at the Bishop's Castle at Le Cateau-Cambrésis in April 1559 Charles v was dead. They spelt the end of the wars, bloody and meaningless, which had ravaged Italy since Charles viii led his Swiss pikemen and Gascon infantry over the Alps, sixty-five years before. The issue between Habsburg and Valois was simple: who was to be master of Italy? Through all the military and diplomatic confusion that characterized the wars, the added complications of the Habsburg imperial responsibilities, the growing religious rifts in France, Germany, England and Central Europe, the major centre of the conflict remained Italy. Ironically, neither Spain nor France had any vital interest, political, religious or economic, in Italy. Neither could claim any higher motive for their rape of Italy than dynasticism or animal spirits. Of rational purpose it was entirely devoid. It merely cost lives and money and passed the time for a military caste who had nothing else to do. In Garrett Mattingly's words, 'War was a way of life, an ingrained habit of late feudal society'. Kings themselves generally welcomed foreign wars which got these troublesome, over-mighty subjects out of the way and could be expected to dispose of a reasonable proportion of them for good.

The settlement of Cateau-Cambrésis registered the results of sixty years of futile conflict in a fashion characteristically irrational and irrelevant. The representatives of Spain and France were in no mood for sober calculation of the balance of military advantage. They only knew that their states were totally exhausted and haunted by the spectre of famine and disease. England, the only other power to be invited, was represented by an unimpressive collection of commissioners including, somewhat improbably, the Polonius-like figure of the Bishop of Ely. The Spaniards, reported by the Queen's agent in Brussels to be hostile to England, were not prepared to allow the English claim to Calais to delay the signing of peace, perhaps because Philip's advances to Eliza-beth with offers of marriage had been rejected. So Calais went.

The English out of the way, the Spaniards and French were prepared to agree on the fate of Italy. Not one Italian negotiator or Papal diplomat was present. Nor did the Emperor have a say in the settlement, even though one decision was that the French should keep the imperial cities of Metz, Toul and Verdun taken by Montmorency before he in turn had been captured. This apart, the French did less well than might have been expected, considering their comparative strength in the field. They lost Piedmont and Savoy to their duke, Emmanuel Philibert, for whom a marriage to Margaret of Valois, sister of the King of France, was promptly arranged. The cession of Siena, captured by Spain in 1535, to Cosimo de Medici was confirmed, making him the leader of the north Italian rulers. The Republic of Genoa won back Corsica. Supposedly to sweeten this succession of bitter pills for France, the hand of Philip of Spain was offered in marriage to the thirteen-year-old daughter of the French king, Elizabeth of Valois.

But even the continuing support for the terms of the treaties could not silence those dissident voices which continued stolidly to assert that after years of glory France had been betrayed and robbed of her rightful rewards. 'By a stroke of the pen,' said one, 'all our conquests of thirty years have been handed back.' Although one of the French negotiators was the Cardinal of Lorraine, the Guise clan – Duke Francis in particular – firmly placed the humiliation of France at the door of the Constable, Montmorency. He did not long survive the death of Henry II. By a swift reversal of court favour the Guises swept into power.

Their first move was disastrous. From Scotland, Mary of Lorraine, sister of the Guise brothers and queen regent, sent an appeal for help against the Protestant 'Lords of the Congregation' and Calvinist iconoclasts roused to frenzy by John Knox. Was not this the Guise opportunity to place Mary's daughter, Mary, Queen of Scots, on the throne of England? They made a bad miscalculation. For once, Elizabeth acted with speed and decision. By January 1560 an English fleet was in the Firth of Forth; soon after English forces laid siege to the French army at Leith. Badly shaken, the Guises concluded that prudence was the better part of valour. A French deputation was despatched to Scotland. By the Treaty of Edinburgh (July 1560) French troops were withdrawn, and with them Mary's claim to the throne of England. Her husband, Francis II, King of France, died a few months later.

For the moment French policy was transposed into a lower key. Resources were hopelessly depleted, the Guises temporarily without allies; Mary back in Scotland was powerless to threaten Elizabeth with her claim. Nor, for the moment, was any help forthcoming from Philip of Spain.

Philip could certainly claim to be the master of Italy from Milan and the Plain of Lombardy to Sicily; with the wealth of the Netherlands, of Castile, the trade of the Indies and the silver mines of the New World, he was – on paper – the richest prince in Europe. But his resources were slow to materialize. Ill at ease in the Netherlands, he decided in June 1559 to return to Spain. His decision was partly connected with the recent disappointingly low yield of his Netherlands revenues. Perhaps his presence in Spain would speed the flow of Castilian taxes and American silver? In August he left for Spain and never returned, despite later promises to do so. His other reason was probably his desire to renew the crusade against the Turk in the Mediterranean, to which he was dedicated by the fanatical power of his Catholic faith and the urgings of his military advisers, who assumed that this was the moment when Turkish power would be weakened by the loss of their traditional ally, France. They were wrong. All the future was to offer was an endless outpouring of blood and treasure compared with which the Italian wars had been insignificant. But the magnitude of the strategic task was still unknown. It was assumed in the autumn of 1559 that all Philip needed was a little time: given that, he could be master of the world.

The other half of Charles's empire – Austria, the Alpine provinces, Swabia and the upper Rhine area incorporating claims to Bohemia and Hungary – was left in an even more precarious condition. In reality the power wielded by the Emperor was less impressive. Since 1541, most of Hungary was in the hands of the Turks and the Prince of Transylvania. Here, and in Bohemia, a powerful nobility was far from unanimous in its approval of Ferdinand's claim. Ferdinand and Maximilian were more attractive personalities than the Spanish Habsburg kings, but with their limited resources they could do little more than discharge their main function: to protect Eastern and Central Europe from the perpetual threat of the Ottoman Turks. A treaty of 1562 officially brought the war with the Turks to an end but left them with their conquests intact and the Emperor under heavy and humiliating annual tribute. Even the peace was precarious, and war flared up in 1566 and again between 1593 and 1606.

On Ferdinand's death the imperial possessions were once again divided, so that Maximilian and Rudolf were left with only Austria and the claims to Bohemia and Hungary. Here, as in most of Central and Eastern Europe, the price-rise of the second half of the sixteenth century, combined with the growing demands for greater supplies of food, prolonged and strengthened the neo-feudal economy as surely as in some areas of the west it accelerated the growth of a capitalist economy. Until around 1550 the feudal lords lived on revenues from the peasant farmers. After that date the share of the nobles in agricultural enterprise rose while that of the peasants declined. Noble demesnes worked by paid labour expanded; wheat and wine output rose. Just as in Poland, where the Vistula and the grain trade it carried northwards became the dominant force in the economy, so in Hungary the nobility took the initiative in demesne farming; so that a modern Hungarian historian has discerned among them some resemblances to the bourgeois, entrepreneurial trading activities of the Tudor gentry of Elizabethan England. Hungary, however, so far as the wild *puszta* was concerned, was to be a land of horses and cattle, symbols of the economy and culture brought by the Magyars after their long wanderings. Now they were depopulated during the wearying struggles against the Turks.

Bohemia experienced similar trends, but was more intimately influenced by the west. The Bohemian kings – Václav II, Karel IV (the first Czech emperor) and Václav IV – had turned Prague into a 'garden of delight' (Charles IV's phrase), a thriving city of forty thousand people by 1400 and second only to Rome. In the mid-sixteenth century Prague was still a flourishing Renaissance city, boasting new Italianate buildings, thriving trade and industry (including an important share of the European printing industry) and a strong, proud spirit of municipal dignity and independence. Round its castle were assembled the great Bohemian lords – the Rožmberks, Pernštejns, Lobkoviczs, Griespeks, the lords of Hradec – while the lesser nobles had their being in the outer bailey of the castle. It was by their election that Ferdinand had been voted into his kingship. He was sustained in power by their purses, and these were protected by the assembly meeting at Prague. The Austrian Habsburgs of the sixteenth century always acknowledged that they had to keep on the right side of the powerful Bohemian aristocracy.

Faced by a rising Protestantism within their own direct-rule areas and by a number of powerful Lutheran princes among the imperial vassals, Ferdinand and his successors had to tread carefully. The Empire had never been 'Holy': it now became less overtly 'Roman' and a great deal more German. The princes (fifty ecclesiastical, thirty secular), the middling nobility (about 150), the two thousand or more imperial knights, and sixty-six cities, still made their views felt through the Reichstag, the Imperial Parliament. But by the later decades of the century, religious conflict between the deputies reduced its sessions to anarchic impotence.

Since the imperial constitution could call upon no sanctions backed by force, power was passing to the more influential of the greater individual states. Of these, electoral Saxony, with its rich mining industry, was Lutheran but usually in favour of compromise in matters of imperial politics. In the Palatine electorate, on the other hand, the ruler from 1559 to 1576 was the vigorous and apparently convinced Calvinist Frederick III. His excursions against the Emperor and in favour of the Huguenots and Dutch rebels were continually fluttering the imperial dovecotes. Bavaria was an equally stout centre of support for the Counter-Reformation. The Duke confronted a strong Lutheran party among his nobles and succeeded in breaking the dissident ring and ending heresy. Protestants had to choose between conversion or exile. Bavaria became solidly Catholic. So did a great part of north-west Germany and the Rhineland, including the great imperial cities of Cologne and Aachen (most of the other free cities were Lutheran).

The prudence and flexibility of the Austrian Habsburgs paid handsome dividends for the Counter-Reform movement and its German supporters, laying the foundations for the later total extinction of Protestantism in Bohemia and Central and Eastern Europe generally. For most of the second half of the sixteenth century it is true that Calvinism continued to grow. Party alignments polarized round this new Protestantism or the new Tridentine Catholicism. But by the end of the century the Catholic position was a good deal less unpromising than would have seemed possible in 1555. How did this change of religious fortunes come about?

No single answer presents itself in either political or socio-economic terms, and even the chronological and sociological detail of the process remains obscure. Rome itself was now reorganized and regrouped for the task of bringing more effective pressure to bear on Germany. The re-Catholicization of Germany and the stemming of Protestantism may have deeper roots than this, but it is enough for our purpose to trace the reform of Rome, the emergence of the Catholic missions and the political reorganization of the Vatican.

Reform and Counter-Reform

In the 1520s Europe had been plunged into its first great religious revolt since Hus. Luther's protest had drawn its strength from a number of sources: from the sense of frustration, parish loyalty and moral outrage provoked by the hierarchy of the Roman Church which seemed specifically designed to drain and exploit Germany for the sake of an Italian Pope; from the biting satire and intellectual breadth of Erasmus and the ideas he had fostered in the cities of the Netherlands and Italy, the universities of England, France and Spain, and in the innermost recesses of the Church itself; from the ambitions of the people of the German cities to control their municipal governments and worship in their own way.

The first reaction of the Church was a shamefaced admission that there was justice behind the protest. This soon turned to a different mood as its consequences for the power and property of the Church and its secular allies were clarified. By the time of the Peace of Augsburg and the emergence of the German particularist 'solution' to the religious problem the Church was pulling itself together, though still hampered by the incompetence, corruption and eccentricity of a series of senile Popes. So far as Lutheranism was concerned it was too late to put out the fire. It had swept through Germany and Scandinavia, appealing to men through its liturgical sense and the warmth of personal piety which was Luther's own greatest contribution to the Church named after him. Then it paused, some would say stopped. Luther had little flair for, or interest in, church organization. His spirit tended to flow, like molten metal, into existing political moulds. So Lutheranism survived, but in a sadly lowered key: as a *religious* challenge it shrank away during the latter decades of the sixteenth century. Its mission was taken over by the followers of John Calvin – 'the most perfect school of Christ that ever was on the earth since the days of the Apostles', as John Knox described it. Geneva was the Holy City for Calvin and his followers. Yet Geneva was necessary as an international centre only because it was impossible for Calvin or his followers to find one in France. Calvinism was totally French in its intellectual precision and its grasp of the importance of administrative organization. Calvin, with his early French legal training, steadily thought through the traditional beliefs of the Church to produce a logical system of theology and church organization. At its heart was the belief in predestination – salvation was for the elect, and this 'election' resided in the inscrutable and timeless will of God himself.

Much has been written about Calvin's 'social' ideas, yet the theories of Max Weber and R. H. Tawney that 'capitalism' found special sanction in Calvin's doctrines is impossible to substantiate either from doctrinal or sociological evidence. Luther had condemned usury, middlemen, banks, luxury. Calvin was equally cautious: gingerly, in two pages out of the twenty volumes of his printed works, he set out his views on 'economic' matters. The gist of his remarks was to put the controversial question of usury on to a basis of simple morality rather than one of theological casuistry. It was no more unjust to charge a moderate rate of interest for a loan than to charge rent for land. But it was 'evil and foul' to wring heavy exactions from poor peasants or shopkeepers. Even in this modest re-statement Calvin was not followed by his disciples. (Voetivs, the doyen of Dutch Calvinist divines in the next century, could still excommunicate a God-fearing woman from his congregation because her husband was a pawnbroker.) So far from being consciously in sympathy with the objectives of new capitalistic modes of trade and industry, Protestants, Puritans and extreme Calvinists were frequently ranged against them as much as the medieval Church itself.

Calvinism swiftly recruited massive support in many countries. Much of it was brutally political, secular and self-interested. In France, Germany, the Netherlands, Hungary, Bohemia and elsewhere its adherents came quite early to include great nobles and hundreds and thousands of minor nobles and gentry. For many, but not all, of them it provided, directly or indirectly, a justification for overthrowing the existing government, central or local, seizing or looting Church property, dressing up in new style an old feud between one *seigneur* and another, one town against another, even one area against another. French tradition distinguished, quite simply, between 'political' and 'religious' Huguenots. Not all noble Protestants were merely destructive or hypocritical. Noble leadership and patronage, exercised for whatever motive, was a vital element in the conversion of Calvinist beliefs into political forms and allegiances. Yet a simple consideration of numbers will show that neither the nobility nor the merchant class of 'capitalists' could possibly have provided a fraction of the many hundreds of thousands who had been attracted into the various forms of Calvinism and its derivatives by the later sixteenth century in the Low Countries, France, Switzerland, England, Scotland, Germany, Hungary, Bohemia, Poland, Scandinavia and, later, North America. Who responded to the appeal of Calvinism and why?

First, it is reasonably certain that the rank-and-file were of humble origin and occupation. Most were urban or sub-urban artisans, though of these some were in the process of becoming petty capitalists. In the Low Countries the congregations were formed from artisans from the textile industries. Here, and farther north in the ports of Zeeland and Holland, Calvinists, Anabaptists and Mennonites (Baptists) were to be found among the fishermen, sailmakers, barrel-makers, salt-picklers, ship-builders and around the inland towns among the market-gardeners and rural craftsmen. Much the same was true in Scotland of the followers of Knox. The Flemish, Walloon and Dutch refugees who settled in Eastern England were mostly drawn from the same type of artisanate. Most probably came originally from the 'new drapery' area of West Flanders round Ypres – weavers, bookbinders, carpenters, gardeners, brewers and the like. There was much coming and going between Flanders, Holland and East Anglia. Not all were necessarily martyrs to their faith. Some certainly left long before the arrival of Alba's army. They were probably 'neutrals' in religion, moved more by consideration of their own safety and employment than by theological conviction. All were much the same kind of men and women who later left East Anglia and other parts of England for North America. Their social ideas also were essentially medieval. The settlers of the Pilgrim Fathers' age were still working for 'social stability, order and discipline of the senses'. It was much later in the seventeenth century that newer, more secular and economically purposeful arrivals (mainly from London) seemed to be aiming at 'mobility, growth and enjoyment of life'.[32]

Nor were circumstances very different in France. Though the location of the later Calvinist communities and *places de sûreté* is no sure guide to the early distribution of Protestantism in France, there is little doubt that the communities multiplied round the ports and up the rivers – the Rhône, Gave, Garonne, Charente, Loire, Upper Meuse – and were composed mainly of the socially humble. At Montpellier, for which precise figures exist, 70 per cent of the Huguenot community were artisans. This was not untypical of the social structure of French Calvinism. Possibly French Calvinism had a larger element of minor professional men – lawyers, scriveners, clerks, apothecaries and the like. In the upper échelons there was invariably the vital adhesion of minor gentry and the indispensable patronage of the great lord. What they emphatically were not, at this stage, were predominantly 'merchant' congregations. This fallacy seems to be the result of reading the social history of Protestantism backwards – from the later prosperous middle-class phenomena of English Dissent or North American Unitarianism of the eighteenth or nineteenth centuries. The true character of a typical Calvinist congregation emerges vividly from the surviving letters written by the Flemish refugees at Norwich to their relatives in the Ypres district. Here is one from a boy, a refugee from Ypres, able to write and describe his family and their circumstances, to his grandmother in 1567:

My dear Grandmama,

Father, Mother and my sisters are all well. We have been at Norwich a little less than 2 years, where we are living in great quietness and peace and the word of God is much preached among us. For half a year I learnt book-binding, but it gave little profit; now I have another trade. My eldest sister works for Peter Bake (of Ypres) who has a brewery here in Norwich. My brother Willekin is learning the trade of a Cutler. Father is working in a thread-twist factory. My little sister spins thread. Little Francis plays all day and little George died in the fourth week after Whit Sunday. I send you my love.

Yours loving Grandchild
Nicodemus Navegeer.

Circumstances varied from country to country. It would be strange if Calvinism proved to have precisely the same social colour in the Hungary of the new, revived feudalism as in bourgeois Holland or England. It did not; even doctrine and organization varied. The 'Helvetian' confession grew more rapidly in the Magyar areas, and in the Transylvanian Principality (ruled by Protestant princes) it was dominant. But from the start Calvinism in Hungary derived more from the 'Court Calvinism' of Heidelberg and the theologians surrounding the Courts Palatine of the Rhine, with their heavy undertow of medieval scholaticism. Its organization remained based on two institutions of which the first was certainly feudal: the rights of the secular patron (landlords in the country, city councils in the towns), which included the appointment and dismissal of pastors; the other was the preachers' synod which determined matters of discipline, liturgy and dogma, with no room for lay control. So the religious orders survived and patrons and preachers divided the Church between themselves. As the pastors' income remained that of their Catholic predecessors, they remained chained to the traditional system of tithes. Hungarian Calvinism was rent by disputes between patrons, pastors and their serf congregations. The farmers living around the market towns seem to have been the main source of lay support for protest against 'Court Calvinism'. Reformation in this neo-feudal area was hampered and distorted by prevailing political and social conditions. What is surprising is that it survived into the seventeenth century to make a contribution to the modified 'Puritan' movement of that century.

In Bohemia, too, the reforming movement took on its own peculiar shape. From the Hussite movement of the previous century it inherited a strong anti-papal, anti-clerical, moralistic tradition. Its theological basis was weak and confused. New and old Utraquists, Lutherans, Calvinists and Anabaptists provided a mêlée of ideas but were unimpressive except in their capacity for internecine warfare. Far the most positive Protestants were the Czech Brethren. Their origins went back to the medieval heresies, and in contrast to the other 'Protestants' they were concerned with discipline, education and organization. This they contrived to blend with a profound belief in personal revelation, private religious decision and a penchant for prophetic Utopianism. They took root in Poland and Hungary too; but in Bohemia, and especially in Moravia, they found their safest refuge under laws which were particularly favourable to dissidents in religion. The Brethren were therefore often confused with Anabaptism and Socinianism. Who the Czech Protestants were is less certain but evidently they were drawn from a wide cross-section of opinion and society. Ferdinand made a start on counter-reform in 1561 by refounding the Archbishopric of Prague and setting up a Jesuit Academy near by. But the Brethrens' emphasis on education made the task of reconversion very difficult in a country where the roots of heresy and anti-clericalism were deep and genuine. In the last quarter of the century a fairly reliable count estimates the proportion of Catholics at only about 10 per cent. Nowhere did the Counter-Reformers find the going more heavy, supported as the heresy was by both popular and noble sympathies.

Neither the 'social response' to the new Protestantism nor its internal, doctrinal, organizational character suggests that simple explanations of its appeal can be entirely convincing. The societies that produced Protestant converts in large numbers were socially diverse, ranging from the 'advanced' areas of the Low Countries to the 'neo-feudal' areas of Hungary and Poland. The teachings of Calvin were modified to include

or exclude relationships with other forms of protest. A few generaliza-
tions are nevertheless still possible. The appeal of Calvinism seems to
have been mainly to urban society. When one says 'urban' one does not
necessarily mean great agglomerations like London, Amsterdam or
Paris, but rather the smaller, still semi-rural towns of between two and
twenty thousand, still closely in contact with the countryside, yet sufficiently urban to permit and encourage a free and critical inquest upon
the condition of the Church, the hierarchy and the local priesthood and
feel dissatisfied with the result. The new Protestants still laid their accent
on the old rules and traditional virtues – work, prayer, abstinence.
Calvin himself had emphasized the virtues of personal character and
conduct which so often seemed to contrast with the contemporary
extravagance, ignorance, immorality and worldliness of the Popes,
bishops and local priests. His version of the Christian religion seemed to
add purpose to humble occupations, so that men who brought sobriety,
thrift and piety to their lives and tasks were as capable of believing they
might be of the elect as the born elite. Here we come to the link between
theology, conduct and social characteristics which has so often been
neglected by those who have concentrated too much on the doctrinal
content or the social relations of the new creed. Why did predestination
not promote complacency and torpor rather than application and
practical energy? The answer was fairly simple. No one could ever be
sure that he was of the elect. In an age where many men steadily became
more convinced that they lived in times of wickedness, the spiritual life
took on the nature of a holy war, especially for example in France.
Calvin and his followers did not treat religion as a comfort and a balm.
Far from it. They played upon the sense of guilt, the certainty of sin.
They made it their business to terrify and denounce: to instil into their
generation (for whom belief in eternal life or damnation was in the
nature of things) the *fear* of God – in the most literal sense. How *could* a
believer be sure that he was among the elect? One means was by the
knowledge of God's favour shown through his blessing in material
matters.

There is little doubt that for many in an easy-going society, little
concerned with efficiency or planning, promotion came to those who
could organize themselves in terms of the traditional virtues that later
came to be called 'bourgeois'. It was not so much that religion organized
on Calvinist principles was, as Tawney suggested, 'designed for a rising
bourgeois class', as that its more energetic enforcement of a traditional

morality helped to turn working artisanates into a middle class. It converted most easily 'the men who were least satisfied with things as they had been or most accustomed to make their fortunes by striking out for themselves'.[33] And of dissatisfied and ambitious men in all classes, the sixteenth-century world was not lacking.

Second only to its fundamental theology, Calvinism progressed by means of its internal organization. Calvin's ambition was to establish a new orthodoxy as strong as that of Rome and enforced by a more efficient congregational organization. The Church was to be governed by its ministers, elders and deacons. The first two orders were the guardians of faith and discipline: the deacons attended to the welfare of the poor, the sick and the orphans. Their work was no less important for it impinged on the educational propaganda that was the main weapon of the reformers. Behind a screen of pseudo-democracy, the order of Calvinism was oligarchical. Each minister was vetted by the body of pastors for his literacy and orthodoxy. The consistory, ministers and elders maintained the moral discipline of the members, turning each Church into a miniature police state, an Old Testament-inspired tyranny. The success of the system is explicable only in terms of the corrupt Church and vulnerable society against which Calvin rebelled.

Geneva, purged of its brothel-taverns and much improved in its sanitation, remained the Utopia and New Jerusalem for puritans everywhere, especially after the foundation of the university under Calvin's disciple Theodore Beza. Beza, like Calvin, was a French lawyer by training who prided himself on being a reformed rake, taking a line a good deal harder than his master. Beza contributed powerfully to the development of Geneva as the centre of training, missionary education and publishing for the new Church. Sharing with relish Calvin's intolerance, Beza in 1564 defended the killing at Lyons of Servetus, born Miguel Serveto, an Aragonese physician who was tortured for three months before being burned (*estre brusle tout vyfz* as the judges briskly expressed their sentence). Calvin had instigated the trial. He would have preferred the victim to be beheaded; Beza disagreed; so Servetus was burned.

The burning acquits Calvin and his lieutenants from any charge of being in advance of contemporary standards of humanitarianism. Indeed, the incident sent a shock of repulsion through reforming circles and completes the analogy with the inquisitorial terrorism of twentieth century fascism and communism. The fears of more liberal minds were

well grounded. The incident marked an important stage in the hardening of Calvinist dogmatism. Sharpened and brutalized by warfare in
France and the Netherlands, the Calvinists of England and Scotland
slid smoothly into the new bigotry of Beza. Here the leading figure was
William Cartwright, Lady Margaret Professor of Divinity at Cambridge, who believed as firmly as Beza that the Calvinist system was
commanded by Scripture. In Scotland, John Knox, who had learnt his
philosophy of life the hard way (he was a French prisoner of war and
galley-slave for two years), believed in matching violence by violence,
revolution with war. Men like Knox, David Black of St Andrews (who
provoked an international incident by calling Queen Elizabeth an
atheist and Kings 'the devil's children') and Andrew Melville (who
addressed James VI as 'God's silly vassal') helped to match Calvinism
with its times, to brutalize, ossify and bureaucratize it into a creed at
once pitiless and cold.

This was perhaps inevitable as its adherents were drawn into the
bloody realities of the struggle with authority, which Calvin himself had
condemned in his *Institutes*. To resist the magistrate was, for Calvin, to
resist God's will. Yet the magistrate also had another obligation: to
establish the true religion and punish the wicked. Was it not therefore
the obligation of society at large to regard the former as a more urgent
duty than obedience to a wicked ruler? By 1579 the Calvinist author of
the *Vindiciae Contra Tyrannos* (probably Duplessis-Mornay) had developed Beza's distinction between the *office* and the *person* of the magistrate into a theory of the state as a mutual covenant between prince and
people for the establishment and maintenance of true religion. If the
prince broke his contract, the people could resist him as a faithless and
unworthy usurper of his high office. Yet the deposition of the tyrant
could not be done by any private person – only by the magistrates in
virtue of their office. Beza and Duplessis-Mornay were still acutely
aware that the problem of total anarchy might always be just around
the corner.

The cutting edge of these new doctrines was still French (Beza,
Duplessis, Hotman) but all were translated into English, and supplemented from Scotland by George Buchanan's early enunciation of
something like a secular theory of the state and doctrines of natural
equality. Paradoxically, the very violence of Calvinist theory as it
developed in the violent world of 1570–1600 helped slowly to substitute
a new preoccupation with individual rights for the old corporate

concern for discipline and authority. Unwittingly, unwillingly, Calvinism helped to refound society on a secular libertarian basis.

The character and methods of Calvinism were both a result and cause of these and other changes in sixteenth-century society. Sociologically minded historians have described the Reformation as a change from an image-culture to a word-culture; from ritualism to preaching, psalm-singing and Bible-reading. Calvinists reflected the new literacy of an urban economy itself needing literate and numerate clerks. Towns were already more literate than country, Londoners, Venetians, Antwerpers more literate than the citizens of smaller, still semi-rural, towns. The literate citizens of these last seem to have represented a similar proportion of the whole population in France and the Netherlands by 1600. France had fewer towns, but the proportion of literacy was high in Huguenot towns like Montpellier or Béziers-Narbonne. The church, the pulpit, the sermon were not only the means of grace but instruments of political indoctrination, orthodox or heterodox. In Amsterdam and London pamphlets, newspapers and books flowed increasingly from the presses. When Jan Comenius, the Bohemian exile and reformer, visited London in 1641 he was astonished to see 'books on sale and congregations taking notes on sermons'. The habit was the product of a long gestation that began after the return of the English Marian exiles from Geneva. In the Low Countries there was a similar progression from the more or less untheological early phases of Protestantism to the complex and today virtually incomprehensible controversies of the early seventeenth century. The progress, despite a relative abundance of printing-presses and paper-mills and widespread urban literacy, was slow. Not until 1650 could Netherlands Protestantism claim 50 per cent of the people. In the early stages of revolt the number was nearer 5–10 per cent. Pastors were difficult to come by, for few priests came over to the new creed, and the magistracy tended to be conservative or neutral. Again, it was through political initiative, education and welfare work that the leaven worked.

The Counter-Reformation was amalgam of many forces. When Cardinal Pole made his exhortation to the second session of the Council of Trent in January 1546, he voiced a sense of responsibility on the part of the hierarchy for the alarming state of affairs in Germany and England: 'We are like salt that has lost its savour.' Yet the purpose of the Council was not merely to respond to protest: it was the total restoration of the historic Church, the restatement and clarification of dogma, the purification of the priesthood at all levels and its liberation from lay influence. From the start it was a vital conditioning factor of counter-reform that Trent was dominated by cardinals and bishops from Southern Europe – Italy and Spain especially – although the heresies and revolts it was supposed to counter had largely developed in Northern Europe. The bias was accentuated during the seventeen years of Council sessions. More and more, the Papacy emerged as the controlling force. This added threat of greater centralization was anathema to the Protestants, for whom the Council portended a new Babylonish captivity of the Christian Church. Even Philip of Spain complained that his bishops returned from Trent with their status reduced to that of priests. The conventionally Catholic faithful in the French *parlements* and the States of the Netherlands likewise complained of the new clericalism. When the Council ended in 1563, the outlook was still gloomy. Protestantism, in ever more violently contentious forms, was still spreading. Even in Italy and Spain heresy was not yet broken. Yet by 1600 France and the Spanish Netherlands had been won back to the Church, Protestantism was at least contained in large areas of Germany and Austria–Hungary and Poland were bitterly divided. Everywhere Protestants went in fear that the Reformation stood in danger of extinction. How had this great reversal come about?

To some extent, the revival of Catholic piety antedated the Reformation and might well have developed strongly without its added stimulus. In Spain and Italy the Counter-Reformation owed its success to the steady, automatic support of the Spanish Habsburgs, the most powerful monarchy of the age, in collaboration with the Holy Office of the Inquisition. Here was a state within a state, a faceless terror – comparable to the KGB in modern Russia – which could outlaw the Archbishop of Toledo and defy even the Pope himself. Dissidence in any form, including racial impurity, was its target; Protestants, heretics, Muslims and Jews its predestined victims. Yet alongside these instruments of retribution were found less repellent influences. Outstanding was the missionary zeal of the religious orders and of individuals like St Charles Borromeo, the Cardinal Archbishop of Milan. Catholic activities in the universities revived and were sometimes strongest among those orders and persons who most deeply distrusted the acknowledged spearhead of counter-reform, the Jesuits. Depending directly upon Rome, the Jesuits provided not merely a new and extraordinarily detailed training for the priesthood in theology, preaching, instruction and pastoral technique, but the opportunity for members of the society of Jesus, future priests and laymen, to receive a liberal education in history, languages, astronomy and mathematics. Influenced to some extent by Calvinist example the Church now recognized more fully than ever before the vital role of systematic training and education in winning men back into the Catholic fold. From institutions like the University of Ingolstadt in Bavaria, strongly under Jesuit influence, came a stream of well-trained Catholics from whom the parish priests and bishops of the future were to be recruited. The stemming of the strong Protestant tide in Germany and Austria by the sixteenth-century Habsburgs could never have been achieved without Jesuit help, supervised from the *Congregatio Germanica*, founded at Rome in 1573 to oversee the Catholic salvation of Germany.

Vital though re-education and decontamination of the elite and masses was seen to be, Rome never forgot that the contemporary world was an authoritarian one. The diplomatic representation of the Papacy through its nuncios in Germany and elsewhere and its agents at the courts of princes everywhere – Protestant states included – reflected the new organization of the Papal States themselves.

It has not been sufficiently recognized how much the spiritual progress of the Counter-Reformation and the diplomatic leverage which the Counter-Reformation Papacy exercised in the Catholic states owed to the administrative reorganization of the Papal States themselves. The sixteenth century realized the Papal dream of ages. Beginning with Julius II – energetic, impulsive, indomitable – successive Popes pushed back the Papal frontiers, incorporating many new enclaves and reducing neighbouring city-states and fiefs to submission. In 1506 it was Bologna, then Faenza, Ravenna, Cervia, Rimini, Ancona and finally, in 1598, Ferrara. The old feudal and military nobility, like the Orsini, and Colonna, were reduced to internecine feuds among themselves, or with newer creations of the Popes, like the Aldobrandini and Peretti. If not bankrupted by war, they ruined themselves by extravagant building and high life.

The revival of Rome after the chaos of the Borgias, the ravages of the French 'barbarians' and the sack of Rome itself by the imperial troops was a truly remarkable achievement, all the greater when one remembers that the Reformation was not only a political humiliation and religious loss. It was also a financial catastrophe of the first magnitude which cut the Popes off from essential sources of income, especially in Germany,

England and the Netherlands. Yet in a hundred years the population of the city more than trebled – from thirty thousand to more than a hundred thousand. New public buildings, private palaces, magnificent churches, new streets, acqueducts and fountains appeared, while dependent cities like Bologna and Ancona were sucked dry. On 18 April 1506 Julius II blessed the foundation-stone of St Peter's, to be built to the grand design of Bramante, embellished and modified by Michelangelo and Raphael. The supreme symbol of the new Papal Renaissance was to take a hundred and twenty years to complete and the cost was enormous. So was the cost of the works by Julius's successors of the later decades of the century, especially Sixtus V (1585–90), a Peretti, who enlarged the Vatican Library, drained the Pontine Marshes, created the Via Sistina, Santa Maria Maggiore, the Felice acqueduct, the obelisks of the Vatican, the Lateran, restored the columns of Trajan and Antoninus, completed the great cupola of St Peter's and the Sistine Chapel. To the costs of what was only a prelude to the great Baroque age of Papal patronage of the arts had to be added those of the Papal wars – against the Turks, French, Spaniards, Huguenots – waged with the new and expensive techniques of infantrymen, artillery and fortifications. How was the money found?

The answer is: by an administration and bureaucracy which for a time turned the Papal states into a model state. Foreign policy was guided by the chief minister and Papal administrator. The Cardinal-Chamberlain controlled domestic affairs. His Vice-Chamberlain was in charge of security as chief of police. Under Sixtus V the Papal States were said to be the safest country in Europe and the 'bandits' who had come into being as a protest against the new order were routed. The whole bureaucracy was taken over by ecclesiastics. Even the remnants of republicanism in the dependent fiefs disappeared. The coinage, the alum mines, prisons, rivers, tolls, food supplies were all (by the standards of the day) unusually well run, under the eye of the Congregation of Cardinals in their regular meetings.

Less desirable consequences were, however, equally inescapable. From being the most lightly taxed of the Italian states, the Papal States became, by 1600, the most heavily taxed, and a vast public debt had been created by means of bonds floated in Italy and abroad (the *luoghi di monte*). Nevertheless, for a time Rome became immensely prosperous. With the monopoly of the alum mines of Tolfa, a large invisible export income from the thousands of pilgrims and tourists, its mints and grain markets, Rome seemed to be set fair for prosperity. In 1595 Giovanni Botero, the Papal administrator, pronounced with satisfaction: 'The Ecclesiastical State is more peaceful today than formerly and the authority of its prince greater than it ever has been.' Up to a point Botero was right. The Pope's domains swept up from the west coast of Italy, skirting Florence (where ruled the relations of Popes Leo x, Clement VII and Pius IV) across to the Adriatic and Ancona, north to Ravenna, Bologna and Ferrara and the Papal fief of Modena. Domestically Rome was safe and well administered. Yet its economic basis was exceedingly narrow. It had few industries or trades, except those which catered for the tourists and the nobility. It was an economy not of manufacturers but of debts and taxes, not of workers, but of consumers. Enterprise that might have gone into production trickled away into pawnbroking, and its archetypes were its idle aristocracy and the Genoese and Florentine bankers who lent not only to the Pope but to the other cities and tributaries who needed money to scrape together their offertory to the Pope. Botero, a politician and leading social propagandist for the Counter-Reformation, was deeply imbued with the doctrines it was his profession to propagate. In his book on *The Greatness of Cities* he assumes that the desiderata of urban greatness are the presence of nobility, of government offices and officers, bureaucrats, lawyers. Geneva and other cities that had grown as centres of trade he dismisses as unworthy of the title. The Counter-Reformation city, in Spain, in Italy, in Belgium, in Austria and Bavaria, preferred grandeur to solvency, display to profit, uniformity of style to the variety required by economic or social realities. They might still have a bourgeois elite, but by 1630 it was to be one of high bureaucrats rather than of merchants.

Rome too kept going. Like other princely states dedicated to the Counter-Reformation, the Papacy was sustained by the temporary largesse which Spain spread among its clientage from its American windfall. Thus a Church once universal became narrower and more parochial. It was now too alarmed by the consequences to indulge its old medieval latitude towards deviants, minor and unimportant though they might be. The Erasmists of Italy and Spain were hounded down and out; so were the Calvinists, Anabaptists of Flanders and Germany (later of France too). And with them went their industries and trades. Even a Catholic state like Venice saw the writing on the wall, risking Papal interdict rather than yield to Botero's idea of the state as a unity of state *and* church. Under the guidance of the Counter-Reformation machine that was Rome, the Catholic Church became politically 'the church of the princely system and, in society, the church of a "feudal", official system: it was exclusively tied to these systems, its old elasticity had gone, intellectually and spiritually as well as politically'.[34] The only discussions of the Congregations of Cardinals that failed totally to achieve anything were those piously but vainly dedicated to the problem of how to reduce Papal taxation and economize Papal spending.

Warfare: New Style

The modern science of history was conceived during the century following the Napoleonic Wars when war intruded seriously on the ordinary life of Western Europeans for only brief interludes. Historians derived from the times in which they were fortunate to live quite erroneous ideas about the past, among them ideas about peace and war. In their own day war could reasonably be regarded as an uncomfortable interlude between long 'normal' stretches of peace. In the sixteenth and seventeenth centuries, on the other hand, the natural condition of 'international' relations – in so far as we can even use the term – was nearer to war than it was to peace: let us say a precarious equilibrium always inclining towards war. Even 'normal relations' (between England and Spain, Spain and the Netherlands, France and Spain) were constantly interrupted by what a later age would have regarded as acts of war – such as, for instance, the English seizure of the Duke of Alba's payships at Plymouth in 1568 on Queen Elizabeth's orders. Medieval wars had been declared, and sometimes conducted, according to very formal conventions – like the tournaments they resembled. But the weakness of the rules governing international relations in general, and in particular of diplomatic procedure, had probably helped to prevent warlike incidents becoming the occasion of widespread and continuous conflict. With the French invasions of Italy, however, war became the norm; peace an unnatural interval in which the breathless but still ardent contestants recovered their wind for the next round.

The new age of warfare was the outcome of many underlying tensions inherent in the structure and psychology of Renaissance society: dynastic, economic, tribal, personal but also – and increasingly as the Reformation and Counter-Reformation came into confrontation – religious. Religion might be a cloak for the material interests of powerful individuals and groups, but the wars of the period cannot be simply 'explained', still less explained away, as struggles for economic objectives. Whether we regard it as deep spirituality or ignorant superstition, religion was the moving force that impelled men into some of the most brutal and bloody wars in history; in Italy, France, the Netherlands, Germany and Bohemia, war was generated by the belief that the most fundamental values of human life were at stake. No considerations of mere pelf could explain their ferocity, even in a ferocious age.

The Treaty of Cateau-Cambrésis ended the Habsburg-Valois wars between these particular combatants only formally. Both they and nearly every other European prince and state were almost at once embroiled in a series of new and complicated conflicts. The Spanish aristocracy were found mangling the Netherlands subjects of Spain in the name of religion and fealty. In France they were allied with the extreme Catholic faction, and opposed by the nobles (both Catholic and Protestant) of the Netherlands and France, who equally claimed feudal and religious sanction for their decisions. Elizabeth of England found herself threatened by the same Catholic crusaders of France and Spain, while the King of France became deeply involved in the complex politics of Poland. For the Guises the peace was 'the peace of the Constable', their enemy Montmorency. For the Duke of Alba, whose military experience had secured for the Emperor and his son Philip a large measure of Spanish military success, Cateau-Cambrésis likewise seemed a betrayal which he openly blamed on the rival Eboli faction at the Spanish Court. The peace, in short, was popular with nobody; it therefore merely inaugurated a new kind of violence dominated by the spy and the assassin and, at sea, the privateer and the pirate. Technically, the Christian world might be at peace. In practice, a series of civil wars spilled over the national frontiers of Europe, bringing international bloodshed with them.

There was, therefore, no interruption in the process which since the late fifteenth century had been transforming the nature and conduct of warfare. Medieval warfare had been dominated by cavalry. Its scale was bounded by the size of the knightly class. All this was ended by the victories of the Swiss infantry and their eighteen-foot pikes over the Burgundian cavalry between 1475 and 1477. The implications of these battles were driven home by Niccolò Macchiavelli in his *Discourses* and *Art of War*, and his opinions were widely influential. Quantity, Macchiavelli argued, had triumphed over quality. Armies would therefore grow larger; warfare would be on a proportionately larger scale. He was right on both counts. Only in his belief that battles would be shorter and more decisive was he wrong.

The Italian wars, as we have seen, were more ferocious and unrestrained than ever. By the 1530s the brakes were taken off the size of armies. To defend Milan and invade Provence, Charles v mobilized 60,000 men – twice the size of the armies of the earlier wars. In the 1570s his son was maintaining an army, in Flanders alone, of 86,000 men. By 1623 Philip IV was to boast of armed forces of 300,000 men. Most of the increase was in the infantry – and the same was true of armies in France, the Netherlands and England. Why did this happen? Largely because the conditions of warfare changed, as the military engineers increased the strength of town defences in siege-warfare.

Previously it had been common for a besieging force to break up the relatively vulnerable walls of a town by mines, gunfire or rams and follow up with infantry assault. The coming of the elaborate defensive works which came to be known as the *trace italienne* from the late fifteenth century switched the advantage to the defenders. Projections from the walls (bastions) were provided with platforms for defence artillery which prevented the attackers from coming within range of the town. It was therefore necessary for them to build a double chain of fortifications of their own round the defenders' perimeter. The inner circle was directed against the defenders, the outer to hold off any armies which might try to relieve them.

Not only was it unlikely that a town defended by a well-designed apparatus on the new plan would easily fall except by total blockade, but the conduct of the action was no longer the old-fashioned quick knock-out, with victory going to brawn rather than brain. It was now a complex game of skill and calculation. After the open battle of Gembloux in 1578, when Don John of Austria and the Spaniards defeated the army of the anti-Spanish Netherlands States-General, William Davison, who was watching the situation in the Low Countries for the Queen of England, reported back to Lord Burghley that things were perhaps not as black as they seemed. For whereas the Spaniards had failed to follow up their victory, the States had taken advantage of the delay to put the defences of some of their cities and towns in the south Netherlands into good readiness. So the Spaniards were faced with

having to expunge one towne after another, the least of a number whereof cannot cost [Don John] less than half a yares' siege with an infinite charge, loss of men and hazard of his fortune and reputation because (as men of warr are wont to saye) one good towne well defended sufficeth to ruyn a mightie army.[35]

Davison's observation was perfectly accurate. The *trace italienne* spread steadily from north Italy after the 1520s until it reached into all the main war zones of Europe. Italian-trained engineers had built bastions all along the Franco-Netherlands border at the instigation of Francis I. Charles V followed with defences on his side – at Charlemont, Philippeville and other towns. The majority of the sieges in the Dutch Eighty Years War were long blockades aimed at starving out the defenders. They were fought largely round the *trace italienne* – infantry duels with only occasional use of light cavalry. Much of the territory, especially in the north Netherlands was intensively urbanized, like north Italy itself. Only farther south, where there was more open country, would cavalry be useful.

Vast numbers of men were tied down to garrison duty. Nearly one-third of the Spanish Army of Flanders was thus engaged, for within the seventeen provinces lay more than two hundred walled cities, to say nothing of 150 chartered towns and over six thousand villages. Sixty massive fortresses guarded the whole area. The cost of these fortifications, often built in brick (which absorbed shot better than stone) was enormous. And, if morale collapsed, even the *trace italienne* was rendered useless in these war-games of time and cunning. Thus in the end Ghent and Antwerp, and many other cities of the south simply surrendered to the Spanish conqueror because, although their defences were still virtually intact, the will to resist had gone. Neither river barriers nor urban fortifications were an infallible shield against defeat. It was not for nothing that the greatest master of warfare in the Netherlands wars of the sixteenth century, Prince Maurice of Nassau, was called the chess-master: for it was by juggling with the mathematical implications of the siege, the tactical possibilities of ballistics and the potential of his sappers that he achieved his victories.

Even Maurice could not take out of warfare the element which characterized it most vividly: its uncertainty and its indecisiveness. In this respect warfare exemplified to the full another feature of the age difficult for later generations to grasp. Naturally, strategy and tactics on land and sea aimed at decision. The pitched battle on land which tried to reach a rapid outcome rested on assumptions somewhat like those of the 'fleet-in-being' in maritime war. In both cases the object was to destroy the striking potential of the other side. But more commonly war had become siege war and therefore, like the kind of maritime war that was directed against trade, a war of attrition. Only rarely could land or sea battles be described as decisive. At sea, fleets could be heavily damaged, but most often were preserved by fog or storm to fight another day. On land armies survived until darkness fell and enabled the near-defeated to creep away and regroup. Naturally, there were local, tactical exceptions to this. Individual sieges were appallingly successful. But generally strategic finality escaped the grasp of commanders whose material resources were invariably inadequate and whose organization was too casual. Thus Farnese's capture of Maastricht in the end meant little. Philip's careful preparation of the Armada ended in catastrophe: but victory did not hand any immediate palm to the English. 'Peace settlements' were usually brought about by exhaustion and the collapse of the will to continue fighting. This was true of Cateau-Cambrésis, Vervins, the Hispano-Dutch truce of 1609 and of the Peace of Westphalia in 1648.[36]

THE GREAT CIVIL WARS

FRANCE AND THE CALVINIST CHALLENGE 1559–1572

Down to the end of the Habsburg-Valois wars the kings of France had managed to hold in check the conflicts inherent in French aristocratic society. Now war was suspended; Henry II was dead.

At the accession of Francis II the problem of maintaining a balance between the great nobles scarcely arose. His wife, after all, was Mary, Queen of Scots, and her uncles were the Duke of Guise and Charles, Cardinal of Lorraine. They formed an invincible combination which neither the old Constable of France, Anne de Montmorency, nor Antony of Bourbon, King of Navarre nor his brother the Prince of Condé could match in courage, skill or intrigue. Guise and Montmorency were originally divided by ambition and tradition more than by religion. The Bourbons were already Protestant, though Antony, as was his nature, was never more than lukewarm and Condé's own views were still unclear to all and suspect by many.

The 1550s had seen widespread conversions to Calvinism in France at all levels of society. Among the nobles there was discontent, some of it perfectly genuine, at the state to which the Church had been reduced under the Concordat of 1516. To the anti-Guise faction the Cardinal of Lorraine seemed the embodiment of corruption and pluralism. Thus concern for the condition of the Church merged with their private and material discontents – inflation of prices, depreciation of the government *rentes* (annuities) into which many had put their capital, and the cramping effects of the *dérogation* system. An alternative form of religion, tailor-made by French minds and skilfully organized on a basis at once flexible and adaptable, had a natural appeal. By 1559 Calvinism was fashionable, and its progress was accelerated by the conversion of some influential figures persuaded by the debating talent of Theodore Beza and the hand-picked team of Genevan missionaries who infiltrated France under his guidance. Women were especially vulnerable to the appeal of Calvinism: Jeanne d'Albret, wife of the King of Navarre, mother of the future Henry IV and a powerful figure in the new movement; Eléonore de Roye, wife of Condé, who in turn converted her impetuous husband, and the mother of Philippe de Plessis-Mornay, one of the most influential thinkers in the French reform movement. Between them, these three women indirectly helped to provide the guidance for the next three or four decades of French Protestantism. Even the staunchly Catholic Montmorency found Calvinism penetrating the Chatillon branch of his family. Of the three Chatillon brothers, one achieved the remarkable feat of becoming a cardinal without ever being ordained and retaining his office and revenues as a prince of the Church after his conversion to Protestantism. The second brother, Gaspard de Coligny, Admiral of France, had been converted while a prisoner in the Low Countries during the recent wars. Conviction, anti-clericalism, humanism, intellectual modishness, material discontents – such were the mixed and sometimes conflicting motives that steered large numbers of the French nobility towards Protestantism in the 1550s and 1560s.

For the moment Catherine de Medici, mother of four boys of whom the eldest was only fifteen years old, could do nothing but capitulate to Guise influence and watch helplessly while their policies of repression provoked the Bourbons into violent revolt. Condé himself kept in the background. It was left to a minor noble, de la Renaudie, to plan the first Calvinist coup at Amboise in March 1560 designed to eliminate the Guises. It failed and most of the conspirators were killed. Condé, continuing to plot, was himself arrested, sentenced to death and only saved by the sudden death of the king himself. The situation at Court was at once transformed. Catherine de Medici swiftly had herself appointed regent to her second son who now became king as Charles IX. Now it was the turn of the Bourbons (Condé and the King of Navarre) to seize power. This was the first of the cox-and-box changes of court influence which were to reduce the government to incapacity for anything but mischief and France itself to misery, violence and poverty for nearly forty years.

The position of Catherine de Medici provides the ultimate rationale for the standard contemporary clichés about the nature of government: the insistence on the weakness of female authority, the importance of establishing accepted orders of succession and authority, the subordination of even the great to the greatest, and the nature of monarchy as the unapproachable pinnacle of political power. All these were thrown into relief by the death of Henry II and the procession of sickly boys who followed him. Catherine's policies were a catastrophe of the first order for France. She learnt only slowly – if ever – that the gap between the Catholicism of Rome, Spain and the Guises on one side, and the Calvinism of Beza, Condé and de la Noue on the other was daily becoming wider and more unbridgeable. The moderates were being silenced and extruded from power during one of those periods of violence and bigotry by which history is from time to time punctuated. She had no understanding of the political difficulties inherent in the theological conflicts when, in August 1561, she summoned Beza and the Cardinal of Lorraine and arranged with them the so-called 'Colloquy' of Poissy to try and thrash out a national religious compromise. Superficially her strategy, even her tactics, were plausible. Why should not Guise and Bourbon live in peace at Court? Why should not the growing number of Huguenots be offered some sort of olive-branch? Why should not everybody sit together in conference and work out a rational, sensible political solution?

Her methods were tested at Poissy; they were found wanting. True, Catholic and Protestants mingled to observe the strange spectacle of the Pope's delegate listening to the Huguenot party sing psalms and hearing Calvinist sermons. Beza dominated the debate, until the Jesuit General Laynez intervened, after two weeks' fruitless argument, to denounce the whole proceedings as an invasion of territory properly the domain of the Council of Trent. Catherine's policy was doomed. The only result of Poissy was to encourage the Huguenots to think of themselves as the soldiers of the Crown; while in deep suspicion of her policies Guises and Montmorencys drew together.

There was a fatal facility about her tactics at Poissy which not only made the tensions appreciably worse but positively emphasized the growing isolation of regent and monarchy. Dominating all other elements in her character was Catherine's intense, ferocious maternalism; for her sons' sakes she was capable of anything. In her favour it must be conceded that the irreconcilability which surrounded her was something new and strange, especially to one coached in the deviousness and expediency of Italian politics. Nor should we read back the neo-Calvinism of the later anti-monarchical, tyrannicidal polemicists into the 1560s. That came only after 1572, and largely as the result of Catherine's failures. In the jealousies and ambitions of Guise, Bourbon and Montmorency she faced not merely the most bitter feud for political power waged anywhere in Europe, but a contest between ex-generals experienced in war, backed by effective private armies, operating from well-organized territorial bases. The prize for which they fought was essentially the control of the king, her son. Finally, as if all this was not enough, her problems were not merely domestic. No sooner had the treaties been signed at Le Cateau-Cambrésis than France became a stage upon which European dynastic ambitions and religious conflicts were to be played out. The politics of France were thereafter inextricably entangled with those of Spain, the Netherlands, England, Germany and even Poland.

Only a spark was needed to set ablaze the combustible material stacked up for twenty years and now exposed by the fiasco at Poissy. It was provided by the Duke of Guise. On 1 March 1562 he found a party of Huguenots at worship at Vassy (in Guise territory). Thirty were killed and a hundred or more wounded. Condé immediately ordered the Huguenots to arms while the Guises and Montmorency seized Paris. More massacres took place, the worst at Sens, south of Paris. Now Catherine called upon Condé and Coligny to help, but in vain. The details of the three episodes of open civil war which followed need not concern us except for a few general observations. For a decade the losses to the leadership of both sides were fairly even. The Duke of Guise and the King of Navarre were killed; Condé and Montmorency were taken prisoner. Catherine, now disillusioned about the power of the Huguenots, made haste to pacify their enemies. Calvinism had already suffered restrictions under the peace of Amboise that closed the first phase of the war in 1563. As the Huguenots' own resentment at her policies grew, they naturally suspected her motives in agreeing to the meeting with Philip of Spain at Bayonne in mid-summer 1565, where Philip was, in the end, represented by the Duke of Alba. Huguenot suspicion, though exaggerated, was natural enough. It became part of the tarred image of Philip II carefully fostered by Protestant leaders that at Cateau-Cambrésis a plot was hatched with Henry II of France to exterminate all heretics in their dominions. If the detail was wrong, the principle was in essence correct. And it was, above all, Alba who had consistently urged

Philip to foment to the utmost the grievances of French Catholics against the Protestant nobility.

As the vendetta grew in France, it became clear that the major struggle was between the Guises and Gaspard de Coligny. Of all the high noble Calvinists, Coligny was the only one whose motives were primarily and sincerely religious. His own conversion had been slow and painful, but once achieved he brought to French Calvinism all his personal courage, commitment, authoritarian discipline and patriotism – as he understood it; and his understanding was that his beliefs conferred on him the duty to secure freedom of worship for the Protestants and deliverance of the king from Guise control. Coligny was marked out by his singleness of purpose. It was this which for a time gave a special unity to French Calvinism with all its strange and varied adherents.

Coligny was no diplomat. He had none of the subtlety and flexibility of mind which enabled William the Silent to fuse together an equally difficult team of opposition long enough to achieve its improbable destiny. Again, it was Alba who recognized in Coligny a man whose principles and character were dangerous. By 1564 he was doing his best to persuade Philip that with Coligny at their head the French Calvinists represented the greatest threat to his plans for a Catholic Europe. Cardinal Granvelle (now removed by Philip from the Netherlands under pressure from the Netherlands nobles) was at one with Alba in marking out Coligny as the major target. Was he not also a cousin of the Baron of Montigny, who, along with Egmont, was the emissary of evil tidings of dissidence from Philip's Netherlands dominions? Were they not both of the apostate branch of the Montmorencys? Events in France seemed to bear out Alba's fears. Despite Coligny's personal antipathy to the idea of civil war, the logic of events was more and more forcing the Calvinists to infiltrate public office and seize control of municipal and provincial government. The Calvinist international, forged as an ecclesiastical reality under Beza's leadership, was now becoming an economic and military reality too.

By 1568 the Huguenots had an army of twenty-five thousand men, while from La Rochelle came forth a fleet of between forty and fifty ships manned by sailors whose theology might be rough and ready but whose hatred of Spain was deep and resolute, rooted as it was in bloody encounters in the Indies and in the knowledge that Spanish seaborne trade offered rich pickings to the bold. In turn, they were in close touch with the privateers whose exclusion from Netherland ports by Spanish forces sent them searching for shelter, maintenance and victuals in any English or French port where they could gain entry.

When in 1567 Philip despatched Alba with an army of ten thousand by the overland route from Italy to Flanders which became known as the 'Spanish Road', there were widespread fears among the Protestant powers or minorities who lined the route that Alba's object might also include the elimination of Protestantism in their territories. But Alba went straight to his target, while in France two more 'civil' wars were fought before peace was signed in 1570. Once again there had been heavy losses. Cities were sacked and burnt in the worst excesses of brutality so far. At Orléans two hundred Huguenots were murdered by a Catholic mob in their prison and others later burnt to death in the blazing building. Condé was shot in the back and killed – after the battle. His counsels were dispensable. He had always been a doubtful asset to the Huguenots. Now that he was gone no one disputed the supremacy of Coligny.

With German mercenary help, the Calvinists had ended the war stronger than they began it. Their reward, in 1570, was the new concession of four *places de sureté* garrisoned for safety and the retirement of the Guises from Court. Their departure marked the revulsion – shared by others besides dedicated Protestants – against Guise arrogance and the growing distrust of their involvement in international plots. Already Alba, their friend in the Low Countries, had beheaded two of the leading Catholic nobles, Egmont and Hoorn. Both Alba and the Cardinal of Lorraine were plotting with a group of dissident nobles in England only too ready to accept Alba's bribes in return for overthrowing Queen Elizabeth. The plan of late 1569, urged on by the Pope (who was preparing to excommunicate Elizabeth) was nothing if not comprehensive: Elizabeth was to be killed; Mary Queen of Scots was to take her place; the northern Catholic earls were to foment general rebellion while England would be invaded by a fleet controlled by the Guises from France.

A decade of bloody warfare and a widespread sense of hopelessness was nevertheless bringing a general change of atmosphere. In France itself, a group of growing influence was forming round François de Montmorency, son of the old Constable. The word *politique* was already in popular usage to describe those who had come to believe that the problem of religion had to be taken out of the hands of fanatics before they destroyed France. Such views were uppermost in the wake of the recent wars, and no one entered into their spirit more warmly than the queen-mother, who envisaged not only France but Europe pacified by a suitable pattern of matchmaking. Her daughter would marry Henry of Navarre, now the leading Bourbon, and thus unite French Catholics and Protestants. Her son, Charles IX, would marry the Emperor's daughter, thus burying the Habsburg-Valois hatchet. Her second son, Henry of Anjou would marry Queen Elizabeth and finally end the ancient rivalry with England.

More immediately, an Anglo-French treaty (Blois 1572) provided in elaborate detail for a defensive alliance between the two old enemies, and economic arrangements which would have replaced Antwerp by Rouen as the Continental market for English cloth. There is nothing to indicate that anything except expediency motivated Elizabeth in putting her signature to the treaty. Nothing came of it. More comprehensive arrangements, including a war to break the Spanish encirclement of France, did not even reach the wastepaper basket. They were merely the stuff of the interminable comings-and-goings within the Protestant international led, not by Coligny, but by Louis of Nassau. Louis was a bold and important figure in these years before his brother, William, emerged from exile in Germany. He was Coligny's intimate, and commander and organizer of the Dutch and French privateers who lived off Spanish shipping plying between the Netherlands and western France. The grand strategy which Louis of Nassau urged upon the impressionable Charles IX was this: Louis, with de la Noue and other Huguenot forces, would join up on the Hainault frontier to capture Mons and Valenciennes – the entrance from France into Flanders; his brother William would advance from Germany via Duisburg into Gelderland. The reward for France? The southern half of the Netherlands would become French. The northern half? Perhaps – if Elizabeth could be drawn into agreement – it would fall under English sovereignty; or, if she hesitated, become part of the Empire.

Louis encountered one insuperable problem: nobody had any enthusiasm for his plan. Even Coligny was unconvinced that French Huguenot resources were sufficient to be divided between France and the Netherlands. Catherine de Medici, though not radically opposed, feared that any move so manifestly pro-Protestant would renew all the factions at the French Court now for the moment dormant. Elizabeth was hesitant to make any move towards opposing Philip overtly in his lawful dominions. Any basis of agreement between such an ill-assorted collection of potential allies had to be tenuous, to say the least. It was also known – in France as well as in England – that Alba had his hands full in the Netherlands and was not anxious to back hard-liners in Madrid in their enthusiasm for an invasion of England. Elizabeth herself had no wish to see a substantial French presence on the strategically vital Netherlands coast. Nobody, in fact, except Louis really wanted decisive action in the spring of 1572.

One important battle remained: the battle for the will of the King of France, now torn between his mother's fears of taking any further action to help the Dutch rebels and the urgings of Coligny, who had now brought himself to believe Spain could be defeated if only Charles would agree to send a French army into the field under his command. Coligny won. Early in August, Charles IX was persuaded to put an army of fifteen thousand under Coligny's command into Flanders and on 11 August he wrote to William the Silent to announce his decision. But before it could be put into practice, Coligny was assassinated and the flower of the Huguenot leadership was lying massacred in Paris.

Much about the Massacre of St Bartholomew remains obscure. First as regards the complicity of Catherine de Medici, to whom total responsibility has often been assigned: this has become increasingly doubtful. The Massacre was neither the first nor the last mass killing in a war fraught with such things. The butchery of two to three thousand Huguenots in Paris and many thousands of others in the provinces does not seem to have been any part of her calculation. Her direct complicity in the affair was limited to her part in the attempt on Coligny's life on 22 August 1572. Injured by a shot from the arquebus of an assassin, he nevertheless survived – firearms were still very unreliable weapons. The act was almost certainly done with her approval if not at her instigation. She had been reported as telling the Spanish Ambassador that he would soon see 'a service to God and this King so remarkable that Philip and the world would rejoice over it'. It was said that she had promised pardon and reward for anyone who would kill Coligny. Such reports may have been true, or partly true; undoubtedly Catherine was in the Medici tradition.

But her plans never allowed for the failure of the assassination. The worst had now happened. Matters were out of Catherine's hands: the Guises took over, and with them the always anti-Huguenot Paris mob. The list of victims, long prepared by the Guises (who continued, wrongly, to blame Coligny for the killing of the Duke of Guise in 1563) was the basis of the Massacre. Swiftly St Bartholomew became a subject of conflicting legends. To the Protestants, Catherine was the villain of the piece, the Machiavellian brain behind the conspiracy; Charles ix the executioner. To the Guises and Catholic extremists, it was the culmination of crusade and blood-feud. A fervently Catholic Paris butcher would boast that he killed four hundred Huguenots by himself. Philip of Spain sent Catherine messages of fulsome praise for her services to God and Christendom. Pope and cardinals chanted a special *Te Deum*. Even such relative moderates as the Venetian Senate and the Duke of Tuscany forwarded polite diplomatic congratulations. Catherine herself showed no remorse. She merely lied to the Protestant powers, exculpating herself from all responsibility.

The black legend of the Massacre wrote itself. Even at a distance of centuries, and with due allowance for the character of the age, it remains horrid witness to the bestiality that always lay just under the glossy surface of the civilization of the Renaissance. As the most recent authority on the subject has said, the fundamental question to be asked by anyone wanting to understand the reasons for the Massacre relates to the principal victim.[37] Why did Coligny have to die? Fundamentally, because he had provoked the jealousy of Catherine by acquiring excessive power over her son and, thereby, over France. His was the first name on the list of those who were despatched on 24 August. With him went the natural leader, of the Huguenot movement, for a large part of the Huguenot nobility were assembled in Paris for the marriage of their young hero Henry of Navarre to the queen's daughter, Margaret of Valois. Of the elite, only Henry of Navarre and the Prince of Condé escaped.

The loss of thousands of leaders in a shock attack changed the character of Calvinism. To this had to be added the demoralizing effects on those less able to contemplate the prospects of an endless fight against hopeless odds. Calvinism in France was purged of the half-hearted. Its continuing support came from the totally committed, especially in the old dissident areas of west and south, like Languedoc or La Rochelle, which now prepared itself for a seven-month siege.

The surviving members of the old Huguenot party saw their ideology undergoing a fundamental change. Between 1572 and 1579, the author of the *Vindiciae contra Tyrannos* and other apologists of militant resistance, worked out their theories which empowered the 'magistrates' (the lawfully appointed civil authority) to authorize resistance to a tyrannical ruler. In some places – as in the *Apology* of William of Orange – this was joined with the older idea that an outraged *feudal* subject could withdraw his fealty. The idea of a contract of government linked the old and new ideas.

The contraction of the Calvinist appeal under threat of extermination, and the new doctrines of resistance, suggest a hardening and sharpening of doctrine. But this change within the Calvinist Church was accompanied by another and quite different development in practical politics and theory. The Massacre gave added force to those *politiques* who felt that the time had come to limit confessional strife. The younger branches of the House of Montmorency, influenced also perhaps by their Netherlands relatives, were already inclining to such views. The second son of the old Constable, Henri Montmorency-Damville, strongly entrenched in Languedoc where he was governor, announced his readiness to support any reasonable moves to end the civil wars. This, as events were to show, was beyond his power; but slowly the area which he governed began to assume something of the character of an independent state. By 1574 a general assembly of Montmorency and Huguenot supporters at Nîmes consolidated this semi-independent group of provinces – Languedoc, Provence and Dauphiné. They had the support of the youngest (and most mischievous) of the Valois, the Duke of Alençon, and of Henry of Navarre, temporarily unemployed and with no visible means of support. The Montmorency move in the south was to demonstrate its own threat to France later. For the moment it provided a rescue operation for the Protestants and Henry of Navarre.

The effect of the Massacre for the Netherlands rebels was shattering. It came at a critical moment in the fortunes of their military operations on land. Both Louis of Nassau and William the Silent were anxiously awaiting help from France to extricate them at Mons and Mechlin respectively. Both were compelled to bow to Alba, whose forces were now freed to move north into Holland and Zeeland. The hopes of the rebels were now pinned on the unlikely prospects of the 'Sea-Beggars', who had made landfall at the Brill on the appropriate date of 1 April. But their numbers were small and the reaction of the Dutch people to their arrival uncertain. Alba dismissed them as unimportant and continued with his policies of terror at Haarlem and Naarden, still satisfied that his troops' dispositions to meet the threat from France were correct.

Many historians have also continued to believe that the French threat to Spain in the Netherlands was the more serious. Recently, one has written of the 'certain' victory of the French that was frustrated by Coligny's murder. This is a doubtful assumption. As we have seen, few things in sixteenth-century warfare were certain, least of all total victory. And even if victory had come it is more than doubtful what its long-term effects would have been. It may be doubted whether, given the balance of social forces in France and the Netherlands, a military victory for a Huguenot army at this stage in the Netherlands revolt would have been desirable. For in France it was already discernible that Calvinism did not command the allegiance of a majority of the nation; in the Netherlands, the 'revolt' was even more of a social and religious mélange. Its support certainly included many (even excluding the nobility) who committed themselves to war only with great reluctance. For them – patricians, magistrates and town officials, merchants – the war was fought *against* despotism, dynasticism, religious uniformity and theocracy. It is unlikely that they would have regarded a victory by a crusading French Calvinist army as supporting their cause or their basic tenets.

✤ 7 ✤

THE SPANISH LABYRINTH[38]

In 1559 Philip left the Netherlands for Spain and never returned. His journey was the first of a series of physical and psychological retreats from the world of his father. It had taken all Charles's tenacity to prevent his universal Empire from dissolving into dreams and fragments, and his last act had been to divide it between his brother and his son. Henceforth the relationship between Philip and the Austrian Habsburgs was purely dynastic. His own 'empire' was Spanish, and as a Spanish monarch Philip could claim to rule over a large part of the known world. After three-quarters of a century of war, France had been excluded from almost all Italy, which was henceforth to be under the rule of Spanish dependants like the Dukes of Savoy and Florence. Only the Papal States and a recalcitrant Venice spoilt the picture of an espagnolized Italy. In the Netherlands, Philip had inherited his father's prestige and a collection of titles – Duke, Count, and other even less exalted titles; but he was King only of Spain. There seemed to be no reason (save perhaps injured English feelings about Philip's failure to secure the return of Calais) why Spain should not be on friendly terms with England. In the tradition of the old Burgundian alliance against France, Antwerp had become by far the largest foreign market for English cloth while England took considerable quantities of Spanish wool, sherry and oil. Each country had an interest in peaceful relations in the English Channel; Spain needed to keep open the sea-lanes to her Netherlands possessions, while England was still (in 1559 and for long after) more worried by the threat of French than of Spanish control of these foreign shores and ports nearest to her.

Nor was there any insuperable difficulty about Spain's American possessions. It was true that Spain and Portugal had agreed by the Treaty of Tordesillas to divide the New World between themselves. But their right to do so rested on the normal claim that the territories concerned were previously vacant. By confirming this agreement between secular powers, all the Pope did was to confer on them the right to supervise Christian churches and missionaries on his behalf. The challenges and conflicts of later decades arose because French, Dutch and English Protestants (though the Catholic Valois also contested the arrangements) refused to agree that the Spanish-Portuguese treaty was more than a piece of private mutual diplomacy. It was not, they argued, part of the public law of Christendom. But in 1559 the entanglements which were to equate privateering and Protestantism as twin challenges to Hispano-Papal monopoly still lay in the future. Except for Brazil, which was Portuguese, the rest of the New World was Spanish, the property of the Crown, where Cortes and Pizarro had constructed a new empire on the ruins of the Aztecs and Incas.

The weaknesses in Philip's inheritance were in Spain itself; but in 1559 they were dormant. The original marriage of Ferdinand and Isabella had united two dissimilar kingdoms. The Castilian ethos differed markedly from that of Aragon, whose prosperity (now sadly diminished) was the creation of the relatively free mercantile society of Catalonia. Already, long before Philip's accession, his predecessors had vigorously purified the Church in Spain, introducing, through the Inquisition, the enforcement of an orthodoxy that was the most rigid in the world.

Even as Philip returned to Spain the Holy Office was still dismantling what was described as a 'terrible conspiracy' against the faith and the state by a handful of harmless Erasmian latitudinarians. Spain, Castile especially, had during the reconquest from the Moors become obsessed with the overriding importance of orthodoxy. Moors, Jews, Protestants were bracketed in many a Spanish mind as offenders against the unity and orthodoxy which alone could enable the king to overcome regional divergences (emphasized by ubiquitous mountain ranges) and forge a collection of kingdoms into a national reality.

To do this demanded a centralized, bureaucratized administration. Philip's withdrawal to Spain meant withdrawal to Madrid, then to the Escorial and the Mausoleum. Though officially the affairs of state were conducted through the Council of State, this body at once fell victim to the law that invariably condemns large committees to impotence and dismemberment. All the more so because it was not only too large to discharge business satisfactorily, but also too divided by rivalries between the great noble tribes. A proposal had only to be made by one such faction for the rest to block it on principle. The only way to circumvent this was for Philip to take refuge in secret discussions with individuals – mostly officials – or with *ad hoc* juntas which dealt with special items of policy such as the Turkish or Netherlands problem.

This coincided altogether too closely with Philip's own psychological propensities. Fear of his father was at the root of Philip's lack of confidence and fundamental lethargy. When he entered into his inheritance these traits were modified but not eliminated. Problems were if possible avoided or passed on to others. No nettle was grasped that could be ignored or handed to a subordinate. Policies were shaped in writing rather than by personal, still less open, discussion. The master of half the world, the perfect model of the centralizing administrator, archetype of the new ruler of the modern state, was still at heart a timid escapist, the ultimate victim of his own anxieties and suspicions. The passage of time did not reduce his problems. His son, Don Carlos, turned out to be a violent and dangerous schizophrenic and died in confinement. The mystery of his death has never been solved. Philip's enemies, including William of Orange, denounced it as murder. Others argued that Don Carlos could as easily have died of natural causes. The death of his third wife, Elizabeth of Valois, in the same year (1568) was also regarded as murder by his enemies: again, the truth remains hidden. What is certain is that the relentless strains of office turned Philip into a prematurely aged recluse, endlessly intriguing amid mountains of *consultas*, reports, briefs, maps and statistics that accumulated in his small private office in the Escorial. The Council of State met without him: officially, because the king did not want to inhibit the members' freedom to speak out frankly. The more likely reason was Philip's instinctive shrinking from human contact and personal responsibility. It was, after all, common knowledge that everything transacted at the Council was meticulously reported to Philip by his officials. The result was that a paralysing indecision slowed down the whole process of government. Every Spanish viceroy knew that the royal spies began work as soon as he was out of range of the Court. Intrigue and distrust were the hallmarks of Philip's 'system'. Commanders overseas in his sprawling empire had to plead for intelligible instructions or watch their advice being mangled or inverted for reasons never disclosed. The monotony and frustration of this perpetual indecision was punctuated only by occasional moments of panic: then he would suddenly order the total evacuation of the Balearic Islands because of a rumoured Turkish raid or command Santa Cruz to hoist sail with the unfinished Armada for England in the middle of the November gales.

The economic and social system over which Philip brooded was correspondingly unsatisfactory. He had inherited a country already bankrupt: its government had, that is to say, by 1557 spent more than it possessed and declared itself unable to repay its debts. This was to be a recurring phenomenon throughout Philip's reign and afterwards. In order to raise money, the debts that could not be paid were 'funded'. From direct taxes the noble class and the Church were exempt; and since the businessmen upon whom they fell most heavily were often able to buy their way out by purchasing *hidalgo* privileges, the main burden fell on those classes least able to bear it. The royal revenue itself was mortgaged a long way ahead to help meet the interest payments on loans.

It has sometimes been argued that exploration and expansion in the New World enriched Spain, widened her horizons and brought a new sense of realism to her rulers. There is little evidence to support any of these assertions. Certainly, Hispano-American trade had expanded until the mid-century. Certainly, after pausing for a decade, it expanded again between 1562 and 1600. But relatively few Spaniards profited by the expansion. The main beneficiaries were Dutch merchants who did well out of the export of goods to America, imports of food and raw materials to Spain and the provision of war stores for Spanish armies and navies. Genoese bankers made high profits by financing loans for the wars. The massive deficit in Spain's balance of payments absorbed most of the surplus silver. Nearly a quarter of a million Spaniards emigrated to America during the sixteenth century to escape from poverty and oppression and look for money or adventure.

In the last analysis, the Spanish economy shrank rather than expanded. And with it shrank Spain's mental horizons. The assignment of new spheres of influence to absolute government encouraged Spain in authoritarianism. Renaissance humanism gave way to a hideously efficient system of repression. Such was 'the closed parish' of Spain in the 1560s,[39] and it displayed features which cannot but call to mind (even to those sceptical of historical parallels) features of Hitler's Germany or Stalin's Russia.

Philip and his Council had also to manage the kaleidoscope of Italian internal politics, especially the problem of a Venetian Republic which had its own, increasingly devious notions of relations with the neigh-bouring Papal States, Spain and the Turks. With the Papacy there might be coincidence of aims in principle: but principle and practice were different things. King and Pope might need each other, but they were as often as not at loggerheads – especially over the royal jurisdic-tion of the church in Spain and Italy. As Professor Elliott has pointed out, the enemies of Spain happened usually to be enemies of the Pope; but successive Popes, Pius v in particular, irritated Philip by exigent demands that the allocation of Spain's resources – against Turk and Protestant – should be arranged with more regard for the well-being of the Church than that of Spain. The Papacy was never satisfied with Philip's efforts against the Turk. The Spanish campaigns had to be crusades against heresy, not merely the repression of overweening sub-jects. Popes, Philip was constantly having to lament, had little con-sideration for the complexity of politics, for the risk that excessive zeal for the faith might be self-defeating if it was pursued regardless of politi-cal or economic realities. Yet for all Philip's caution, it was difficult to discern how the interests of Spain were involved in those battles on land or sea paid for by her and waged by her forces but dictated by the need of strict religious orthodoxy and little else.

East of Gibraltar, all around the Mediterranean coasts, on into the Middle East and northwards to Central Europe, the strategy of Spain, now the dominant Christian power, was conditioned by the presence of the Ottoman Turks. From the mid-sixteenth century until well into the seventeenth, the world power-structure presented a strange paradox. Spain and the rival powers were boldly expanding overseas into the Americas, Africa and Asia; but along the eastward frontiers of the European land wars, Europeans were retreating under Turkish pressure. Serbia had been lost in 1459, Bosnia-Herzegovina in 1463–6, Negro-ponte followed in 1468–70, Albania in 1468. The Knights of Rhodes had been expelled in 1521. In 1526 a large part of Hungary had gone. By 1529 Vienna was under siege (it was besieged again in 1606 and was still to be threatened as late as 1683).

The chronology was important. By mid-century the Austrian Habs-burgs were the main bulwark on land. The overseas possessions of the

Venetian Republic, much as Cyprus, depended on sea power. Philip of Spain, therefore, as champion of Christendom, saw his natural ally in the Venetians, with their traditional role as the chief maritime power of the eastern Mediterranean. But the Venetians were unenthusiastic allies. Like the Netherlands, and for similar reasons, they mistrusted the rigid stance of Spain. Moreover, the Mediterranean states were beginning to lag in the techniques of shipbuilding and maritime war. War and trade, warships and merchant ships, were still closely related. In the second half of the century, the new galleons of the northern powers were invading the old trading monopolies of Italy, and of Venice especially. Venice had experimented in a half-hearted way with the new types of ship, but quite early in the sixteenth century gave up the attempt. Spain herself was likewise comparatively backward at sea. Her war fleet still relied heavily on oar-propelled galleys, a kind of floating barracks – forty of these were still included in the Armada against England as originally planned. Spanish ships were said to stand too high out of the water. Italian ships were condemned in 1617 by Fynes Moryson, the keen English observer, as 'heavy in sayling and great of burthen'.[40]

Fortunately for the Christian powers, the Turks – so successful with their use of massive artillery on land at Constantinople and elsewhere, as with their superb deployment of cavalry – remained equally, if not more, old-fashioned at sea. Yet Turkish resources seemed inexhaustible. About half the people who lived around the Mediterranean were subjects of the Porte – perhaps thirty millions. They had evolved a style of land war which made war largely pay for itself: at sea, piracy and privateering played a similar role.

Even today much of the domestic history of Islam in this period remains obscure and will remain so until the relatively recent opening of the Turkish archives bears fruit. All that can be said is that when Philip returned from the Netherlands the Turks were still strong enough to repulse with ease his attempt to recover Tripoli. A much larger Turkish fleet fell upon the attackers and captured twenty-seven Spanish galleys. The entire garrison of six thousand Spaniards at Djerba, the island guarding its approaches, was forced to surrender ten weeks later by hunger and thirst. For the next few years the Turkish fleet roamed the western Mediterranean unmolested. Philip had to bide his time till 1564 when a Spanish fleet threw the Turkish corsairs out of their lair at Peñon de Vélez, west of Tangier. The next year a Spanish fleet with ten thousand soldiers came to the relief of Malta, the last stronghold of the Knights of St John, where a large army of Turks had landed. The Turks finally withdrew: but the battle was not over. They merely shifted their ground to prepare the next land attack against Austria. Once again it was checked largely by the dogged resistance of the garrison of the Hungarian fortress at Szigeth in south-west Hungary. The major land war thereafter petered out.

The next episode took place in Spain itself. After the conquest of Granada it had been official policy to encourage the assimilation of the Moriscoes into Spanish Christian society. It did not get far. The Moriscoes remained second-class citizens. Their special industries, like silk manufacture, groaned under heavy taxation. Their titles to land were subjected to continuous and harassing investigation. As the Ottoman threat grew, rumours that the Moriscoes were a Turkish fifth-column blighted their relations with ordinary Spaniards. Cardinal Espinosa, Philip's leading adviser on religious policy, insisted that the lax Christian observance of the Moriscoes must be stiffened and reformed. Philip agreed, against the advice of those (like the Marquis of Mondijar) who knew the Moriscoes best. Terrified, the Moriscoes rose in a bloody and prolonged revolt. The rebels fled to the mountains, pursued by Spanish troops. Would the rumours which had done much to provoke the conflict prove true? Would the Turks land in Spain in support of their semi-brethren? Was Morisco Granada the predestined bridgehead of the Turks? It was not. In May 1570 the Moriscoes surrendered and 150,000 or more of them were expelled from their villages in Granada and dispersed throughout Castile to await their final expulsion from Spain in 1609. There was not the slightest evidence that the allegations that the Moriscoes were a Turkish fifth-column was anything more than a part of the hysterical scaremongering, racialism and bigotry by which Philip's Spain was now deeply infected. The case for driving this poor and hard-working minority north into Castile rested on the danger they posed near the coast in the event of a Turkish invasion. But their removal did nothing to stem a tide of prejudice and persecution which was as benighted as most other aspects of Philip's police state.

It is, in fact, unlikely that the Turks ever seriously intended any invasion attempt. Spain was too far from a major Turkish base for anything bigger than raiding parties to be practicable. Sulaiman the Magnificent, under whose ambitious military genius the advances of the

Ottoman Empire in recent years had been achieved, was now dead and his successor Selim II was more aesthete than warrior. In any event there were more obvious targets for the Turks nearer home: Cyprus, for example, with Corfu and Crete one of the richest outposts of the Venetian trade empire.

Venice was now deprived of the traditional help of France. She was weakened by the explosion of the Venetian *arsenale* and apparently serious damage to her fleet. Now was the moment for the Turk to strike: the blow fell early in 1570. An ultimatum demanded the delivery to the Grand Porte of Cyprus, Venice's 'Levantine jewel'. By a fairly narrow majority the Venetian Senate rejected the demand. In July the Turks occupied Cyprus with ease, while Venice argued with the Pope and Spain on the terms of an anti-Turkish alliance.

It was nearly a year before the Holy League came into being. The largest share of its funds came from Spain and its commander was Don John of Austria, Philip's half-brother. The two great fleets, of approximately equal size, met in the Gulf of Patras. The battle of Lepanto was a decisive but costly victory for Don John, who replaced the Ottoman Crescent on the Turkish flagship by the Banner of the Cross and, in another Christian gesture, cut off the Turkish commander's head and set it on a spike on the prow of the flagship.

Christendom seemed to be suitably avenged for nearly a century of Turkish advance into Europe. But the initial cheering quickly died down as the diplomatic consequences were revealed. Venetian realism swiftly despatched the Holy League by making a treaty which handed over to the Turks Cyprus and the Venetian territory along the Dalmatian coast, plus a large money indemnity.

Lepanto was a classic illustration of the limited consequences of apparently major and decisive victories in this age. The Turkish fleet was swiftly rebuilt and remanned. The Turks did not retreat from the western Mediterranean but their main thrust was now limited to North Africa, where the capture of Tunis strengthened their grip.

A tendency to disengagement in the Hispano-Turkish conflict was nevertheless evident. A new division into spheres of influence opened: Iberia was to be for Spain, Africa for Islam. This was the drift of the truce of 1578 which in turn reflected growing Turkish concern for the Middle Eastern situation. The settlement of the Turkish frontiers with Austria persisted as defeated Hungary continued to develop Turkish characteristics. The progress of Hungarian Calvinism itself owed something to Turkish tolerance, which contrasted markedly with the increasing bigotry of the Christian dogmatists. Sweden had sought Turkish aid against Muscovy. England sold them raw stores and cloth. Poland-Lithuania and Venice traded metals and food. The Turkish state that ran from Hungary through the Balkans and the Levant to the Caucacus and Ukraine promised to form an economic and strategic unity. This became less and less probable in the west, where to cover great stretches of ocean or occupy vast arcas of unpopulated desert in North Africa created insuperable problems of strategy, expense and manpower for the Turks.

From the mid-sixteenth century signs began to multiply that the great phase of Turkish expansion might be reaching its peak. The earlier flexibility of Turkish organization gave way to a more centralized bureaucracy. Population growth and the increasing burden of taxes provoked peasant and artisan emigration to Persia. Turkish fortunes still fluctuated down to 1578, but between then and 1606 the Ottoman state ran itself into a civil war, two major foreign wars and rampant inflation. Corruption in high places squcczcd out the earlier system of opening careers to talent and provoked more discontent, more emigration. Malaise enveloped the ruling class as dreams of an ordered Islamic state steadily faded. In the western Mediterranean, Turkish maritime power turned into privateering as Moslem corsairs from Tunis, Tripoli and Algiers plied a profitable trade raiding Dutch, English and French shipping or forcing the maritime powers to make treaties of convenience with them. Elizabeth's policy, and the attempts to negotiate trade treaties with the Turks, illustrates the new opportunism of the western powers. By the early seventeenth century the label 'Turkey merchant' described Jacobean London's equivalent of a millionaire.

By 1612 the Turkish empire was crumbling beneath the growing burden of war with the Austrian Habsburgs, the Persians, under Shah Abbas, and the pressure of Muscovite expansion. Decline was still only incipient, but in retrospect we may see clearly the growth of pressures on the Turks which in the end were to bring them to a halt and turn expansion into retreat.

The events of the second half of the sixteenth century east of Gibraltar certainly promised to relieve the pressure of the Turk on Spain's resources, military and financial. This favourable trend seemed to be steadily reinforced by the growing yield of silver bullion from the New World. Silver mines were opened up successively in Mexico (Zacatecas 1546,

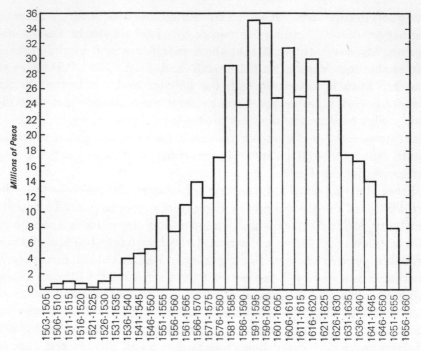

Total Imports of Treasure

Compostela 1553, Sombrete and Durango 1555, Trestrille 1562, Parral 1598–1600) and Peru, where the rich lodes of Potosi were found in 1543. New methods of extracting the silver from the ore by mercury (from 1556 in Mexico, from 1572 in Peru) steadily raised the quantities of bullion landed on the wharves of Seville and passed through the Casa de Contratacion, reaching a peak somewhere between 1591 and 1609. Before the mid-sixteenth century quinquennial silver imports from Spanish America had risen to a record level of ten million pesos. By 1600 the figure stood at over thirty millions. Of the total import a *quint* (approximately one-fifth) went to the Crown. The gross resources of the Spanish Crown increased enormously, not only from the bullion receipts but also from taxation. The main source was Castile, to which was given the privilege of ruling the Spanish Empire, along with the duty of financing it. To the existing direct taxes was added the notorious *alcabala*, an indirect sales tax now converted into an annual lump sum worth approximately half a million pounds sterling. By funding its debts the Spanish government increased its purchasing power far above its immediate resources of cash. Tax yields were used to pay the interest on a growing volume of loans raised from the bankers (mainly foreign). By 1573 these stood at fifty million ducats – two and a half times their volume at the death of Charles v.

Such was the strategic and financial background against which Philip turned to deal with the problems of the Netherlands. There seemed little reason to doubt that any troubles that might arise there were well within his capacity to handle.

8

THE NETHERLANDS: PROTEST
AND TERROR

The complex problems of Philip's Netherland inheritance were already apparent before he himself stormed out of Brussels in 1559, enraged by the noble censure of Spain's war with France in 1556; by the insistence of the States-General in 1558 on their right to raise the subsidy he had demanded only through commissioners appointed by and responsible to the States; and finally, just before he left, by their stipulation that three thousand Spanish troops stationed in the Netherlands should depart forthwith.

It was not lost on Philip that this last demand came from the States-General in session at Ghent. Was it not Ghent where Philip's father had encountered and crushed revolt only twenty years ago? The Ghent revolt reflected the unwillingness of its governors to finance war against France, their determination to maintain local and exclusive control of manufactures in the countryside around the city. In the reforms that followed Charles had abolished local gild and municipal privileges, freeing the countryside from urban restrictions and building a citadel from which a garrison would keep the turbulent city in order. Did not these events prove that strong central government was essential for these overweening tradesmen?

It was certainly true that in the Netherlands was to be found one of the most complex economies and societies of Europe – more complex perhaps even than that of north Italy. Its ruling class, outside the towns and to some extent over them, consisted mainly of the great noble Walloon families. Most were French-speaking and had their estates in the south. Hainault was the home of the great clan of the Croys who had served faithfully both Philip the Good and Charles v and been suitably rewarded: Aerschot, Chièvres, Roeulx, Chimay; of the Lannoys, Lignes, Lalaings, Hennins, Glymes, Montignys, Berlaymonts. Often their estates stretched into Brabant, Limburg and Gelderland. Not all were Walloon. William, Prince of Orange (a small sovereign state on the Rhône) was eldest son of the Count of Nassau, in Germany; his first wife was daughter of the Elector of Saxony, though most of his own large estates were in Brabant. Of the other two leading nobles, Egmont and Hoorn, the first was of a Holland family but much of his property in Flanders and Luxembourg came from his wife who was a Walloon. Hoorn, like Montigny, came from the Netherlands branch of the great French family of Montmorency. Count Mansfeld, like Orange, was of German blood. And so on: a large, powerful group, Catholic certainly but in an undogmatic, latitudinarian fashion. If there had been more philosophical colouring to their beliefs they might have been called Erasmian. But there was little; for the most part, they were characteristic of the landowning nobility of their day: extravagant, martial, proud, quick to anger and fundamentally unconstructive and short-sighted politically, always ready to defend the privileges of their class, normally loyal to the princes by whose favours they had acquired or expanded their lands and wealth.

From their ranks were drawn the stadholders for the different provinces. Thus Egmont was stadholder in Flanders; Aremberg (a Ligne) of Groningen, Friesland and Overysel; Orange of Holland, Zeeland and Utrecht. The largest concentration of the higher nobility was in the south – Hainault in particular. Farther north, in Gelderland and Friesland, there was a large class of minor gentry – a sort of squirearchy – but few great lords of the standing of the Walloon nobles of the south. They were also, for the most part, 'local' squires without the network of international kinship – with France and Germany especially – that characterized the great nobility. They shared nevertheless some of the attributes and attitudes of their greater neighbours. For the most part they were Catholics, but untheological ones. They too lived cheek by jowl with the urban patriciate which governed the towns. They shared, directly – as property-owners and developers – in urban prosperity. They intermarried with the families of the merchant oligarchs. Their own farms and those of their tenants supplied the townspeople with food. As a class they were alive to the complex nature of Netherlands prosperity and equally distrustful of the rule of dynasts, whether home or foreign-bred.

Both south and north of the estuaries of the great rivers which flowed through the middle of the Netherlands from east to west, trade and industry were growing fast in the first half of the century. The south, with its richer variety of land and industry, was still far and away the more prosperous half: in area, what was later to be the modern Netherlands and modern Belgium were roughly the same size, and the whole Netherlands was approximately three-fifths the size of England. But the northern towns were still relatively modest compared with the great cities of Antwerp, Ghent, Bruges or Mechlin.

While the treaties of Cateau-Cambrésis were signed and Philip left for Spain, important changes were taking place in the Netherlands. Antwerp was overtaking Bruges, where the harbour was markedly less busy than formerly. While Ghent had been fighting its neighbour, Bruges, and both had suffered by the restrictive and short-sighted rule of the craft gilds, Antwerp had forged ahead under the more liberal, plutocratic rule of its merchant and financial capitalists. Ypres, Brussels, Leiden, Bruges, Ghent were either on the wane or holding their own only with difficulty. In most of the old urban centres of cloth manufacture in the Netherlands (as in north Italy) the preceding years had been times of decline. Looms had dwindled in numbers or disappeared. The old *lakens* (broad cloths) made at Leiden shrank from over twenty thousand in 1528 to a mere thousand in 1572. But from the small towns and large villages of West Flanders came a different story. Here the enterprise of a new breed of clothier, much freer of the heavy hand of gild control than the broadcloth-makers of the old cities, was making new types of cloth. At Hondschoote, Armentières, Poperinghe and other towns around Ypres and Lille was the home of the *Nieuwe Draperijen* – bays and says, serges, perpetuanas, twills, and many kinds of light worsted and stuffs. These new cloths were of cheaper wool and easier to make. They were bright, attractive and inexpensive. They could be used for men's clothing, women's dresses and for furnishings. Antwerp, now also became the market centre for these 'new draperies'. No wonder the old cloth towns of Flanders and Brabant maintained continuous pressure on the government to prohibit the new domestic manufactures and to keep out the rival products from England.

The northern economy moved more slowly. The towns most characteristic of its style were smaller – Leiden, Haarlem, Middelburg, Alkmaar, Groningen. The north lived by agriculture, by fishing and by trade based on ports like Amsterdam, Hoorn, Enkhuizen (on the Zuider

Zee) or Middelburg, Rotterdam, Flushing, farther south on the great estuaries of Rhine and Maas.

An important trade was growing up between the Baltic and the Bay of Biscay. Its freight was grain, timber, wine, salt, iron, ships' stores; but its scale and operators were still modest. In all the correspondence of Sir Thomas Gresham, who was England's economic agent in the Low Countries from 1540 to 1570, Amsterdam, so soon to be the world's greatest entrepôt, is mentioned only once and then casually: as a place a man might go to to buy wainscoting. Yet Amsterdam's economy was soundly based; rooted in a merchant fleet which already promised to rule the trade routes from the Baltic to the Mediterranean.

Shifts in products, manufactures and materials, in industrial location, the expansion of overseas trade in some sectors, the hesitations in others, the marked sagging of yet others (the Italian connexions at Bruges) – all these changes were moulding and remoulding the economic and social shape of the Netherlands. Not only did economic growth reflect the growing influence of the merchant groups in the cities. It also called into being something more like a modern proletariat than could be discerned in any other contemporary society. At the top were the weavers, carpenters, printers, bookbinders, sugar-boilers, cloth-dyers, brewers: the artisans and craftsmen, diligent, skilled and often literate. Below, in descending stages of poverty, the casual labour of the wharfside of Antwerp, Amsterdam, Enkhuizen and a score of other ports; unskilled workers who handled cargoes, sorted fish, mended sails and nets. With the – by contemporary standards – fairly rapid increase in the population and its growing density in towns, this floating mass of labour, often only half-employed, presented a serious social problem. Weavers and other cloth workers in the 'new drapery' areas were less protected than the crafts of the old towns against the bleak winds of this world of change and competition that was replacing the old social collectivism. Men were in work or out of it according to the whim of the merchant capitalist-entrepreneurs.

To economic instabilities was added the new disturbing, critical self-awareness of an urban society that was not prepared to swallow its discontents. A man might farm, sow and reap, without having to read. But tradesmen were literate by reason of their trade. The belief that 'printing leads to heresy' was as commonly held as the modern assumption that a popular press or television encourages protest, subversion of authority and attack on established values. Literacy was high in these

Netherland towns and it undoubtedly encouraged the spreading criticisms of a lax, corrupt Church and a luxurious church hierarchy.

In previous decades this had taken the form of Anabaptism, a collection of beliefs and practices to which no precise definition or doctrine
could be attached. Many Anabaptists had been killed – perhaps two to
three thousand between 1523, when Charles v introduced the Inquisition, and 1566. By the 1560s Calvinism had left Anabaptists, Lutherans
and Mennonites well behind. As we have seen, it recruited its greatest
numbers from the urban artisanate. The Calvinists did not, during these
early phases, represent more than a small minority – perhaps 5–10 per
cent of the total population; even by 1650 the figure was probably only
50 per cent.

Calvinism added a new dimension to the Netherlands problem. It
attracted few recruits among the patrician class of magistrates who
governed the towns, and, in large measure, the Netherlands as a whole.
As a class they inclined to tolerance. Most were still Catholics (especially
at Amsterdam, where they were to remain obstinately pro-Spanish).
They did not as a rule like the new pastors who held dangerous sway
over their congregations and whose theocratic and intolerant doctrines
diverged as much from their habitually easygoing ways of running local
government as those of Philip and his Spanish advisers. Protestant progress itself depended on their tolerance; but, as the Calvinist grip on
opinion, through churches, schools, orphanages and alms-houses
tightened, the inherent conflict between Erasmian tolerance and
Calvinist dogmatism, even to the death, came more and more to the
surface. Nevertheless, the empirical, self-interested belief in freedom was
strong enough to encourage the magistrates openly to grant freedom of
worship to Jews, Protestants of all kinds and, later, Catholics.

As a group the magistracy was not vocal, breaking silence only when
Calvinist arrogance went too far. The role of the town rulers in the
impending struggle was to be enigmatic. They formed, politically and
socially, part of that large body of 'middle opinion' which historians
now recognize in this (as in many other revolutions) as a vital, if
indefinable factor in the unfolding drama.

In the 1550s and 1560s distrust and hatred of Spain, the Inquisition
and the government in Brussels and Madrid united many nobles and
magistrates, with a vociferous element among the artisan and even
humbler classes, in their determination to resist. Each group had its
special grievances: often there was really little in common between

them. Each town had its own viewpoint. So that the States-General throughout the sixteenth century remained largely a collection of 'voices' from the provincial estates. They, in turn, were merely delegates of the towns whose instructions strictly governed what they were allowed to say. Cities from Flanders, the richest province, or from Holland, really ruled the proceedings in a way not found elsewhere. Although the voice of the gilds and craftsmen had been largely eliminated by Charles v in 1540 the meetings of the estates and States-General remained exercises in frustration – especially of the government's plans to raise money. They did not challenge the government's right to control policy; but increasingly the States were voicing the discontents which inflation, economic change, foreign wars and new taxes were arousing in one class after another. The troubles which culminated in 1566 were cradled in fear. How was it bred? We must look back at politics for an answer.

When Philip left for Spain, he placed the government in the hands of a regent, Margaret of Parma, Charles's natural daughter born in Flanders. She undertook her duties without enthusiasm, knowing only too well the seething jealousies and intrigues which disfigured relations within the nobility. She was aware of the rising tide of dissidence. She knew her own weakness, her hesitancy, her lack of resources and support. She knew the even more malevolent forces at work in Spain. She knew, though she might be regent, where the real power would lie: with Antoine Perrenot, the Besançon lawyer who, together with his two brothers, entered the service of Charles v in 1550, rising swiftly to be Bishop of Arras. The Perrenots were a shrewd family, smoothly bureaucratic, diplomatic, not tyrannical by nature. Antoine simply deemed it his duty to the king to do his will. First as Archbishop of Mechlin, then as Cardinal Granvelle, Perrenot was to provoke the jealousy and hatred of the entire noble class, to say nothing of widespread distrust among the merchant class of the great cities, all of whom equated him with attempted usurpation of local privileges through centralized, alien rule. Even loyal nobles like Berlaymont and Mansfeld, ordinary conservatives, regarded Granvelle as a dangerous upstart. Many of the nobles suspected that he was the leader of an informal inner junta – similar to those through which Philip covertly ruled in Madrid – which really dictated policy for the Netherlands.

A split rapidly developed between Granvelle and the man who was already emerging as the leader of the noble faction: William of Orange.

In rapid succession, a series of crises broke: in each there was the inevitable clash between the 'privilege' issue and the government. For instance, did the king have the right to nominate (via Granvelle) to the governorship of Franche-Comté, or was this a noble perquisite? Had he the right to reorganize the bishoprics of the Netherlands, reducing their number and grouping them under three archbishops, making the new bishops royal nominees and Granvelle Archbishop of Mechlin, so that he would be superior to the Council of State?

In such arguments, there was always a case – sometimes a strong one – to be made for the royal policy. Equally, the noble or municipal insistence on their 'privileges' could often be criticized as selfish, particularist, even corrupt. The reforms could be defended as the rationalization of a debased ecclesiastical organization. But this was not enough. The 'reforms' immediately provoked spectacular and almost universal disapproval. Nobles, magistrates, even abbots and thousands of ordinary people, joined in denouncing the reorganization as the work of Granvelle. The critics turned a deaf ear to rejoinders that Granvelle had little or nothing to do with the matter. It was enough that he emerged from it enhanced in rank and power.

To most Netherlanders the reorganization was merely a preparatory step towards persecution and inquisition. Orange, Egmont and Hoorn withdrew from the Council of State. Montigny was despatched to Spain to petition Philip and make contact with the Duke of Eboli's faction at Court who were believed to be hostile to Granvelle. Philip bowed – if only for the moment – to noble pressure. First Granvelle, then Viglius, President of the Council of State, was removed from office. The nobles resumed their offices. But the problem was not solved so easily. The agents of Spain in Brussels were more active than ever. The magistrates continued their fight, with Bruges in the lead, to assert secular control of education and social welfare. But perhaps most serious, the nobility now found themselves, willy-nilly, the heroes of the Calvinists. The junction was in one sense natural; in another, highly embarrassing. To Orange in particular, Calvinist intolerance and violence was repellent. Yet what alternative had he to Spanish brutality? He knew that a man like Viglius, though a moderate, would be terrified by the implications of his words. Yet on New Year's Eve 1564 he told the Council that the king was wrong if he thought Netherlanders, used as they were to religious freedoms, would support his sanguinary edicts: 'However strongly I am attached to the Catholic religion, I cannot approve of princes trying to rule the consciences of their subjects and trying to rob them of the liberty of faith.' That, for him at least was the heart of the matter. In February 1565 Egmont, a soldier, simple and impressionable, was sent to Spain to plead the nobles' case with Philip, hoping undoubtedly, to benefit from his supposed friendship with the Eboli faction and Don Carlos, Philip's eccentric son. Naïvely Egmont thought he had made real progress. The king was sympathetic outwardly at least. What Egmont did not know was that his Spanish friends at Court were themselves slipping. In one of those intrigues that ended in a reshuffle Eboli had to give way to Alba, now, as ever, the leader of hard-line argument against the Netherlands nobility. He had the help now of Antonio Perez, the Council Secretary.

Their case was supported by despatches from the Netherlands, where Villavicencio, an exigent Augustinian friar of deeply fanatical Tridentine views, was whipping up government opinion in favour of a necessary Spanish intervention in Netherlands affairs. There was, for example the curious – and significant – controversy at Bruges over the disposal of the mortal remains of an English merchant who had died while visiting Bruges. Should he be buried with Christian rites? No, said Villavicencio: to do so was against every Catholic belief. Yes, said the magistrates: not to do so would be un-Christian and inhumane. It would also set Protestant Europe by the ears and be disastrous for trade. There, in miniature, was the whole dilemma, of principle and interest. In both, Spain and the Netherlanders were irreconcilably divided.

Egmont returned to Brussels only to find he had been sadly deceived. The entire Spanish Council of State had unanimously rejected his plea for toleration. Orders for the persecution of Anabaptists and other Protestants had outpaced him. On 5 November letters reached Brussels from the king. Peremptorily, the magistrates were ordered to enforce the edicts against heresy. Egmont, discredited and disillusioned, withdrew from the Council of State. With him went Orange and Hoorn, while stadholders like Meghen and Bergen asked to be relieved of office. By the autumn the lesser nobles, guided by Orange's brother, Louis, the brothers Marnix, close friends of both, and the blustering, ungovernable Culemborch and Brederode, formed a 'league' of their own. Its members were drawn more from the northern than the southern provinces. In April 1566 several hundred of them rode into Brussels to petition the Regent. *'Gueux!'* ('beggars'), cried Berlaymont as he saw them. But his contemptuous phrase was taken up with enthusiasm by the crowd and by the nobles themselves. '*Vive le Geus*' became the cry in Amsterdam, Delft and Antwerp.

A revolutionary moment: but where were the revolutionaries? Were they more than a few hundred nobles, largely motivated by their own economic problems? This was the conviction of Granvelle who was already preaching his own economic interpretation of the troubles. It would be simple, he told Philip, to buy them off. He had heard from his brother, who was Orange's steward, that Orange's estates carried an insupportable load of debt. And Orange was the richest of all. The others, with smaller estates but equal burdens, were even worse off.

Granvelle's analysis was plausible. The Netherlands nobility, like their counterparts elsewhere, *were* high-living and extravagant. They had been hit by rising prices, by the loss of jobs in the army since Cateau-Cambrésis and by the prospective loss of jobs in the purified, espagnolized church. But that was not all. They shared, perfectly naturally, in the broader view which was labelled 'Erasmian' but had deeper roots and a longer history than half a century. Their ambiance was the world of towns, trade, manufactures and commercial farming. Like the Venetian aristocracy they lived close to business and they did not like Spanish bigotry and intransigence. *Politiques* by nature, they might in the end prove to be divided, unconstructive, unreliable. Land, office, the traditional love of power and a need for royal patronage provided strong natural links of loyalty to the king. But for the moment they were angry, apprehensive and mutinous. But though their influence was great, their numbers were too small to provide the rank and file of a national movement against Spain. This had to come from the people. By mid-summer 1566 it was forming. Camp-meetings of thousands took place outside cities like Ghent and Antwerp. The preachers and women sat in the centre protected by a ring of stakes, cords and soldiers and Calvinist sermons alternated with the cries of '*Vive le Geus*'.

How and why the camp-meetings became the orgies of image-breaking of August 1566 will never be known precisely. But the riots which culminated in the sack and desecration of scores of churches, including Antwerp Cathedral, were certainly closely connected with the steep rise of corn prices in 1565 (rye rose from 78 to 141 groats a quarter) and the near-famine that followed. A crisis in Anglo-Netherlands trade simultaneously caused unemployment and an unprecedented fall in wages. This all came after a quarter of a century of fairly steady economic expansion. It hit not only casual labour. Skilled men of modest substance, most vulnerable to the appeal of the Calvinist sermon, were even more affected. That they were egged on by professional agitators and mercenaries, paid for from France, England and Germany, is also likely. But the rioters needed little encouragement from outside.

Only a month or two passed before the weakness of the opposition became apparent. Nobles and worker-Calvinists? It was an unnatural alliance. The opponents of Spain and persecution were soon quarrelling and fighting among themselves. Recovering her shaken nerve, the regent rallied the naturally loyal supporters among the nobles. The Lord of Noircarmes annihilated the protesting bands at Valenciennes with exemplary brutality. Others followed his lead until peace was restored. Thousands went into exile. Over thirty thousand left the ports of Flanders for Kent and from thence found their way to London, Colchester and Norwich, though the greatest influx awaited the more horrific persecutions still to come. Among the refugees who streamed eastwards to Germany were Brederode and Orange. The first phase of revolt was over. It had failed; but it had added the first of two new dimensions to the movement. Down to 1566, the resistance had been 'a revolt of medievalism' (in the late Professor Renier's phrase) centred upon largely noble grievances. The 'hunger-year' of 1566 had combined these with popular revolt and Calvinist ideology. There had also been hints of international co-operation. Little had come of them so far. But it would not be long before religion, popular support and hostility to Spain in France and England all became linked in a renewed national and international revolutionary movement.

The Terror 1567–1573

The 'Segovia' letters of 14 November were the symbol for a radical enforcement of orthodoxy. Never before had the edicts against heresy been applied more than spasmodically. Nor had the Inquisition been free to act as in Spain. Fanatics urged upon Philip the need to visit Brussels. The people, they said, were Catholic and loyal and only a mischievous group of nobles was exploiting the king's absence. In July, Philip yielded to these voices – which probably included Alba's. He would go, at the head of his troops, and convert humiliation into victory. As always with Philip, the decision was soon reversed. News of the outbreaks of the summer began to trickle in. Would it not, after all, be better if Alba went at the head of an army large enough to crush and annihilate the rebels? So, later in August 1567, Alba arrived in Brussels with his army. They had marched, as many later contingents were to march, along the route mapped out probably by Philip himself for his own projected journey: what was to be called 'the Spanish road', from Italy by way of the Mount Cenis pass over the Alps, west of Geneva, Franche-Comté, Lorraine and Luxembourg. Europe, Protestant and non-Protestant, shivered. But Alba went straight for Brussels, presenting himself to an apprehensive Margaret of Parma on 22 August. He was far from satisfied with his lot: in the end Philip had cut his 70,000 troops to 10,000. The Netherlands would be brought to heel by a salutary dose of terror. The so-called 'liberties' of lords and cities would be eliminated; the Tridentine decrees, edicts and placards properly enforced with the help of an unfettered Inquisition.

Once again Philip had run away from reality. Brusquely Philip ignored the fact that here he was not king, much less emperor, as his father had been. Of the four languages the Netherlands people spoke – Dutch, Frisian, Low German and French – Philip was innocent of all save a smattering of bad French. Of their unique culture, their idiosyncratic political and social structure, he knew and cared nothing. He was understandably unpopular with all classes.

Alba was unperturbed by such considerations. His methods would be independent of loyalties or sentiments, and he began as he meant to continue. Egmont and Hoorn were arrested within two weeks of his arrival. The arrests deeply shocked public opinion – as they were intended to. Alba's first two victims were Knights of the Golden Fleece, entitled to require a warrant signed by six members of their most elevated Order, the creation of the Burgundians and Habsburgs themselves. By its rules members were entitled to be incarcerated not in a common goal but in the 'amiable companionship' of their Order. Alba's roughshod behaviour was a deliberate insult to the highest nobility and was treated as such. Immediately, the ranks of the Netherlands resistance, sadly shaken by the iconoclasts and by Margaret's astute handling of them, began to close again. Everywhere the Calvinist nobles – of France as well as the Netherlands – began to draw together as Alba's Council of Troubles (called by Netherlanders the 'Council of Blood') began its work. During the next five years there were to be 12,000 trials, 9,000 convictions, over 1,000 executions. While Catholic nobles and Calvinist weavers came closer together again for support, Alba's financial moves also consolidated the commercial classes of the cities against him. Elizabeth's seizure of his bullion – £85,000-worth – at Plymouth in

November 1568 left him hard-pressed for cash. Away in Spain his enemies were already putting any administrative obstacles they could devise in his way. Castile's revenues, it was urged on Philip, could cover only half of his war costs. Alba must make the Netherlands pay their own way. This was his excuse for demanding a subsidy of the 100th, 20th and 10th penny in March 1569. The States-General's consent was essential: they agreed to the first but flatly rejected the second and third, which would have constituted a permanent tax on the turnover and export of goods. A prospect so disastrous united all classes, even the prudent oligarchs of the cities. In the end Alba got a reluctant once-for-all grant of four million florins. The permanent *alcabala* he envisaged faded before his eyes and was never collected in Brabant or Flanders.

The cash did not go far. Alba was an efficient commander: if total ruthlessness had been enough for victory, the revolt would have been quickly over. But it was not. He might defeat Louis of Nassau at Jemmingen, outlaw Orange, kidnap and deport his son to Spain, execute Egmont and Hoorn in the Grand Place at Brussels, persecute, torture and burn – but somehow the war dragged on. The international ramifications of the noble rebels enabled Louis to reappear on the French border in the south, Orange from the east, while Coligny promised aid from France. Such dangers prevented Alba, whether he liked it or not, from supporting any move against the other enemy, believed by many of Philip's advisers to be the root of his troubles – Elizabeth and England – or from burning out of their holes the 'Beggars' of the cities and towns of Holland, Zeeland, Utrecht and Groningen. The Massacre of St Bartholomew afforded him marvellous relief. Now at least he seemed to be free to tackle the north.

The following months were the most heroic and bloody phase of the revolt, when the unbelievable obstinacy of the resistance was revealed. Its details have been frequently narrated. It is enough here to recall a few of the high points: the three-day sack, by Alba, of Mechlin which had surrendered previously to Orange; the sack of Zutfen and then of Naarden by another Spanish army under Alba's son, Don Frederick of Toledo. The butchery at Naarden was as horrific as anything in the entire war. Haarlem, besieged by Don Frederick from winter 1572 to summer 1573, finally gave in, but the siege had cost the Spaniards more than half a year and twelve thousand dead and wounded. Would its loss, and the continued Spanish hold on Amsterdam, cut the northern Netherlands in two? It seemed likely. That it did not was due to the heroic and skilful resistance of Alkmaar a few months later. Here the local Beggars flushed the Spaniards away from the town by opening the sluices, cutting the dykes and flooding the surrounding countryside. It was a decisive action: as the saying went, 'at Alkmaar began victory'. It signalized the Beggars' growing skill at putting their knowledge of the watery terrain to good use. The Spanish *tercios* were tough and well trained but they were increasingly poor in morale, unpaid and mutinous. Above all, they were frightened by the hazards of war in flood, mud and quicksand.

Successful defence was not the whole story, nor the most crucial part of it. All unconscious of events, Alba found himself facing a new force: the so-called 'Sea Beggars'. And it was the Sea Beggars whose enterprise was to prove one of the most critical factors of the whole war. Their disorderly squadrons consisted of some two hundred or so captains, many of them minor nobles, from north and south alike. Others were drapers, bakers, soap-boilers, sailors – there was even a painter. They were a rough crew, well fitted to deal with their opponents, as were their leaders, the Lord of Lumey and Lord of Treslong. Motley has a portrait of Lumey which catches the tribal violence of the Beggar movement:

A wild, sanguinary, licentious noble, wearing his hair and beard unshorn, according to ancient Batavian custom until the death of his relative, Egmont, should have been expiated, a worthy descendant of the Wild Boar of the Ardennes, this hirsute and savage corsair seemed an embodiment of vengeance. He had sworn to wreak upon Alba and upon Popery the deep revenge owed to them by the Netherland nobility; and in the cruelties afterwards practised by him upon monks and priests, the Blood Council learned that their example had made at least one ripe scholar among the rebels.

The Sea Beggars had come into existence some five years earlier. Like the Huguenot fleet operating from La Rochelle, they were privateers, dedicated to pillaging the enemy (and neutrals too). The sixteenth-century privateer was often indistinguishable from a common pirate, but in theory he had his legal justification in his licence or letters of marque. These could be issued by a prince who had no warships of his own (or not enough) and authorized the bearer to act in his name. Orange had done precisely this, and the profits of his privateers came to represent an important part of his revenue in these critical years. They also enabled the rebels, in his name, to harass shipping off the coasts of Holland and Groningen, and help in projected attacks on the province of Groningen. But by 1569 the Sea Beggars had had little success. One squadron based in northern waters was still raiding in the Ems estuary. Another was fitting out on the Thames with financial support from the Dutch congregation established at the Church of the Austin Friars in the City of London. The following year they continued to threaten Amsterdam and Antwerp and the shipping entering and leaving those ports; but of any grand maritime strategy there was no sign. Orange and Alba were at least agreed on that. Elizabeth even ordered them out of her ports in October 1571. It was not until the end of March 1572 that Lumey finally agreed to go. Suddenly, after attacking some Spanish ships off Dover, on 1 April he landed at the small port of Brill on the south side of the Maas estuary. With him were four hundred men, starving and desperate. By a mixture of bluff and force they seized the town, threw out the terrified magistrates, requisitioned billets, sacked the church and appropriated chasubles and chalices. Finally, with barbarous relish, they executed thirteen monks and priests.

Such was the episode of the Brill, a mélange of bravery and barbarity, idealism and greed, characteristic of the Eighty Years' War. To Lumey it was nothing more than a raid of vengeance and booty. Even to Orange it seemed a dangerous and premature diversion of scarce resources. In any case he detested the picaresque Lumey, condemning both man and methods. Treslong, on the other hand, seems to have grasped the potential importance of the Brill. Instead of re-embarking, as Lumey wanted, the Beggars stayed, fanning out through Holland and Zeeland. In this way the revolt obtained what it conspicuously lacked: a firm military, naval and commercial base.

Geldorp, friend and follower of Orange, had seen in 1570 that the best centre of resistance to Spain was not the south, resting on the traditional political axis of Brussels, but the north, with its rivers and islands. Here was the great redoubt: not a prison in which the rebellion could be caught and trapped but a *place d'armes*, filled with supplies, arms and ships, connected by river and sea with the outside world. So, in one town and port after another, the Beggars took over. Flushing fell first, then Enkhuizen, Medemblik, Hoorn, Brouwershaven. At Middelburg and Zierikzee the Spaniards were besieged and were soon to fall. Meanwhile the Beggars were raiding island after island from their bases at Brill and Flushing.

But contrasted with this rising tide of victories were setbacks inland. In March 1574 Prince Louis of Nassau and his younger brother, Henry, were both killed in the battle at Mook, near Nymegen, where the rebels suffered a shattering defeat: in ordinary land warfare they were still inferior to the Spanish *tercios*. Leiden lay under siege by the Spaniards for months in this same critical year. Orange's supporters desperately tried to relieve the starving citizens by flooding the countryside and sending in supplies. Its relief was vital to the future of the revolt in the northern provinces, for spectacular though the success of the Beggars had been, the Spaniards still occupied much of Holland north of Rotterdam in 1574, including the important city of Amsterdam. If the Spaniards could have brought up more cannon and conducted an assault-siege, the town would have fallen and Holland might still have been theirs. But the flooding and their lack of artillery had forced on them a long drawn-out blockade. It also put a fearsome strain on the magistrates of the town, essentially cautious and judicious men. True, the sturdier spirits among them like Douza (a noble, a philosopher and scholar), Van Hout (the town secretary) and van der Werff (Orange's friend, an underground fighter, very brave and tough) complained of the unfaithful among the upper classes who incited the common people to give up the struggle. Robert Fruin, the great nineteenth-century Dutch historian, believed that at Leiden the basic opposition to Spain came from the lower orders: 'The higher the social status the greater the indifference.'[41] Yet the crucial decisions rested, as on so many occasions, with the minority. The men whose leadership saved Leiden might be exceptions to the rule of caution, timidity or indifference. The arguments in favour of resistance and against compromise were not always as self-evident to contemporaries as they were to be to historians in comfortable retrospect. Even a close and trusted friend of Orange like Marnix often pleaded with the prince to allow him to try to mediate with Philip. It seemed often to be only Orange himself who recognized that compromise with that obstinate recluse was not within the bounds of the possible.

It was only on 3 October that a great autumn tempest of wind and flood swept the relieving fleet up to Leiden. As on earlier occasions the Spaniards fled before the rushing tide, plagued by terror and mutiny. They did not stop until they reached Utrecht. The raising of the siege was rightly regarded as a great victory for the forces of freedom and humanism. It was celebrated by the foundation of a university, and from the beginning Leiden was no mere theological academy: it was also to be a meeting-place for humanists (especially Protestant humanists) of

England, France and Germany too. What Louvain was to the south, Leiden would be in the north. Its network of cultural relationships was to be an important factor in the future of the rebellion.

Even before the relief of Leiden Alba's spirit was broken. In November 1573, at his own request, he was allowed to return home. Six years, in which every step forward had been followed by two steps back, had been too much for him. Ill, exhausted and broken he left for Spain. Alba had performed financial miracles in making the Netherlands pay for the war between 1569 and 1572. Altogether he had bled them of some thirteen million florins: more than Castile had sent in the same period. But his merciless tactics had provoked an apparently inconquerable spirit of resistance. His six disastrous years of failure was reflected, temporarily at any rate, in the change of policy which seemed to be contemplated under Don Luis de Requesens, who succeeded him as Spanish governor from 1573 to 1576.

Requesens disagreed with Alba on almost every issue of importance concerning the Netherlands troubles. Alba had believed the root of the trouble domestically was religion: only its drastic excision would cure the disease. The nobles he despised as unreliable or incompetent – Aerschot was lazy, Mansfeld a good soldier, Viglius a reasonable administrator – but they were dwarfs. Only Noircarmes and Berlaymont could be trusted. The Sea Beggars were insignificant: they were a tool of France and she was a worse enemy than England, who would be brought to heel in good time.

To Requesens this was all dangerously misconceived. Religion had been exaggerated as the cause of the trouble: 'I do not hold with the view that religion has been the cause of the uprising. Rather, the people have rebelled against the new taxes which have been imposed and the ill-treatment . . . which they have received at the hands of the soldiers.'[42] He proposed therefore to achieve mastery of the sea with the aid of a great fleet carrying six thousand infantry. Prudent concessions would be made to the rebels, but the Beggars would be smashed.

Requesens failed as miserably as Alba: for several reasons. The early successes he achieved in Zeeland, where he tried to drive a wedge between the Beggars north of Zierikzee and south of it, aborted. Like Alba, Requesens was enormously expensive; but he failed to extract from the Netherlands anything like the cash Alba had managed to squeeze from them. His demands on Spain grew alarmingly. Some seventeen million florins were sent to meet Requesens's demands while little more than six million was extracted from the Netherlands. His attempts to negotiate with the rebels at Breda in 1576 broke down on precisely the issue of religion which Requesens had been convinced was negotiable. Neither Orange nor Philip would give way.

When Requesens died suddenly, in March 1576, Philip was relieved to see him go. A general pardon had failed to pacify the country. Philip had been forced into another decree of bankruptcy when a wild orgy of destruction by mutinous Spanish soldiers who had received no pay for nearly two years broke out. Known as the 'Spanish Fury' it began near Zierikzee, spreading through Zeeland into Brabant, and ending in a week of plunder, murder, rape and general barbarity at Antwerp. All told some eight thousand people were massacred. It was not an isolated incident: over forty of these concerted Spanish mutinies took place in the Netherlands in the last quarter of the sixteenth century. Its immediate effect – like the calculated outrages by Alba nine years earlier – was to unite the entire Netherlands in angry indignation.

The Requesens governorship was not without its effects. For some of Philip's advisers, if not for Philip himself, it gave due warning that the costs of Spain's wars against Netherlanders and Turks must, at current rates of expenditure, bring economic ruin. The costs of Philip's imperialism in 1571–5 were fourteen million ducats. Total royal receipts from the Indies covered about a quarter of this. The rest came from taxes, in the Netherlands or Castile. And since the Netherlands would neither pay nor obey, it was the peasants of Castile who did. Castile was to become the most heavily taxed country in the late sixteenth-century world. Requesens's failure probably persuaded many intelligent Spaniards that the best hope for the future was to seek agreement wherever there was a prospect that obedience and orthodoxy could be re-established. In this sense, Farnese was to be his pupil. More immediately, the consequence of Requesens was a federation of Holland and Zeeland. At its head as commander-in-chief and stadholder was William of Orange. Thus the two provinces were consolidated as the heart of the resistance. They were to remain so as the province of Holland became increasingly the principal source of financial support for the revolt. For the moment the energies of the whole fatherland were harnessed against the invader. Yet without Orange's leadership the nobles would have sacrificed even the temporary unity of wrath to their personal feuds. When the bad news came through that Requesens's successor was to be Don John of Austria, Philip's bastard brother and the formidable victor of Lepanto, the Lords of Hèze and Bergen still found time to throw the Duke of Aerschot and the Council of State into prison. Only the skill and eloquence of Orange restored order and promise of better times in the shape of the Pacification of Ghent. This was an attempt to establish a religious settlement based on the status quo, an end of prose-lytizing by both sides, and the recognition of Orange in all those offices from which he had been expelled by Spanish decree. Its essential aim was to unite all the provinces, north and south, on an anti-Spanish platform.

These were to be the years of opportunity for Orange. The new Spanish governor quickly dissipated any goodwill he might have retained. He broke the uneasy peace that had reigned since the Fury by seizing the citadel at Namur. Civil war broke out again, but now it was a civil war in which the whole Netherlands was committed and in which an embryonic Netherlands State came into being.

There was no doubt who was its head. Out of the leaders – good, bad and indifferent – who emerged from the resistance, Orange was the only one capable of unifying the revolt at all levels. He had become a Calvinist in October 1573, having for some years been inclined to Lutheranism, like his brother Louis. This did not prevent fellow-nobles and Catholics like Philippe de Lalaing, Rennenberg (also a Lalaing), the young Egmont, even Aerschot himself (though *au fond* deeply jealous of Orange) from paying repeated tribute to him at this critical phase. His prestige reached its peak in the summer of 1577. In September when he came to Antwerp and Brussels he received a tumultuous hero's welcome as he rode, with Aerschot beside him, though city streets filled with cheering crowds and gaily decked with flowers.

William was now in his forty-fourth year. He was no longer the care-less young noble who had endeared himself to Charles v. His life had been saddened by troubles domestic as well as public. The Spaniards had kidnapped his son and carried him off to Spain. He had had to endure the misery of one wife who was schizophrenic and unfaithful; he was to lose the next two through death. He had been defeated in the field, condemned to the life of a wanderer, and reviled for failures for which he was not responsible. Yet his spirit was unbroken, his character had gained in depth and resilience and his mind sharpened by constant vigilance. In many ways he conformed to the norms of noble behaviour in his day, but he was exceptional in several profoundly important respects. He was acutely sensitive to injustice and persecution; he never exceeded his powers; he never avoided his duty. Finally he possessed in abundance the gift of attracting men to him for discussion and advice. Wherever he went he talked naturally to people of all estates, high and low. He became *pater patriae*, 'Father William', living in a comparatively modest town house at Delft. No doubt his written works, especially his famous *Apology* (1581) in which he defended himself against Philip's calumnies (and for good measure threw some of the mud back where it came from), owed something to the advice of his friends; but one cannot read the verbatim accounts of his recorded audiences with foreign diplomats without realizing that his voice and mind were essentially his own. He was perhaps the only political leader of the age who foresaw the need for statesmanship in the modern sense. His blend of natural authority, integrity and opportunism was his own; his basic principles were immovable but he knew that politics was indeed the art of the possible. His ideas were in a sense feudal: he saw himself as a loyal subject outrageously wronged by his lord. Yet mixed with this was a habit of discussion and persuasion that was partly instinctive, partly learnt. For in this fragmented country, where every lord, province and town fought for individual privileges, this was the only way in which he could survive politically. He was, therefore, different from the dynasts, despots and demagogues who surrounded him; neither spotless, nor without error, nor pretending to be; he was complicated, serious, and tough: a man undoubtedly great.

Orange had no more illusions than Philip, Alba or Charles v about the reliability of the Netherlands nobility. Nor had he been blinded by the progress since 1572 into believing that his 'redoubt' in any way enjoyed automatic security against invasion, capture and defeat by reason of its natural defences of river, ocean and wind, useful though these were. He would have been sceptical of later theories that attributed the survival of the Dutch Republic to the 'defence line' of the great rivers or to any other *deus ex machina*. For him the struggle must be unremitting. Only thus could victory be possible. Above all, in the years after the Pacification of Ghent it seemed to him that victory against the committed resources of Europe's greatest power could only be assured with the help of another great power. There were only two candidates: it must be England or France.

9

THE DUTCH REVOLT BECOMES EUROPEAN

Between 1576 and 1609 the Revolt of the Netherlands, always a potential international explosion, became ineluctably a European imbroglio. Orange sought for foreign allies to bolster the slender advantage given him by the nation-wide indignation over the Spanish Fury. Refugees from the southern provinces continued to pour over the Scheldt. Some of them were Calvinists whose primary goal was freedom to worship. Others were tradesmen, capitalists, manufacturers or artisans for whom Alba and Spain promised only economic ruin. But the diaspora was also a cultural movement. Among the migrants were scholars and artists who disliked and mistrusted the kind of society which seemed likely to emerge from the Spanish occupation. The contribution of the southerners to the creation of a northern state can hardly be exaggerated. The next century was to find them and their descendants spread throughout the activities of the republic. Their international connexions, Calvinist or Sephardic (for many Portuguese and Spanish Jews also left Antwerp) were to prove especially valuable in creating Amsterdam's international network of entrepôt trades.

Northern economic strength was growing. It remained to find strong allies. Yet France was more than ever disrupted and devastated by civil war. War and plunder had become a way of life; the central government was powerless. Spinning her webs of intrigue the queen-mother still exercised her malign maternal influence over the king; even more over his next brother, the Duke of Anjou and over his third brother, the Duke of Alençon. The second she had busily and successfully urged into the contest for the throne of Poland in 1573, though Anjou himself was

157

reluctant to leave France. He was relieved of his role in what was never more than a farcical proceeding when the king died in 1574. One prospective crown was thus removed from Catherine's dream of a Medici Europe.

Another still remained: for could not Alençon, who now succeeded his elder brother as Duke of Anjou, be held in reserve as consort to Elizabeth of England? Insignificant and misshapen he might be; 'ferocious without courage, ambitious without talent and bigoted without opinions' (in Motley's phrase), but Catherine was used to making bricks without straw. The new king, on the other hand, was as versatile intellectually as he was sexually. Dominated by his mother, he had some of her female energy and cunning but this alternated with bouts of depression or frivolity: dancing and feasting in bizarre costumes of mulberry satin and coral bracelets was interspersed with spells of flagellation and psalm-singing. His bosom companions were familiar to the satirists as the 'Princes of Sodom'. Early in life he had been obsessed by Calvinism. Now a chance meeting with Cardinal Borromeo brought him under the spell of that impressive eminence of Counter-Reformation piety. Henry took to works of penitence and self-mortification as a small girl might play with dolls. From 1575 to 1589 he was to be victim of his mother's intrigues; France was to be victim of his own mixture of intelligence, vacillation and weakness.

The first sign of the new order was the formation of the Catholic League in 1576. Just as the Huguenots had armed and consolidated their supporters into a separatist, dedicated military order, the extreme Catholics now did the same. And Henry, Duke of Guise was more dangerous than the Huguenot leaders, closely linked as he was with Spain and financially supported by Philip. Thus the crisis which had been growing in France since Cateau-Cambrésis seemed to be reaching its climax. These were the conditions in which Orange turned to the other source of help: Elizabeth and England.

In 1576, the outlook for an Anglo-Netherlands alliance was not inherently promising, but neither was it hopeless. There was no doubt where Elizabeth's sympathies lay. She detested rebels and rebellion especially when they were associated with Calvinism. If she could have made her own choice she would, in her own words, have hanged them all. But her problems were more complex. What was the future of the Netherlands to be? Commercially, this was a vital problem for English trade and prosperity depended in a large measure on Antwerp. Strategically, it would be disastrous if the Netherlands were to be occupied by an enemy, whether the 'ancient enemy', France, or an aggressively Tridentine imperialist crusader like Philip. What was needed was a reformulated version of the old Anglo-Burgundian alliance. And it was this to which Elizabeth and Burghley now dedicated themselves. Month after month, year after year, Burghley penned scores of memoranda addressed to the Queen's ambassadors, agents, secretaries, privy councillors, as well as to foreign princes and diplomats, proclaiming the English policy: she would acknowledge Philip's rights in the Netherlands provided he would recognize and restore their ancient liberties' and reconcile himself to the nobility and his other subjects. The justification was the threat which would be posed by France if Spain should be expelled, leaving a vacuum in the Netherlands. The objection was that France, torn to pieces by one civil war after another, unlikely to pose was such a threat: in any case, Elizabeth at this very time proclaimed herself ready to sign treaties of alliance with France, even to coquette with Alençon as a suitor. On the best interpretation, her 'policies' from 1576 to 1585 were a clever deception imposed on Western Europe with the aim of easing Spain out of the Netherlands while preventing France from getting in; they also had the merit of preserving the Queen's reputation for being the least demanding prince of the century where her subjects' pockets were concerned. On the worst interpretation, her policies were a disastrous muddle, a succession of contradictory, confusing stratagems which all failed, lowered the reputation of the Queen and her state, lost the southern half of the Netherlands to Spain and still left her to bear the burdens of a war on behalf of the north from 1585 to 1604. On this reading, the Burghley formula was merely one of inaction, in practice meaningless.

If Burghley shaped the Queen's mind towards prevarication, he was not without his critics. Sir Francis Walsingham, joint Secretary of the Queen's Council, his partner, Sir Thomas Wilson, and Daniel Rogers, an important diplomatic agent who shared the task of conducting the Queen's relations with Orange in these years, formed the nucleus of the Queen's permanent staff dedicated to the plan of an Anglo-Netherlands alliance, if necessary to English military intervention. With them stood others of the gentry and nobility including Philip Sidney and his uncle Robert Dudley, Earl of Leicester, the Queen's favourite. Leicester – ambitious, uncontrolled, choleric – had his own reasons for joining the Protestant group: for if an expeditionary force should set out, or if the

Queen should take the Netherlands under her wing, who more fit for high office than Leicester?

The interventionists were strongly pro-Orange. Those who met the prince and saw him in action on their visits to the Low Countries were confirmed in their faith. One and all, they laboured to put his case to the Queen. It was for the sake of the safety of England and her throne that the Queen should support the revolt. This, too, was the case put by Orange in seeking the Queen's help.

If there was a case for intervention it was probably strongest in this period, between 1576 and 1579, when the Netherlands most nearly approached unity, when Spain had its own difficulties in abundance, when Orange's prestige was high, offering a chance that he would be able to consolidate the Netherlands nobles, towns and Calvinists behind him. More than once it seemed that the die was cast, that the Queen was in agreement with the unanimous views of her council and that action would follow, rejoicing the hearts of the stoutly pro-English party in the Low Countries which centred on Orange himself and found its strongest support among the magistrates and intellectuals of Leiden – men like the Pensionary of Leiden, Paul Buys, Janus Dousa, Jan van Hout, Hubert Languet and others.

It was not to be. Since 1572 England had infiltrated small bodies of troops into the Flushing area. But they were not enough to give the rebels decisive help. Probably their intention was more to give England a say in the control of the vital traffic along the Scheldt to Antwerp. This was one of the trump-cards which the Beggars' capture of Brill and Flushing had put into Orange's hands. But the operations of his privateers, who took both Spanish and English ships in prize, were a constant provocation to both powers and a constant irritant to Anglo-Dutch relations. Despite the urgings of the Protestant party at Court and Westminster, plans for more decisive help for Orange came to nothing. Even Burghley was now converted to the view that it was important to keep Orange 'in hart and lyf': but all to no purpose. The Queen (possibly going through the change of life in these critical years) was at her most capricious and irascible.

Meanwhile Spain had recovered her strength. She had acquired one other priceless asset. Still under the erratic authority of Don John, the Spanish high command now included a general of outstanding skill, gallantry and intelligence: Alexander Farnese, Prince of Parma and future Governor of the Netherlands. His presence did much to explain the resounding defeat inflicted on the Netherlands States' forces on the last day of January 1578 by Don John, a mixture of Spanish, loyalist Walloon and German officers (like Mansfeld), with twenty thousand veterans. The engagement took place at Gembloux, a village about nine miles from Namur. The States' forces were a mixed bag of rebel nobles, former *Gueux* and others fighting without much spirit or conviction. The defeat, a shattering blow to the morale of the opposition, fore-shadowed the end of the temporary unity that had marked the period since the Spanish Fury. True, the Spaniards failed to follow up their victory but Gembloux had a traumatic political effect. The nobility of the Netherlands, like those of other countries, were torn between private interest and loyalty to the King of Spain. Gembloux deepened their fears about the possible consequences of disloyalty. Where was the revolt leading them? The leading members of the great clans – Croys, Lannoys, Hennins, Lalaings and Egmonts – were troubled men; as Orange's difficulties grew and Elizabeth's promises faded, they became more worried about the retribution that might fall upon them.

Against this background of a crumbling noble front, no error of the Queen's was more serious than her decision to reduce her costs by sub-stituting a German mercenary troop for an English expeditionary force under Leicester. Her choice of a Commander was not fortunate. Duke Casimir, son of the Elector Palatine, was not only a representative of the most decidedly Calvinist of German states – a strange choice for the Queen, it might be thought – he was also a singularly brainless soldier devoid of tact or judgment. He had, however, the merit of having eleven thousand troops behind him, including cavalry, and he was going cheap.

Orange was appalled by her decision. In an interview which he granted to her agent Daniel Rogers, he indicted the Queen mercilessly. She had broken promises which would have bound the Low Countries to her for ever:

Now all the fault wilbe layd upon me (quoth he) and thei which are myne enemyes wilbe glad thei have gotten an occasion to saie that if the Prince of Orange hadd not willed the Estates to depende upon the Quene of England, thei had receaved succour from other places, or otherwise provided for themselves. . . .[43]

Orange realized more clearly than the Queen the implications of her actions. Posing as the hero of the Calvinist theocrats and demogogues,

Casimir took his troops away from the battle to Ghent. Here the Calvinist extremists had already aroused the anxieties and anger of the Walloon nobility by arresting the Duke of Aerschot, leader of the House of Croy and Orange's most jealous rival. Orange had at once ordered his release, but the damage was done: the gulf between the Catholic nobles and the Calvinist rebels was dramatically widened. Orange's policies of moderation were thwarted. Thereafter Casimir departed, leaving his German troops, without food or pay, to ravage the countryside and incur the general hatred of the people until they were commanded by Farnese to leave the Netherlands under pain of extermination.

All this caused grave anxiety among the Protestant party in England who were as bewildered as Orange by the Queen's irrational behaviour. Burghley, equally anxious, persuaded her to despatch a mission headed by Walsingham and Lord Cobham to see whether 'a good and sure peace between the King of Spain and his subjects' could not be reached. It set off, a grand and – for once – extravagant procession, a hundred and twenty strong. One of its members reported encouragingly. There was in the Netherlands a majority of moderates, Protestant and Catholic. The extremists – 'passionate Papists', 'Pater Noster Jacks' – were a minority, but more numerous as one went south. But the Queen was no longer interested in reaching a settlement. By the autumn, Walsingham (and Cobham too) were begging to be brought home. The mission ended in failure and humiliation; God had 'closed up Her Majesty's heart from seeing and executing that which may be for her safety'. Walsingham doubted if she was quite sane.

What had happened? The party of 'malcontent' nobles, sulking after defeat at Gembloux, were no longer reliable. At this critical moment Don John died, unpaid and unrewarded, like Philip's other faithful servants. His successor was Alexander Farnese, a far greater danger to Orange and to Elizabeth. A great soldier, he was too clever to rely simply on force of arms or the evanescent glory of victory. He set to work to achieve what Requesens had failed to do: to win over the nobility. And he quickly spotted their most vulnerable point. One after another they were plied, through 1579 and succeeding years, with offers of money, office, honours. And one after another, they fell – abbots, bishops, town governors, Lalaings, Croys, Montmorencys. By summer 1579 there were few nobles left in the revolt.

Now the Netherlands divided into two parts. The Protestant Union of Utrecht, formed in January 1579, still included a large area of the 'south' – that is, the area south of the great rivers which were to be the broad line of division of the later partition, Ghent and Antwerp still being in the Union. The Catholic Union of Arras, formed in May 1579, was not 'Belgian' in the modern sense for it was limited to the Walloon states. In any case, the military developments of the next five years were to change these boundaries. Meanwhile Orange was now under the ban proclaimed by Philip, who not only armed assassins to kill him but promised rich rewards to anyone who should succeed. It was urgent to fill the gap in the Netherlands constitution left by Philip's betrayal of his duty (as the rebels saw it) and by Elizabeth's refusal to replace him. From the German princes nothing could be hoped. That left only one hope: France. And, divided and distracted though she was, Orange persuaded the States-General in 1580 to open negotiations with the Duke of Anjou. If the Netherlanders were lukewarm and suspicious about accepting a Catholic Valois as their sovereign lord, Anjou himself was at first eager and full of zeal.

Any hopes pinned on him soon faded. His army, such as it was, busied itself mainly with the siege of Cambrai, which was more a French than a Netherlands concern. His troops were unpaid and mutinous. Many faded away when the States-General declared they could not pay them. Relations with Anjou became increasingly strained, despite the super-human patience Orange showed in handling his hypersensitiveness and petty jealousies. Bored and frustrated in the Netherlands Anjou departed in 1581 to resume his ridiculous wooing of the Queen.

Elizabeth had entered into the courtship with her 'dear Frog' with a zest which drove her advisers to distraction. They need not have worried. She had no intention of contracting a marriage, least of all one with a French prince which would have destroyed her personal authority and jeopardized her throne. If there was any point to the proceedings it was perhaps merely to enable her to keep an eye on Anjou. But we may leave the last word with Bishop Creighton: politics had 'never sunk to a lower level of absurdity than in these ridiculous proceedings'.[44]

Early in 1582 the States-General enticed Anjou back to Antwerp with the title of Duke of Brabant. But the tragi-comedy was near its end. Less than a year later his troops invaded Antwerp. But in the fracas that followed they were thrown out. The failure of the *furie française* (as it was called) was the end of Anjou. He returned to France, to die in 1584 from a sudden fever. His departure went unlamented in the Netherlands, where few had seen the 'Defender of Netherlands Liberties Against the

Tyranny of Spain' as anything more than a dangerous nuisance. Indeed Orange's patience, which arose from his conviction that the revolt must have outside support, did him serious damage with his supporters. It also spelt the beginning of the end of the long and fruitless search for a foreign sovereign for the new state.

And now, from 1584 to 1588, the condition of the Netherlands was to reach its most critical point since the time of Alba. The Peace of Arras had effectively divided the Netherlands in two. Since 1580 Parma was engaged in restoring popular, and especially noble, confidence in his ability and good faith. His methods were those of studied moderation, consideration of local interests, applied with liberal doses of material incentive. They were conspicuously successful. By 1582 he was able to win the approval of the Walloon states to the return of the Spanish troops who had been sent home under the terms of the Peace of Arras three years earlier.

Reinforced by his Spaniards, Farnese began to make military as well as political progress. So far he had had an uphill climb. Contrary to theories that the great rivers were the only serious obstacle, the period since the Peace of Arras had proved how strong the fortifications of the Netherlands cities were. It had taken Parma four months of heavy preparation and fighting to crack the defence of Maastricht. Low morale, rather than inherent military weakness, was the risk in this siege warfare. Now, with his *tercios* back, Parma could speed the pace. Learning from his experience at Maastricht, he carefully isolated one great city after another – Ghent, Dendermonde, Mechlin, Brussels. Everywhere treachery, bribery and the fury of opposing bigotries (as at Ghent) did more than guns or valour to end the revolt. By 1585 only Antwerp remained, the last and richest prize.

Even as Parma prepared his *coup de grace*, the rebels suffered their greatest blow. In June 1584 William of Orange – the Silent, the *pater patriae* – was assassinated in his own house at Delft: 'So long as he lived he was the guiding star of a whole brave nation, and when he died the little children cried in the streets.' Motley took the last sentence of his epic *Rise of the Dutch Republic* directly from a contemporary description by the recorder of the States-General. They convey the sense of shock at his assassination. It jerked back to reality many who had vented their discontents on the Prince. Since 1579 he had become the scapegoat for the errors and crimes of everyone else as the south had stumbled through barbaric anarchy back to Spanish obedience. It was inevitable that in this land, where fragmented authority was the key to economic success and political failure, Orange's position should be precarious. But it was a singular misfortune that had made it for the last five years of his life virtually untenable. The wounds inflicted on him are visible in his famous *Apology* (1580). In it he attacked not only Philip but – with almost equal contempt and bitterness – his fellow nobles:

They serve the Duke of Alba ... like scullions. They make war on me to the knife. Then they treat with me, they reconcile themselves with me, they are sworn enemies of the Spaniard. Don John arrives and they follow after him: they intrigue for my ruin. Don John fails ... they turn incontinently and call upon me.... Are the waves of the sea more inconstant ... than the councils of such men?

He was spared the blow of seeing the loss of Antwerp. He had always held that its defence was perfectly practicable: indeed he had set out its main principles. Antwerp lay on the edge of the water area. The dykes must therefore be opened and the surrounding land flooded. Antwerp could then be supplied by sea from neighbouring Zeeland and the besiegers' task would be impossible. But in practice, local feuds between commanders made it impossible to implement the grand plan. Marnix, whom William had sent to prepare for the defence, was by temperament unfitted to impose his authority. The butchers' gild objected to flooding the pastures that provided fodder for so many cattle! The attacks on Parma's bridge across the Scheldt were bungled. After a summer of total confusion, Antwerp finally surrendered on 17 August. Ten days later Parma entered the city. Its capture crowned nearly six years of achievement during which the whole of the south, as far north as the rivers Maas and Waal, and a great band of northern territory including Groningen and Drenthe, as far south as Deventer and Zutfen, had been recaptured for Spain. The revolt was contained, virtually imprisoned, within Holland, Zeeland, Utrecht, Gelderland, Overysel, Friesland and the chain of northern islands.

The Netherlands were now divided; and the fighting of the next sixty years and more were to confirm – with some modifications – this broad division into the Dutch Republic and the Spanish (later Austrian) Netherlands – later Belgium. Why had the attempt to create a single Netherlands state failed?

The Dutch historian Pieter Geyl, propounded the theory, widely accepted by many other scholars for many years, that the unity was split largely because, once the Spanish attack got under way, the south was

The Dutch Revolt

indefensible while the north was protected by the line of great rivers – Maas, Waal and Lek. Most historians today would agree that this is an oversimplication. The rivers and sea were certainly an important aid to the northerners; but their survival as an independent state did not depend on these factors alone. The dogged resistance of the Calvinists, slowly concentrating in the north; the equal concentration of trade and industry in the north by immigration and growth; the leadership of Orange; the distractions affecting the more feudal and agrarian social structure of the south – these were a few of the other factors behind northern survival. Equally, the genius of Parma does much to explain the return of the south to Spanish obedience. Certainly the result was the polarization of economic and social forces to create two states increasingly different in structure and outlook after 1585.

10

THE EUROPEAN POWERS AND THE
NEW NETHERLANDS STATE

FROM NONSUCH TO VERVINS

The fall of Antwerp followed hard on other disasters – the death of Anjou; Parma's military and political successes; the blitzkrieg by Alba on Portugal which united the whole Iberian peninsula (on paper at least) under Philip; and the growing volume of American silver arriving at Seville – all of which necessitated important realignments in the policies of the European powers.

Elizabeth was badly shaken by the fall of Antwerp. Whether her conscience was troubled because she had failed to give Marnix the help which might have saved the city is anyone's guess. The fact was that the key to the old structure of England's overseas trade had been lost – and lost while a Netherlands delegation was discussing renewed and extended English help. The Queen hastened to conclude the Treaty of Nonsuch with the rebels. England was to maintain an army of five thousand foot and a thousand horse in the Netherlands. The Dutch were to repay the costs within five years of signing a peace with Spain (it was assumed that the war would be a short one). The strategic ports of Brill and Flushing were to be garrisoned by English troops and serve as security for English military investment in the new state. In November 1585 the Queen even issued a declaration in four languages justifying her abandonment of neutrality to Philip of Spain and the world. At long last she was committed; but she would in no way accept the sovereignty of the rebel provinces. That was too much for her conservative conscience.

After much havering, the choice of commander of the English forces and the Queen's viceroy in the Netherlands fell upon the Earl of Leicester. He was not much of a soldier and his political and personal record was ambiguous. But he was rich and ambitious, and the Queen's favourite. This was enough to eliminate other candidates. Just before Christmas his force landed at Flushing from fifty ships carrying 'the flower and chief gallants of England'. One of the veterans voiced stoutly, if ungrammatically, the convictions of Protestant patriotism which animated so many of the gentlemen in and out of Parliament of the day: 'This war doth defend England . . . the fire is kindled; whosoever suffers it to go out, it will grow dangerous. . . . The whole state of religion is in question . . . The whole freehold of England will be worth little if this action quail. . . .'[45]

At Flushing, Middelburg, Delft, Leiden, the Hague and Amsterdam the English military procession was cheered and feasted with stupendous entertainments. Their popularity was in no doubt. Leicester himself wrote home that everywhere the crowds cried 'God save the Queen', 'as if we had been in Cheapside'. Alas! these happy relations were not to last long. It was largely, but not entirely, Leicester's fault. His instructions were far from clear and he quickly incurred the severe displeasure of the Queen by accepting the title of 'Absolute Governor' without royal approval. But he had his own troubles; and his troops were left without pay. Parma was attacking along the Maas while brawls broke out among his discontented commanders. Yet Leicester remained optimistic. After repulsing Parma's initial attacks on the Maas fortresses he was confident he would soon have Antwerp and Bruges back. It was not to be. And in Europe political developments were threatening.

Anjou's death raised the awkward problem of the succession to the French Crown. Was it Henry of Navarre? Or was it the Duke of Guise? Legal niceties aside, Guise had powerful support – Paris itself, large areas of Normandy, Champagne and Picardy were for him; so were many of the great nobles. In 1584 their support was crystallized in the renewal of the powerful Catholic League, silent since 1577. Later in 1584 Guise signed a secret treaty (of Joinville) with Philip of Spain. This promised Guise substantial help in return for a pledge to exterminate heresy in France and to support the Cardinal of Bourbon's claim to the throne in place of that of Henry of Navarre. Under irresistible pressure the king surrendered to the Guises while the Pope excommunicated Navarre. In the civil wars which were now renewed, Henry of Navarre turned to England for help. He had few other tangible assets; but his own resilient spirit was unbroken – and he could now appeal to a growing feeling in France that her people were being exploited by a foreign power (Spain) and a Pope for whom the Guises were merely tools.

It was the same brand of patriotism to which Elizabeth was also able to appeal in face of recent Catholic risings and plots in Ireland launched with the Pope's help, and, nearer home, the recurrent intrigues on behalf of the imprisoned Mary, Queen of Scots. These had culminated in 1584 with Walsingham's uncovering of the Throckmorton plot. The confessions of Francis Throckmorton implicated the Spanish Ambassador and Mary, Queen of Scots. Coming on top of this the fall of Antwerp brought the Spanish-Catholic menace too near. A wave of Protestant patriotism demanded action: the growing intimacy of the leading Dutch statesmen, the Queen and Henry of Navarre promised that it would not long be delayed. Indeed, Spain's seizure of all the English shipping in Spanish and Portuguese ports gave the Queen her excuse for making an immediate start. The declared object of Francis Drake's voyage which she authorized in September 1585 was to release the English ships immobilized in Spain. The real object was to intercept the Spanish silver fleet. Meanwhile Philip was beginning to plan seriously for a major 'enterprise against England'.

His decision was hastened by the discovery early in 1586 of yet another plot to assassinate Elizabeth. A letter was found in which Mary, Queen of Scots, offered to transfer her rights to the English throne away from her son James to Philip of Spain. Nothing loth, Philip had accepted. Elizabeth finally signed Mary's death warrant and she was executed at Fotheringay on 18 February 1587. Mary's death gave Philip the excuse he needed. He was her appointed successor, the champion of Catholic orthodoxy, close ally to the new and vigorous Pope Sixtus v, the Guises, and the newly fortified Catholic League.

Behind the growing preparations for a major confrontation between Spain and her chosen enemies lay another development: the tide of silver from the New World was rising towards its peak, to be reached in the 1590s. These staggering windfalls were reflected in the rising investment in the Spanish Army of Flanders. In 1583 and 1584 Spain had remitted a mere 2½ million florins to the Netherlands. In 1587 the remittances rose to nearly 14 million: only in three years before the end of the century were they to fall below 11 million, and in the remaining years they were above that figure. For the die was now cast: Parma's forces in the Netherlands were engaged not merely in trying to bring back the king's subjects to obedience; they were committed to a desperate battle for Catholic-Spanish hegemony in Western Europe.

Spain had no reason to be dissatisfied with Parma's progress down to 1587. The Earl of Leicester had fulfilled all the worst fears of his critics. He repeated the blunder committed by Duke Casimir at Ghent of allying himself with the extremist Calvinists, this time at Utrecht, and thereby grievously undermining the confidence of the most influential class of the Netherlands – the Holland Regents. With incredible ineptitude he thus managed to identify the Queen with the religious sect she most disliked and involve her in the inter-provincial rivalry of the Holland States with the Utrecht dissidents whose major motive was jealousy of Holland's power and wealth.

Nor were his political bunglings offset by any military glories. On the contrary, his own nephew, Philip Sidney, was killed in the pointless and unsuccessful action at Zutfen. At Deventer, the near-by town which had acted as the supply depot for the Spanish army operating in this northeast area, Leicester installed as protector Sir William Stanley, a Catholic soldier of fortune who had previously fought with Alba for Spain. The command of Zutfen fort was entrusted to Rowland York, a desperado ready to join any cause which offered the highest pay. Leicester's maladroit appointments had an inevitable conclusion: Stanley and York both deserted, surrendering Deventer and Zutfen to the enemy for suitable financial compensation. Thus two vital strong-points on the right bank of the River Ijssel, the eastern frontier of the north Netherlands state, were lost to the Anglo-Dutch forces and a severe blow struck against Dutch confidence in their new ally. It was fortunate that, at this critical juncture, the unlucky Parma became the victim of another disastrous piece of strategic rethinking by his master in Spain.

In November 1586 Leicester had returned to England. In his place went a very different personality, Thomas Sackville, Lord Buckhurst. Where Leicester had spread only friction and hysteria, Buckhurst succeeded by his prudent and conciliatory policy in recreating confidence. He called firmly on the Queen for pay for the troops, for sensible attitudes towards her Dutch allies and for an end to the quarrels among her commanders. But his very success doomed him to suffer the Queen's displeasure. In London Leicester managed to wheedle his way back into the Queen's favour. In July 1587 he returned to his command. His second spell of office was as disastrous as the first, culminating in the loss of Sluys to Parma in August. By this unlikely success, the Spaniards had acquired another valuable base for Philip's 'enterprise of England'; to this all Spain's resources were now to be directed.

The original plan, as conceived by the Marquis of Santa Cruz, a veteran of Lepanto, was that a great fleet with sixty thousand soldiers, would make a direct landing in England. Drake's raid on Cadiz, which did severe damage to the Armada building there, and his subsequent harassment of Spanish ships bringing timber and supplies, drove one fatal nail in the coffin of the original plan. Philip's habitual indecision did the rest.

Against the desperate pleadings of Parma, he devised, in concert with the Duke of Medina Sidonia (whose naval experience was nil) a new plan. The Armada, much reduced in size and carrying only a minimum force of landing troops, would rendezvous with an invasion force provided by Parma from his Netherlands resources, collected at Nieupoort and Dunkirk. Time and again Parma urged upon Philip the hazards of the plan. He had no deep-water port in Flanders: galleons drawing 25 to 30 feet of water could not safely approach a coast lined with dangerous sandbanks when the prevailing wind was as likely as not to be blowing them on to a lee shore. As for the flat-bottomed canal barges which would carry his invasion troops, 'four ships of war could sink every one of my boats'. He was correct: the whole Flemish coast and Scheldt estuary were controlled by a fleet of nimble men-of-war commanded by Justin of Nassau, natural son of William the Silent.

The defeat of the Great Armada was not a foregone conclusion. True, Philip had done his best to devise the worst possible strategy. But fortunately for him and Medina Sidonia, Anglo-Dutch preparations and operations were almost as haphazard as those of the would-be invader. When the tortuous peace negotiations which Elizabeth had chosen at this point to conduct with Parma were broken off in mid-July, the Armada was at the mouth of the English Channel. By the end of July it was at Calais roads and had not lost a single ship by gunfire. Only the brilliant improvisation of the fireships by Drake saved a situation in which the allied fleet was completely out of ammunition. That, with the English and Dutch patrols of the Flemish coast and the impromptu initiative of individual commanders, saved the day until the wind blew the Spanish fleet north and away from the sandbanks of Flanders. Two-thirds escaped, and of these a number were wrecked on the route home via Scotland and Ireland. But no professional sailor was under any illusion that it was a great English victory. Roger Williams, the Welsh veteran of many Netherlands campaigns, was probably right: 'miracles alone had saved England from perdition'. In Flanders, Parma and his troops, emaciated after a year of famine and decimated by disease, knew that their best chance of victory over Dutch or English was lost.

There was still hope for Spain in the east, thanks to the betrayals by Stanley and York, now compounded by the surrender – traitorous, as the Dutch inevitably believed – of the strategically important city of Geertruidenberg, just south of the Maas and north of Breda. But providence smiled on the rebels. First, Parma fell sick. Then his troops suffered one of their regular attacks of mutiny. By winter the Spanish war effort was deadlocked. And no threat was now more serious than that from France.

Here 'the war of the three kings' had taken some abrupt turns. Henry III had hoped to defeat Navarre, but in October Navarre turned the tables by defeating and killing the royal favourite, Joyeuse, at Coutras. But a month later Navarre's German mercenary army under Baron von Dohna (partly paid for by Elizabeth's subsidies) was in turn routed by the Duke of Guise. The League was triumphant, especially in Paris where its militant priests and friars whipped up the mob against Henry III and his *mignons*. Guise and the Spanish Ambassador meanwhile concerted plans to seize Paris and the Channel ports against the arrival of the Armada. This would be the signal for the assassination of Henry III and the invasion of England to avenge Mary, Queen of Scots. Henry, who was no coward, moved his Swiss guard into Paris, but the Day of the Barricades left the city in the hands of the Catholic mob. Henry took to his heels. In July the Catholic League forced him to agree to their demands, including the appointment of Guise as military commander of France and the Cardinal of Bourbon as heir. The Estates-General, which met at Blois in September, was packed with a large majority of League supporters. It rubbed salt into the royal wounds: a dangerous thing to do, especially since the disaster of the Armada had deprived the League and Spain of their former power of blackmail. Henry summoned the Duke of Guise and his brother, the Cardinal of Guise, for a royal audience. In the antechamber the duke was assassinated. His brother was murdered a week later in prison.

It was now the turn of the League and its supporters to answer violence with violence. Throughout the civil wars, France had been scarred by 'religious' massacres, almost invariably linked with urban festivals, holy days, heresy trials. Protestants deliberately desecrated religious objects to prove that their magic was fraudulent; Catholics attacked Protestants, regardless of class, as devil and anti-Christ. St Bartholomew had incorporated much of this ritualism. The new wave of violence similarly whipped up purely religious hysteria against leaders both Catholic and Protestant, goaded by Papal blessing. The towns were always the scene of these wild outbreaks. In Paris the Catholics appropriated the weapons of the Huguenots. On 1 August, in a Paris seething with Catholic hysteria and besieged by the troops of Henry of Navarre, Henry III was himself assassinated by a young friar. He had just time, before he died, to recognize Navarre as his successor. Three days later Navarre simultaneously threw down the gauntlet to Spain and made his bid for the support of moderate Catholic patriots by promising to maintain the Catholic faith and to this end call a national religious council. In a beleaguered Paris, men, women and children were dying by the thousand from famine.

Once again, a harassed Philip switched his strategy. Parma was abruptly ordered to withdraw enough troops from the Netherlands theatre of war to march to the relief of Paris, the League and the faith. Reluctantly he agreed. With characteristic brilliance, he forced Henry IV to raise the siege; more Spanish troops landed in Brittany, followed by others in Languedoc. Once more Spain seemed ready to dominate Europe: but this time the strategic centre had moved to France. And the diversion of Parma seemed unlikely to be the temporary matter it had proved for Alba in 1572 or for Parma himself in 1581. For three years he remained in France; but without achieving any decisive victory. In 1592 he died, in disgrace and despair. Philip might not be able to defeat his enemies: he was master of the art of defeating his friends and lieutenants.

Philip's handling of the war between 1588 and 1592 provoked a rising tide of criticism that found expression in the Cortes of 1590, from which Philip was now compelled to demand new and unprecedentedly burdensome taxes. In Aragon it combined with protests against Philip's tactless appointment of a Castilian viceroy – against all precedent – to provoke general discontent. And matters went from bad to worse when Philip's former confidant and secretary Antonio Perez absconded with state documents and took refuge in Aragon early in 1591. Was the ensuing riot in Zaragoza the signal for an Aragonese revolt? A Spanish army made sure it was not, but the episode was disturbing. It was not only discontented nobles and over-taxed tradesmen who were increasingly apprehensive about the country's fate. Five years earlier old Granvelle had died, equally disillusioned. Spain, he had said, was sinking into the mire beneath the burdens of corruption and maladministration. Each year that passed seemed to confirm the truth of his prophecy.

The Netherlands remained a vital area. If they had collapsed, as some had forecast they might in 1589, Philip would have been free to concentrate his total effort on France, with incalculable consequences. But the Netherlands had benefited not only by the death of Parma but by the comprehensive reconstruction of the whole political and economic system since William's death in 1584.

Leicester's brief and disastrous stay in the Low Countries had taught the Dutch ruling class one prime lesson – that it was time to put behind them all idea of according supreme authority to a foreign ruler. The States were now sovereign. True, this hydra-headed kind of sovereignty was unfamiliar and would doubtless be unpalatable and incomprehensible to dynasts like Elizabeth. But it was time to prove that the Netherlands could stand on their own feet. Indeed their peculiar economy – advanced, international, commercial – demanded freedom from dynastic caprice and manipulation if it were to survive, let alone prosper.

During the contest with Leicester, one man had emerged capable of expressing and executing not only this view, but also its complement: that power must reside in the Province of Holland, which as chief paymaster must call the tune. The man was Johan van Oldenbarneveldt, Advocate of the States of Holland. The agents of his policy included the son of William the Silent, Maurice of Nassau, and his nephew, William Louis of Nassau, a loyal supporter of his young cousin. Maurice was a student at the newly founded University of Leiden when his father was assassinated. His father's experiences and disappointments and his own odd and disturbed childhood (he was son of the schizophrenic Anne of Saxony) left him reserved and suspicious. But the States of Holland elected him without delay into their stadholdership. Later Oldenbarneveldt moved skilfully to have him similarly elected to another five of the seven stadholderships. With William Louis as stadholder in Friesland the situation was safe and tidy.

In the year of the Armada, Maurice had just attained his majority. He was already brooding over the principles of the military reforms which would be necessary if the great counter-attack were to be launched against Spain: increased firepower for infantry and cavalry alike, more scientific development of siege warfare, more sappers, more spades, more training, more discipline – above all more pay, for Maurice had seen how fatal the mutiny of unpaid troops had been to the best-laid plans of Alba, Requesens, Parma and Leicester alike.

While these ideas were maturing, Maurice badly needed the political experience of Oldenbarneveldt, nearly twice his age and a seasoned political campaigner. With his stamina and optimism, Oldenbarneveldt set to work to realize the full potential of his office as political chief of the Province of Holland, providing as it did between half and two-thirds of the federal budget of the new state. Ironically, he swiftly achieved a personal domination of Netherlands affairs which dwarfed the Caesarism attempted by Leicester against which he had earlier led the opposition of the decentralized States. In proportion as the power and confidence of the Holland States waxed, so that of the mixed Anglo-Dutch Council of State, which the English had insisted on since 1585, waned. In the flexibility, astuteness and doggedness of Oldenbarneveldt, Elizabeth met her match.

Even Oldenbarneveldt would have been powerless if the wealth of the north had not expanded rapidly in the 1580s and 1590s. Its roots were in the great trade of the Baltic. The 1590s saw this traditional area of Dutch trade expanding and becoming more diversified. Great pathfinders – Barents, Heemskerck, Linschoten, Houtman, Tasman – were thrusting out and away into the extra-European world: to West and South Africa, India, Ceylon, Java, Australia, Tasmania, New Zealand, Spitsbergen, North and South America. Tropical spices, sugar, tobacco, cotton, whale oil joined the flow of traditional products from the old European trades. Specially designed cargo ships (flyboats) lowered costs.

The rising tides of trade brought with them a rising tide of revenue. It was Oldenbarneveldt's task to see that it was applied to war and disbursed in a manner that would not shame a careful merchant. The republic was not to suffer the recurrent declarations of bankruptcy that disfigured the haphazard financial chronicles of Spain or France. The costs of the war were enormous. Land operations alone cost £600,000 a year, borne in the ratio of three to one by the republic and England. But that took no account of sea war, the loss of life, the long drawn-out agony of the war, the destruction of property, crops and livestock by enemy action and by flooding.

If the north had suffered martyrdom, the plight of the south was even worse. Its cities were in ruins, its capital and labour force sapped by emigration; inertia and apathy had replaced the once eager spirit of resistance to Spanish oppression. The south was, for the moment, tired and broken: a point that neither Oldenbarneveldt nor Maurice fully grasped. Granvelle's younger brother, Champagny, was by now a waspish but still lucid old man. All through the revolt he had played a curiously ambiguous role, but he spoke up plainly at this point. The south, he declared, was 'administered without justice or policy, exploited, plundered, demoralized, empty of trade or hope'. But his proposed remedy showed how little the Perrenot brothers had learnt. Let more priests, more monks, he urged, be injected into this corrupt society and rules for the confirmation of bishops be tightened up.

With the help of some capable English commanders, Maurice launched his great counter-attack in 1590. His best *aide* was Francis Vere, of an Essex gentry family descended from the Earls of Oxford, and gifted with an arrogant self-confidence. Sir John Norris was of an earlier vintage; a vigorous, headstrong soldier who had incurred Leicester's deadly enmity for his plain speaking.

It was Vere who resisted Elizabeth's anxious nagging to reduce her costs in the Netherlands – theoretically in favour of more help to France, perhaps aimed at recovering Calais (the injury of 1558 still rankled). No, said Vere; the Netherlands were 'the very root' of English strategy; France was only 'the topp branches'. Perhaps he was right. The Dutch, dogged fighters that they were, were proving themselves the most reliable heirs to the ancient Burgundian alliance. Now that Spain had disinherited herself, the rebels must be recognized *de facto* as the new bearers of the traditional partnership. Even Elizabeth began to change her mind about those she had dismissed as 'tradesmen'. Their powers at sea impressed her. Now they were about to show their paces on land.

With an uncharacteristically dramatic gambit, Maurice began with the capture of Breda, his family seat. Zutfen, Deventer, Groningen and Nijmegen followed, until he had won back a broad band of territory that stretched from west Brabant (north-west of Breda) along the Hollandsch Diep, past Nijmegen and Arnhem, turning north with the river Ijssel and including most of the land between that river and the German border as far north as the estuary of the Ems.

Maurice won these victories by uniquely careful preparation. This was the nearest thing to calculated, planned warfare a casual age had seen. He liked to operate as near as possible to his supply bases. There were no fireworks. Parma's successors in the south – first, the fat and melancholy Archduke Ernest (brother to the Emperor Rudolf), then the Count of Fuentes – were in every way inferior to him, Maurice could not afford to drop his guard. A major problem was France.

Since his accession Henry IV had faced two closely connected tasks: to restore political and religious unity and to drive out the Spaniards. In meeting the first, Henry's strongest card was his hereditary claim to the throne. For all the anarchy of the preceding thirty years, the sense of fundamental law remained strong in France – indeed it has been seen as the basis of all French political institutions. These included the strictly hereditary conception of the monarchy: no French king was deposed or executed, and no king succeeded in defiance of the hereditary law, from the accession of Hugh Capet in 987 down to the French Revolution. This was a far stronger argument for Henry IV than his heresy was against him. And, as the unanimity of the Catholic League crumbled visibly before the force of his hereditary claim, Henry played his trump card. In July 1593 he renounced his Protestant faith. His coronation at Chartres in 1594 proved to all that he had carried the Church with him, and within a month Paris followed the Church and capitulated. In an extraordinary mood of relief, gratitude and affection, the French people surged forward to declare their loyalty. When bribes were needed to grease noble palms within the League, Henry did not hesitate to provide them. He had spent his life since the age of fifteen in war. He was shrewd, tough and unscrupulous, with men as with women. His conversion bore no comparison with, for instance, Orange's change of faith. Religion meant little to him and politics were an unending game of wit and force. Henry was a realist, without illusions or scruples. Paris was worth a Mass; the League was worth a bribe.

France understood him, his strengths and weaknesses. Opportunist he might be; but he was not unreliable, and in the last resort he had a deep sense of responsibility to France. That was enough. The last symbol of the bad old order was gone: almost unnoticed Catherine de Medici had died. The event 'made no more stir than the death of a goat',[46] as an observer unkindly remarked. Henry's order was new and different, for the time being at least. But his problems were by no means ended.

He declared war on Spain in January 1595. Within a year Spanish troops had captured Calais and Philip was fomenting the revolt of O'Neill and the Irish nobles in Ulster. Was a new Armada on the way?

Nobody could be sure, but Henry and Elizabeth hastened to close ranks, along with the Dutch, in an anti-Spanish coalition. The Spaniards, though visibly flagging, managed still to capture Amiens in September 1597; but Philip knew as well as Henry that his strategic position was now gravely undermined by the collapse of the League. Spanish penetration of France and England since Cateau-Cambrésis had depended on presumed *local* resistance to the monarchy: a Spanish invading force would rally, support and place in power this local fifth-column. Without it, even Philip knew his hopes were doomed. Half the resistance – the half that really mattered to Philip – had now crumbled away. The other half, the Huguenots, remained. Henry wasted no time in opening negotiations with them, and in the spring of 1598 these were concluded by the Edict of Nantes. By sixteenth-century standards it was an enlightened settlement. Calvinism was not given equal rights with the Catholic Church, but the Huguenots secured full civil rights, including the right of public worship in their designated towns, to say nothing of the protection given by their *places de sûreté*.

The new Pope, Clement VIII, might protest piously, but he too was a realist. So, in his last months of life, was Philip of Spain. Neither allowed the settlement at Nantes to hold up the Treaty of Vervins concurrently being negotiated which brought the Franco-Spanish war to an end. Spain pulled her troops out of north France and abandoned the fruits of the recent battles in the Netherlands–French frontier areas. The clock was put back exactly forty years, to Cateau-Cambrésis; but the relative strength of the two powers was much changed. Behind a resurgent France lay the potential strength of a vast, rich agricultural land; a large, industrious population; an economy and society still vulnerable to nature but of unlimited promise. Spain, under Philip's rule, had suffered the apparently impossible extremes of government by prevarication, rashness and obduracy in equal doses. The result was to drain the country of most of her windfall from America; to create intolerable tax burdens, especially for Castile; to discourage enterprise and work; to breed excessive numbers of useless mouths, subsidize vagabondage, and conjure up a world that combined the picaresque and fantastic.

But Spain was nothing if not obstinate. The French campaigns had cost Philip enormous sums. He died, after an agonizing illness, in September 1598. He had made characteristically detailed preparations for his end, in the knowledge that his life's work had failed. From 1598

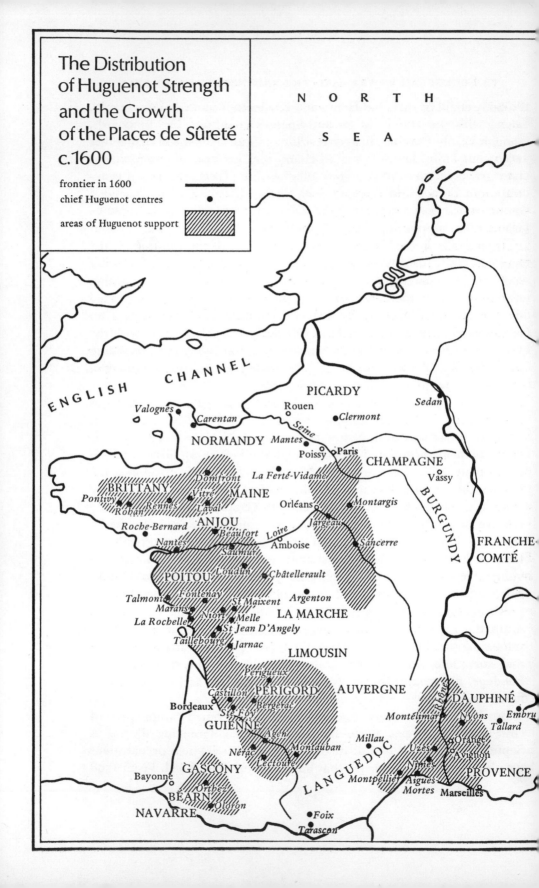

The Distribution of Huguenot Strength and the Growth of the Places de Sûreté c.1600

frontier in 1600 ——————
chief Huguenot centres •
areas of Huguenot support ▨

N O R T H

S E A

E N G L I S H   C H A N N E L

PICARDY

Valognes
Carentan
Rouen
Clermont
Sedan

NORMANDY
Mantes
Seine
Poissy
Paris
CHAMPAGNE
Vassy

Domfront
La Ferté-Vidame
BRITTANY
Vitré
MAINE
Pontivy
Rennes
Rohan
Laval
Orléans
Montargis
BURGUNDY

FRANCHE-
COMTÉ

Roche-Bernard
ANJOU
Beaufort
Loire
Jargeau
Nantes
Saumur
Amboise
Sancerre

POITOU
Loudun
Châtellerault
Talmont
Fontenay
Argenton
Marans
Niort
St Maixent
La Rochelle
Melle
LA MARCHE
Taillebourg
St Jean D'Angely
Jarnac

LIMOUSIN

Périgueux
Castillon
PÉRIGORD
AUVERGNE
DAUPHINÉ
Bergerac
Rhône
Montélimar
Nyons
Embru
Bordeaux
Ste Foy
Tallard
GUIENNE
Agen
Millau
Orange
Avignon
Nérac
Montauban
Uzès
Lectoure
Nîmes
PROVENCE
GASCONY
LANGUEDOC
Bayonne
Montpellier
Aigues-
Orthez
Mortes
Marseilles
BÉARN
Oloron
NAVARRE
Foix
Tarascon

the financial succour to the army in Flanders fell spasmodically. Spain's control over Savoy, the Swiss cantons, north Italy and north-west Germany was becoming precarious. Communications with Italy and the Low Countries also: in 1601 the road to Flanders, main artery of her strength, nearly fell into French hands. The Army of Flanders itself grew weaker while the Dutch grew stronger. In every Spanish theatre of war, discontented, unpaid troops were in constant mutiny between 1598 and 1607.

The only comfort Spain could claim was that Oldenbarneveldt's plan to recover the southern Netherlands totally failed. The south had no spirit left for war, a fact which all Maurice's military reforms had failed to reveal. 'Intelligence' had escaped his careful eye. After a military failure at Nieupoort, an approach by the southern States-General to Oldenbarneveldt ran into the ground at the attempted conference at Bergen-op-Zoom. Not even Oldenbarneveldt's sumptuous hospitality could conceal the lack of any basis for agreement. Since 1585 and the fall of Antwerp, too many vested interests had been created in the north to allow the *status quo ante* to be restored. Thereafter deadlock became complete. The Dutch had enough strong-points on the south bank of the Scheldt to maintain a stranglehold on trade: they could not relieve the Dutch in Ostend. Spinola, the new Spanish commander, finally compelled surrender of its burnt-out shell in September 1604. But the victory was hollow. Spinola could not shake the Dutch grip on the Scheldt, nor satisfy his troops, for whom victory was no substitute for pay. In 1606 some four thousand of them made off for Diest to try and recover their pay – nearly a million florins. Still no offer of a truce from the Dutch: the new king, Philip III, decided to cut his losses and abandon his Army of Flanders. Its provisions were halved. Then something like a miracle intervened: the Dutch offered to discuss a ceasefire. Fighting ended on 24 April 1607.

Disasters continued to fall on Spain – a renewed quarrel with Venice, the destruction of the Spanish fleet under the batteries of Gibraltar by Jacob van Heemskerck, another Spanish decree of bankruptcy. Both sides were now exhausted; the generation that had typified the old contest was dead: Philip, Elizabeth, Orange, Burghley, Walsingham. The new men, Philip III, James I, Robert Cecil, were ready for a pause – at least. Even so, the speed with which an Anglo-Spanish treaty was negotiated and signed on 30 May 1604 surprised and shocked Oldenbarneveldt. Rambling and inconclusive the peace might be: both

France and England were still left free to send volunteers to help their Dutch allies. But, officially, as states, France and England were out of the war.

The negotiations between the Dutch, Spain and the Spanish Netherlands began at the Hague in February 1608. The Spanish representatives were Spinola, victor of Ostend, and Jean Richardot, of Franche-Comté, President of the Brussels Privy Council: they represented both Philip III and the archdukes, Albert and Isabella (Philip II's daughter), who had been left the southern Netherlands as a sovereign possession and had even achieved a degree of independence of Spain in the eyes of their new subjects.

The negotiations were protracted and suspicious. Influential interests were concerned to keep the war going – professional soldiers, privateers who had made large fortunes out of it, war-contractors, Calvinist fanatics preparing a colonial counter-attack against Spain in the New World. Maurice of Nassau was aware of an unexpected gulf widening between himself and Oldenbarneveldt, who now seemed ready to accept something less than a complete declaration of northern independence. The hint of bitterness in Maurice's arguments owed something to the less-than-glorious nature of his recent campaigns, something to a growing reluctance to endure the continuing tutelage of his old master. But, for the moment, the frictions were smoothed out. By the final truce, signed in April 1609, the seven northern provinces achieved an almost complete victory; on northern independence, colonial trade, the position of the northern Catholics, the control of trade in the Scheldt estuary – on all these Spain and the archdukes gave way. To the southern Netherlands 'the treaty gave nothing but twelve years of rest'.[47] To the northern Republic it marked the beginning of a glorious half-century of economic and cultural expansion. The reversal of Dutch fortunes was not lost on Elizabeth. In one of her last recorded utterances she exclaimed:

The sagacious administration of the States Government is so full of good order and policy as far to surpass in its wisdom the intelligence of Kings and potentates . . . we Kings understand nothing of such affairs in comparison, but require – all of us – to go to school to the States General.[48]

Coming from the 'dowager' of the old order, it was an impressive tribute.

II

ADVENTURES OF IMAGINATION
AND REASON

In order to consider the relations between creative thinkers, artists and society in 1600, a modern mind must disencumber itself of at least three centuries of modernity. The historian of ideas must put behind him current assumptions about toleration and humanitarianism. The historian of science must dismantle the framework of rationalism and quantitative calculation that has steadily become his second nature since the Enlightenment, and re-fix the boundaries separating science from superstition. The economic and social historian must adjust his theories of the relationship between science, technology and industry. The musicologist must re-tune an ear conditioned by four centuries' evolving technique of instrument and voice.

The artists and philosophers of this period inhabited a world that was timeless and personal, developing their creative ideas from within themselves. Yet they were also a part of society and subject to its movements, and impressions. Paolo Sarpi was official theologian to the Venetian Republic, yet his philosophy was of a breadth and profundity that promoted him high above his local responsibilities. Grotius could evolve a science of international relations out of a brief which he wrote as the paid advocate of the Dutch East India Company. Like his great predecessor, Erasmus of Rotterdam, Grotius was thoroughly Dutch: like him, he was a citizen of the world. Velázquez was, *par excellence*, a Spanish court painter, yet his portraits have a detachment which lifts them on to a universal plane. The ecumenical appeal of the Dutch painters derived from their intensive exploration of their own microcosm – Saenredam's unadorned interiors of Dutch churches,

Avercamp's stately Dutch skaters, Bosschaert's orderly Dutch tulips and roses, Vermeer's neat gabled house in a Dutch street. By 1650 the influence of Dutch style, like the influence of Dutch trade, was all-pervasive. It extended from England up to Scandinavia and eastwards as far as Prague. In each case universal influence stemmed from a purely local intensity – sublimest witness, the Rembrandt self-portraits.

The artist's response to nature was as old as the idea of art itself. But in this period it was changing along with society and social rhythms. Medieval 'art' had signified the 'treasuries' of churches, abbeys and cathedrals; then the movable painted panel depicting religious themes; then the collective commissions of gilds and companies that were to reach their climax in the great *Night-Watch* of Rembrandt (in reality a dramatic collective portrait of Captain Banningh Cocq's company of the Amsterdam Civic Guard as it lined the streets during the visit of Marie de Medici in 1638) or Frans Hals's *Banquet of the Officers of the Civic Guard of St George at Haarlem* (1616). Medieval collectivism slowly gave way to individualism; religious to humanist, secularized art. Where group painting continued it was at new levels of brilliantly detailed technique. The stiff, formal, gild portrait becomes in reality a collection of individual portraits on a single canvas. (The artists' fee was paid from individual contributions by the sitters; they varied according to the prominence of the individual sitter in the final picture.) Saints and martyrs gave way to kings, queens, popes, bishops, lords and great merchants. Landscape, which had formerly served as a backcloth for historical episodes based on biblical or classical legend, now emerged as a genre in its own right in the canvases of Ruysdael or van Goyen. It was not 'romantic' in the later sense of the word. Sixteenth- and seventeenth-century artists, patrons, readers and listeners all saw nature in the works of man just as they saw man as a divine creation. Landscape, sun, cloud, light, darkness, flowers, trees, insects were only an aspect of the world to be portrayed through word or image. They were not the whole of it: modern iconography has revealed the world of symbolism the artist inhabited.

The passing of the 'primitives' made way for representational art, but there was still a wealth of allusion behind the apparent 'literalism' associated especially with Netherlandish art: the artists had their own private theology. Peter Breughel the Elder (1525–69) has been called the most Netherlandish of painters. A North Brabanter, he came from the heartland of the Netherlands and remained intensely Dutch in feeling despite his international wanderings. Yet one may guess that when Rudolf II chose Breughel's great *Tower of Babel* for his imperial collection at Prague it was not for the Scheldt-like river with its docks, ships and thousands of dockside workers that he wanted the picture, but for the visionary, grandiose splendour of the great tower piercing the clouds to the sky, its hundreds of windows redolent as much of the mystical 'theatres' of Camillo and the occultists as of the Babylonian temple known only from the scattered ruins.

Towns might grow in size and multiply in numbers but men remained countrymen who took nature for granted in a way the town-dweller of the post-industrial age would not be able to. The romanticism of the nineteenth century would have seemed meaningless to the sixteenth-century mind and eye. The proper study of mankind was man and God: but God dwelt more in man himself than in the mountain and flood. The world inhabited by the thinkers and artists was cruel and brutal; its rulers – their patrons – materialist, irresponsible and trivial. The task of artist and poet was to console, flatter, divert, amuse and sometimes frighten them by lifting a curtain on a world of ideals, dreams and nightmares. They compassed therefore something of the functions of both priest and jester. In any age, art must reflect something of the nature of the society in which it is formed; but there is probably no other period in history in which its social content is so rich and varied, or so necessary an aid to an understanding of contemporary society, as in this century.

The French invasions of Italy since 1494 had inaugurated a train of disasters. *Le Calamitá d'Italia* became a melancholy theme of political observers and historians. No doubt much of the lamentation over the demise of republicanism and civic virtue and the victory of tyrants was nostalgic exaggeration or *ex parte* judgment. None of the supposed victims among the city states was felled at a blow. That Italy was entering a phase of decline was true, but the northward shift of Europe's centre of gravity – political, economic, cultural – was slow and protracted. Within Italy there was a local shift of power – from Milan, Genoa and Florence to Venice and the Papal States. The nature of genius was also transmuted, so that specialist art historians are sometimes unreliable guides to the great cycles of growth and decay. The first phase of destruction was past its worst by the 1530s and was succeeded by something of a revival. True, of the greatest Florentine geniuses of the representational and plastic arts, only Michelangelo and Benvenuto

Cellini, with his epic loves, hatreds, extravagances, survived into the second half of the century; and even Michelangelo was attacked by Pietro Aretino (of all people) for the obscenity of the nudes in his greatest masterpiece, the *Last Judgment*.

By 1580, nevertheless, Florence itself seemed grander than ever, gay and vigorous. Its economy flourished as the new tyrants primed the pump, drained swamps and dug canals with Dutch help. Was it true, as later critics would allege, that Florence had become tame, provincial, smug? That intellectual vitality had withered and died? Perhaps, but other facets of Florentine culture remained bright. Was not the Palazzo Pitti still growing, were not the Boboli Gardens larger and more splendid, the Uffizi and the Colonnade still embodying Vasari's command? One contemporary at least, Giacomini, was unworried. 'The greatness of Florence and its inhabitants', he wrote in 1587, 'has been and still is such that the largest discussion could touch upon only a small part.'[49]

Was the explanation simply that Giacomini typified the smugness that had enveloped Florence? Or was genius flowing away into new channels – for example into architecture and music? Was there a subtle change in the context, social and cultural, in which artists had to work, sell their products, make a living? For art coalesces and grows around great patrons and great teachers or inspirers. Genius, like fever, is infectious. It may spread with prosperity; or it may not, as Graham Greene observed of the Swiss and the cuckoo-clock in *The Third Man*. Economic decline may bring artistic decline as patronage shrinks; or 'style' may become stereotyped. Florentine decadence has doubtless been exaggerated; there can be little question that the culture of the Venetian Republic was comparatively more versatile and vigorous.

Economically, Venice had run into great difficulties and was to suffer worse: but Venetian tenacity was remarkable. She had survived the French wars, the Portuguese development of the route to India round the southern cape of Africa and the partial diversion of the spice trade that followed. Contrary to once-received doctrine, the Venetian spice trade had enjoyed an unprecedented revival between 1500 and 1588. Then came sharper rivalry from Dutch, English and French. The great oar-propelled galleys became more costly to build as timber became scarce with the dwindling of the forest area of the Veneto. The English and Dutch could sail and carry faster and more cheaply.

Yet once again the Venetians showed extraordinary resilience. They switched their capital and energies into cloth-making and agriculture. In the second half of the sixteenth century Venetian cloth output doubled, reaching a peak in about 1600. Venice now outpaced Milan, Florence, Genoa, Como, Pavia. Between 1550 and about 1630 Venice seems to have achieved an economy in which advantages and disadvantages for a time cancelled each other out. Even virulent attacks of plague and heavy mortality brought an uncovenanted benefit: they reduced the risk of famine and kept down food prices.

To the outward eye, Venice was free, rich and thriving. So too was her cultural life. Whether we look to painting, sculpture, architecture or music, Venice seemed supreme. The malaise that had fallen on Florentine painting left her untouched. The second half of the century found three of the greatest Venetian artists still at the height of their powers; Tiziano Vecelli (Titian) (c. 1477–1576); Jacopo Robusti Tintoretto (1518–94); and Paolo Veronese (1528–88). Titian, the old lion, somehow symbolized the creative fury which was still Venice. A pupil alongside the great Giorgione and Palma Vecchio, he was still writing to Philip II in 1571 claiming to be ninety-five years old. True or not, his pride symbolized a life of incessant creative genius. His artistic powers were matched by a commanding personal charm and distinction, but this only underlined the supreme professionalism which secured him a continuous stream of municipal, ecclesiastical and private commissions. The greater part of his staggering output (running into seven or eight hundred known and extant works) was devoted to biblical or mythological subjects, but he also brought new vitality to landscape (especially the mountain scenes of his native north Italy) which he was virtually the first painter to 'isolate'.

Tintoretto, unlike Titian whom he greatly admired, was self-contained, ungregarious, shunning casual contacts, as if to reserve his energies for the prodigious canvas he left to posterity. A true Venetian he hardly ever left the city and his greatest works, culminating in his vast *Paradiso* (said to be the largest canvases ever painted), were also mainly biblical or classical in subject-matter. Many were commissioned by one or other of the great *scuole*, those lay religious societies for promoting piety and providing mutual aid and welfare. Vasari, the great historian and painter and a quintessential Florentine, might not altogether approve of Tintoretto's imaginative audacity; but even he had to confess that this was 'the most awesome mind that ever was in painting'.

If a single laureate were to be required for late Renaissance Venetian art, however, the choice would surely fall on Veronese, the last of the great cycle of painters to the republic. In some senses a pictorial rather than an intellectual genius, he was well suited to proclaim the splendours of the city to the world. Producing stupendous effects of colour and combining these with a supreme talent for vast crowd scenes enriched with a profusion of draperies, luminous atmosphere and transparent shadow, he became the personification of Venetian civic pride, preferring to paint his great *Venice, Queen of the Sea* for the Doge's Palace rather than to decorate the Escorial for Philip II.

Much of the work of the Venetian school, Veronese in particular, provided interior decoration for buildings designed by their architect contemporaries which still form the rich framework of Venice. Of these the greatest and most influential was Andrea Palladio (1518–80), born in Vicenza but trained in Rome. Here he was fascinated by the style and proportions of the buildings of ancient Rome and his *I Quattro Libri dell'architettura* (1575) reflects his absorption in Roman remains and the writings of Vitruvius, the Roman architect and engineer whose work inspired the classical revival. After his return to the Veneto, Palladio and his famous pupil Scamozzi set to work on designs for churches and palaces, especially in Vicenza and Venice. Their slightly older contemporary, Jacopo Sansovino, by origin a Florentine and a sculptor, meanwhile achieved fame by his more decorated and freely designed public buildings in Venice, including the public library and the mint, the Scuola della Misericordia and a number of palaces.

Drawing their inspiration from classical models, the Venetian school – Palladio especially – were to exercise a unique influence on European architecture. By the early seventeenth century the designs and measured drawings of Serlio, Vignola, Palladio and Scamozzi were being brought back to the Netherlands and translated into Dutch by architects like Danckerts and Hondius; while Jacob van Campen, architect of the Royal Palace at Amsterdam, and Philip Vingboons, designer of the Amsterdam palace of the Trips (the great Baltic merchants) closely followed the new Italian styles. John Evelyn, the diarist, bought some of these books in Holland in 1641 and they were certainly known to Christopher Wren.

The influence of Vitruvius came to England more directly with Inigo Jones – the 'English Palladio'. His work in Venice on Palladian principles gained him a reputation which took him to Denmark on the invitation of Christian IV in 1604. Here he is supposed to have designed the great royal palaces of Frederiksborg and Rosenborg. After a second visit to Italy in 1612 Inigo Jones became surveyor-general to James I and was kept in office by Charles I.

Linking the often disparate conceptions and inspirations of the post-Renaissance artists and architects was the prevalent style that came to be known as 'Mannerist' (from *manière* or *maniera*: 'style'). Mannerism was the 'style of stylishness'. Impossible to define with precision, this search for conscious style can be sensed in such works as Ammanati's great ornamental fountains, the Boboli Gardens, or Vignola's Villa Farnese at Caprarola with its curving, theatrical staircase. Elegant strangeness and cultivated distortion became a source of grace that gave life and force to works of art. As one writer, Calcaginin, put it: 'There are certain things which are beautiful just because they are deformed and thus please by giving great displeasure.'[50] Like its successor, the Baroque, Mannerism originated in Rome and through Roman, especially Papal, patronage. Then it swiftly spread to Florence, Venice and elsewhere. Yet the Counter-Reformation, with its new, built-in puritanism, was distrustful of the Mannerists. They outraged the newly assumed sense of propriety and decorum that dwelt in the Vatican. The re-grouping of the forces of aesthetic orthodoxy between the Council of Trent (1563) and the death of Clement VIII in 1603 involved little direct dogmatic guidance on art in its religious aspects. The final session of Trent had touched but gingerly on the matter: 'The Council forbids placing in churches any image which illustrates false doctrine and may mislead ... [or] any unusual image, unless ... approved by the Bishops.'[51] El Greco, one of the few who attempted to strike out on new paths in religious art, quickly found himself in deep theological trouble with the chapter of Toledo Cathedral.

But it was not long before a Roman Church more confident and stable under Urban VIII was ready in the 1620s and 1630s to approve an aesthetic offensive on the pilgrims and visitors to the Holy City. Under the autocratic leadership of Bernini, architects were to aim at buildings which would be 'immediately striking'.[52] They were to appeal to the unsophisticated as much as the educated, to emotions as well as the intellect. Their style was rhetorical. They employed large designs, irregular and complex forms, combining movement in line, mass and space. They fused the arts of painter, sculptor and architect with the artful use of illusion – directed and hidden light, their dramatic content 'extended through architectural space and the richness of materials'. Almost all these qualities were embodied in St Peter's and were to be found in abundance in Bernini's design for the Louvre. Thus Baroque became the dominant style in Rome until the mid-eighteenth century, spreading to Piedmont, Austria, south Germany, Bohemia, Poland, even to Russia. Venice and Florence remained mostly outside its influence.

At the centre of the Baroque movement in Rome was the Pope, whom the re-organization of the Papal States had turned into a dictator of taste and fashion. Each new Pope-patron brought in a tribe of painter-protégés. A Bolognese like Gregory xv would bring to Rome painters from Bologna. A Barberini from Florence like Urban viii would bring artists of Tuscan descent like Bernini. Swiftly Bernini became the artistic Commissar of Rome, spitting poison everywhere (as his enemies said) if he thought patronage was being bestowed without his sanction.

A virtual 'spoils system' came into being, for a Papal election closely resembled that of an American President, with new friends, relatives and favourites scrambling for commissions to paint, sculpt and build. Urban's close friends, the brothers Sacchetti from Florence, did much to encourage the Baroque through their patronage of artists like Cortona. A tribe of Barberinis provided rich pickings for Poussin, Guido Reni, Maderno, Lorrain, Van Dyck and others. The Barberini Palace was rich with artistic treasures, allegorical ceilings, a vast library and an elaborate theatre. With the end of the Barberinis in 1644 came the exile of the family, followed by many of their dependent artists. Bernini survived. He had known how to assuage Urban's bouts of bad temper with suitable flattery (mirrored in his busts and bronzes of his patron); now he prepared himself to please a new dynasty – the Pamfili – and control a new flock of dependants.

Bernini had been to Urban what Michelangelo had been to Julius ii. But the Papacy was no longer what it had been. The manner was as grand as ever, but Rome's old troubles were starting up again. Banditry and mob violence returned. Plague attacked. The See was feeling the pinch of its own extravagance. There was a depressing lack of opportunities for raising its income. Its external importance and prestige had faded.

The stature of the sixteenth and seventeenth centuries in the visual arts has always been recognized, even though taste and fashion has swayed between one school and another. The same cannot be said of music. Only comparatively recently – since the pioneer work of Donald Tovey and E. H. Fellowes in fact – has the unique quality of both church and secular compositions been appreciated. The music of the time, whether of Byrd or Tallis, Arcadelt or Bull, Monteverdi or Palestrina, has a unity of conception and a degree of expressive humanism hardly surpassed since. One of the most perceptive critics has written: 'The second half of the sixteenth century seems to me the most *fundamentally* musical period in European civilization; at no other time do we find such subtlety and maturity of technique functioning as naturally as the human organism.'[53] The general level of taste was high and critical. The extraordinary poignancy of the music was heightened by the contrast between its own internal tranquillity and the social and political tensions of the time. The function of art and artist, as of religion and the religious, was to point the contrast between the violence of St Bartholomew or the Spanish Fury or the rape of Italy, and the peace after which men sought – vainly as it most often seemed.

This is not the place for detailed musicological analysis; but, historically, two points emerge. The first is the secularization of music, as of the other arts. The development of the madrigal in the sixteenth century was based on the contrapuntal forms of two centuries of church music, adapting an old technique to secular use. Most of the composers of madrigals were also church composers, choirmasters, singers, organists. The development of opera took secularization a step further, discarding in the process the elaborate choral polyphony of the madrigal, setting solo or dialogue in melodic form, and generally emphasizing harmony at the expense of counterpoint or fugue to heighten the dramatic effect. Secondly, no branch of art was more thoroughly international. Italy learnt its madrigal techniques from the Netherlands. A long succession of Netherlanders of sublime talent were employed in Venice at St Mark's, among them Willaert, Arcadelt, de Rore, Waelrant. Greatest of the Flemish school was Orlandus Lassus (Orlando di Lasso or Roland de Lattre, 1530–94), a genius of commanding personality, composer, teacher, choirmaster for a time and maestro at the Lateran: 'He gave the time with such steadiness that, like warriors at the sound of the trumpet, the expert singers needed no other order than the expression of that powerful and vigorous countenance to animate their sweetly sounding voices.'

If one line of development ran from Antwerp to Venice, another ran from Amsterdam to London. The greatest of the Dutch composer-performers of the late sixteenth century was the Amsterdam organist Sweelinck, the founder of the organ repertory and a composer of much choral music of high quality. The organ in Holland survived Calvinism, at least to the extent of being retained as a kind of public recreation between services, if not during them. Sweelinck's pupils came from many parts of Europe and among his close friends were the English musicians John Bull and Peter Phillips, organists respectively of Antwerp Cathedral and the Royal Chapel at Brussels. Sweelinck brings us back to Venice, for his teacher was Andrea Gabrieli, organist of St Mark's, himself a pupil of the Fleming, Willaert. Andrea's nephew, Giovanni Gabrieli (1557–1612), succeeded his uncle at St Mark's, having as his most distinguished pupil the German composer, Heinrich Schütz. All over Germany the 'Venetian style' spread, to Protestant and Roman churches alike. Gabrieli's lavish arrangements at St Mark's paled beside the eight choirs that inaugurated Salzburg Cathedral in 1628. Could any art be more cosmopolitan or underline more clearly the dominant position of north Italy and the Low Countries in musical history?

The visible and audible consequence of the Late Renaissance in Italy was the opera. The topical infatuation with classical models fired ambitions not only to revive the reputed emotional effects of the musical accompaniment to Greek drama but to study the whole relationship between words and music. This led scholars like Vincenzo Galilei (the scientist's father) to question the effects of polyphony. Was it not too disturbing and distracting to convey the passions of gods and mortals which ought to be the stuff of an integrated music-drama? Vincenzo was a member of the Florentine *Camerata*; its president and patron was grandmaster of ceremonies at the Grand Duke of Tuscany's wedding in 1589. One entertainment on this occasion was provided by Jacopo Peri, who later wrote the operas *Daphne* (1597) and *Euridice* (1600). This last was written to celebrate the marriage of Henri IV of France to Marie de Medici and was first performed in the Pitti Palace. Peri's operas were a breakthrough, followed up by a genius of an altogether higher order, Claudio Monteverdi (1567–1643). The year before he died, and to crown thirty years as director of music at St Mark's, Venice, he produced his masterpiece, the opera *The Coronation of Poppaea*. It signified not only the triumph of the singer and the aria, of melody over polyphony, but a new phase of Italian dominance in a new kind of music.

One key to the international character of musical development was its universal language. This was no longer true – if it had ever been true – of literature or drama. When Nicholas Yonge, a 'singing-man' of St Paul's in London, published a collection of Italian madrigals (*Musica Transalpina*) in 1588 and 1597, he translated the words into English. Conversely, few of the four thousand English madrigals extant can ever have been sung outside England. It was music and ideas, not words, that transcended national boundaries. When ideas were of fashionable interest, for instance those of civility and gentility in Castiglione's *Courtier*, they were translated into other languages. Works on religion and political thought spread widely. But literature, drama and poetry remained little known except to those who spoke or understood the language in which they were written.

The two greatest literatures of the age were those of Spain and England. Few countries could boast a trio of geniuses such as Lope de Vega, Calderón and Cervantes. *Don Quixote*, Cervantes's greatest and most renowned work, was licensed to be printed in 1604 and enjoyed an immediate vogue in Spain. It reflected the nature of Spain and Spanish society amid the remains of imperial glory and the clear intimations of decline. Here nobility and gentry, poets and priests, farmers and barbers and high-born ladies of talent, all mingled with the picaresque elements that increased daily as the economy of Spain relapsed into chaos – the scullions, convicts, muleteers, Moorish sirens, kitchen-maids of doubtful virtue, vagabonds and professional tarts. Oddly, for Spain lay in many ways outside the mainstream of European culture, Spanish drama exercised a powerful influence abroad – on Corneille, for example, whose *Cid* (1636) is sometimes taken as the beginning of French tragedy. In England, Thomas Kyd's blood-curdling revenge melodrama, *The Spanish Tragedy*, had a similar provenance. On the other hand, the genius that inspired English poetry and drama from Wyatt to Donne and Herbert, from Udal through Marlowe and Shakespeare to Ben Jonson, Beaumont and Fletcher, Ford and Webster was plainly local. This is not to say that it did not draw on, for instance, Italian example, as did many Shakespearian comedies and the tragedies of Webster, Ford and others. Nor did it ultimately prevent the unexcelled profundity of human passion, the delicacy and understanding of English lyric poetry, sonnets and verse plays communicating themselves to the world: all the more because they achieved universality through an intensity of feeling which could result *only* from the personal and the local. These last years of the sixteenth and early decades of the seventeenth centuries were the richest in the English heritage. Both Shakespeare and Marlowe illustrate vividly the tension between the growing humanist belief in the capacity and duty of the individual consciousness to explore its own destiny, even into the darkest places, and the pull of ancient Christian belief and morality which drew back from the consequences of such explorations.

Nevertheless, to Shakespeare and his colleagues, the drama (even the sonnets) were also their bread-and-butter. Unlike Ben Jonson – who, as John Aubrey tells us 'acted and wrote, but both ill, at the Green Curtaine ...' – 'Mr. William Shakespear ... did act exceeding well ... and his playes tooke well. He was a handsome, well-shap't man: very good company and of a very readie and pleasant smooth witt.' He was also a sufficiently astute businessman to see to it that his audiences got what they paid for. The Curtain and the Theatre were in the theatrical area of Moorfields. Here, tradition would draw audiences composed of citizens of standing and education from the counting-houses and fair residences of the bourgeoisie in the neighbourhood. At the Globe on the South Bank, a less respectable audience might be expected in an area well-provided with light entertainment, brothels and taverns, suitable for young bloods on a night out. The influence of such 'market' forces on Shakespeare's public remains a matter of speculation, but they remind us that literary genius is not wholly to be considered in terms ineffable or divine. Without patronage, individual or collective, the idea might have remained unrealized, the genius unknown.

How accidental the creative process could be was illustrated by John Donne, whose passionate, tortured, ratiocinatory poetry was to shape the character of Caroline verse in England and strongly influence poetic evolution in Holland. His unique fusion of scholastic thought and new learning, occultism and science, with febrile emotional energy and odd, perverse wit was the outcome of a harassed life spent on the fringes of high politics and society. A life less contorted by tribulation could hardly have produced this unique genius.

The philosophic and scientific thought of the age was still bedded in the international reputation and influence of the Italian universities. Here a specifically 'humanist' conception of learning had permeated the culture of the sixteenth century with Greek and, to a lesser extent Roman, example. The major intellectual focus of the epoch was 'the purpose of human life and . . . the place of man in the universe . . .'[54] The pithiest expression of the new ideal was Montaigne's observation that 'his own self was the main object of his philosophy'. The obstacles to the acceptance of such ideas were formidable. Theologians of the old school still ruled at the Sorbonne, Oxford and Cambridge and their continuing influence was buttressed by the intellectual poverty of a society where the possession of twenty books was a rare luxury. A few continental cities – Nuremberg, Leipzig, Frankfurt – had public libraries; but most great libraries were accessible only to licensed scholars. Nevertheless, painfully and slowly, the Erasmian leaven worked. 'No one', Erasmus had said, 'will ever understand any other person's opinion without knowing the language in which that opinion was expressed.' Thus the study of *language* – the means of communication – was the starting-point for reforms aimed at the self-improvement of the individual. Improvement or perfection? Would the new aspirations lead to a reformed Christian religion based on conviction rather than outworn ritualism? Or would they erode the essence of religion and lead only to a self-indulgent, pagan humanism? Was a 'Christian humanism' a contradiction in terms? This was the point at which, unwittingly, the extremes of religious conservatism and 'new' puritanism met.

Humane studies broadened along a wide international front. The principal contacts lay within the area between north Italy, the Low Countries and England, as if rational thinking did in a measure turn upon trade routes, entrepôts and the stimulus and challenge of social change created by economic advance. Paolo Sarpi (1552–1623) the Venetian polymath – astronomer, historian, mathematician, linguist, lawyer, theologian – was a shining example of the new learning. Originally a Servite monk he became a member of the *Ridotto Morosini*, a club of young nobles united in their aim to reform the republic and free it from the cramping influence of Spain and the Papacy. When Venice was put under Papal interdict in 1606, the fundamental conflict between Venetian empiricism and Papal dogmatism came to a head. Sarpi was appointed official theologian to the republic. His tranquil life as a scholar was at an end and he threw all his formidable intellectual energies into supporting the claims of the republic to exercise its own sovereign rights, limited only under God for the common good.

To ask whether Sarpi was a Catholic or Protestant, a Christian or a *politique*, is to put the wrong questions. Certainly he distrusted much that passed as counter-reform. He was realist enough to see the weaknesses of Venetian policy; but for him the republic was (not without reason) the lesser evil in a world which he viewed with a genuine Christian resignation. He was sincere in his belief that only faith could lead the way to salvation. But if it turned into an oppressive bureaucracy, it forfeited any claim to moral superiority over the 'state'; for the state too was an instrument of God, in religion as well as in secular affairs. These ideas were developed in his *History of the Council of Trent* (1612–15), a triumphant exercise in concrete, systematic, critical history aiming at truth, if necessary in defiance of the claims of the Pope: 'To some who read this it may seem to give excessive attention to trivial things and causes. But the writer ... has thought it necessary to show what tiny rivulets caused the great lake that occupies Europe.'[55] Sarpi – Venetian, republican and historian – looked back to the older Italian traditions of urban freedom and humanism of which Venice now seemed to be the last defender. His *History* was published under a pseudonym in London in 1619.

Not unnaturally, Sarpi looked for allies. He found them not in Italy but in France, the Dutch Republic and England: the same countries in which he pursued Venetian plans for a union of the anti-Papal powers. In France, Jacques-Auguste de Thou, the eminent historian and Bodin's heir as leader of the humanist *politiques*, was a man of like mind, working under the patronage of Henry IV. De Thou, anxious to recruit local material and authority for his great *History of his Own Times*, mobilized Sarpi's help, along with that of Grotius, Francis Bacon and William Camden. Hence Sarpi's voluminous correspondence with all three. Like Sarpi, Camden – already well-known for his *Britannia* – was in a sense a 'commissioned' historian, working with the encouragement of Burghley and the Queen herself.

Like the rulers of the Venetian Republic, Elizabeth also sensed the value of historical support for her claim to authority. But by the time Camden was ready to print, the Queen was dead. Her successor had no love of eulogies of her memory. Just as Sarpi had published in England, so Camden was compelled, in 1625, to publish in Leiden. Like Sarpi, Camden hated intolerance and lies, sorcery and magic, and that 'accomplished courtier ... cunning time-server and respector of his own advantages', the Earl of Leicester. Almost equally he hated that destructive poltergeist, the Earl of Essex. A loyal disciple of the Renaissance, Camden took as his model 'the great master of history': Polybius. And he faithfully followed the maxim of his classical mentor: 'Take away from History *Why*, *How* and *To What End* . . . and all that remains will rather be an idle sport and foolery than a profitable instruction.' Elizabethan England he saw as the product of an historical process that was not simply 'a series of decisions or indecisions, not as a drama of persons . . ., not as a morality play or the exemplification of a political thesis but as a living political and social organism whose political acts were contained and must be understood within a wider context'.[56]

Camden in turn leads us to the Netherlands, home of his friends Janus Gruter and Abraham Ortelius, the learned merchant and cartographer who in his turn was closely connected with the Dutch agent-general in London, the Anglo-Dutch historian, Emanuel van Meteren, and indeed with the whole influential London-Dutch colony that centred upon London's Dutch church at Austin Friars.

At the centre of the humanist connexion in the Dutch Republic was the University of Leiden, founded in January, 1575, to celebrate the end of the siege. Its charter read like a defiant fanfare to academic freedom:

A free, public School and University, founded in order that in the said School . . . the Sciences of Divinity, Law, and Medicine, as well as Philosophy and all the other liberal Arts and also the languages of Latin, Greek, and Hebrew be known, read, and taught by Doctors and Masters qualified therein.

As if to underline the university's liberal purpose it was made possible, three years later, to register as a student 'without having to swear any oath of allegiance to the religion adhered to there' – only a promise to obey the university statutes was required.

Before long young English and Scots students were flocking to hear the formidable philologist Scaliger, the theologian Lipsius, the humanist Janus Dousa, the mathematician Simon Stevin and the numerous philosophers and scientists whom Leiden swiftly drew into its teaching staff. The future which Orange's friend, Philip Sidney had foreseen for the foundation was to be richly fulfilled, in the humanities and the sciences. By the seventeenth century, its alumni were finding their way to England to strengthen the links first forged in Leiden in the 1570s and 1580s. One was Constantyn Huyghens, son of William the Silent's personal secretary, soon to become one of the most versatile scholars and poets of the republic and the father of Christiaan, the distinguished physicist. Upon Leiden humanism and science not a little of the future of European learning was to turn.

European 'science': the universities and their reformers had been more successful in promoting humane studies than in reforming the antique pedantry that passed for science. It was not all, however, equally bad: once again, north Italy, the Netherlands, England and– in this case – Denmark and Germany, were interlinked in a progressive scientific movement. Hieronymo Fabrizio at Padua was the greatest anatomical teacher of his day. Bologna, Pisa, Rome and Florence all had schools of medicine, physiology and mathematics. Leiden had outstanding mathematicians in the persons of Willebrord Snell and Simon Stevin. Utrecht followed Leiden in developing medical studies. Until the Thirty Years War suspended their work, German universities like Marburg, Würzburg, Giessen, Jena, Altdorf and Freiburg had courses in medicine and chemistry. Migrants from Padua brought its medical techniques to Copenhagen and Basel. At Gresham College, London, founded out of a substantial legacy from Elizabeth's former financial expert, Thomas Gresham, the statutes ordained that seven professors should read lectures – one each day of the week – on astronomy, geometry, physic, law, divinity, rhetoric and music. They began in 1597. Here the nucleus of scientists who later formed the Royal Society first met; and it was here, or at the Royal College of Physicians or the College of Barber Surgeons (rather than at Oxford or Cambridge), that men came for serious medical and scientific training. Both the old universities had chairs of science, but their incumbents frequently had to go elsewhere to learn their mathematics.

This pinpoints the major weakness in the unreformed university curricula: they reluctantly allowed the new knowledge to be inserted into their existing structure; it was much longer before they adapted organically to fundamental change. Hence the importance of extra-mural associations – like Duke Federigo Cesi's Accademia dei Lincei at Rome (1603) – which met to witness experiments or hear papers, and of which Galileo was a member for some years.

The first prerequisite for true change was a new philosophy capable of reorganizing three major areas of knowledge – cosmology and the science of motion; optics; anatomy and physiology. To investigate these further, more precise, and more effective tools were necessary.

Down to the mid-seventeenth century, the new philosophy was more successful in suggesting the potential of the new tools – telescopes and microscopes, barometers and time-keepers – than in applying them to specific problems. That was to be the work of the second half of the century. This was true of mathematical tools also: mathematics was studied widely, but for its own sake rather than for applications to science or technology. Logarithms, invented by Burgi and Napier in 1614, and the slide-rule, based on the same principle, were exceptions.

The common objective of those who attempted to isolate and identify scientific method was 'to show how to establish undeniable causal relationships between phenomena'.[57] This was the object and to a certain extent the achievement of both Bacon (in his *Novum Organum* of 1620) and of Galileo in his *Dialogo IV*. Descartes went further: to equate the laws of nature with the laws of motion: 'I have described the whole visible world as if it were simply a machine in which there was nothing to consider but the shape and movement of its parts.' The nature of the world could be understood only in mathematical terms. Descartes has been called the first master of the hypothetical model. By origin a French squire, he moved to Holland partly because, as he said, he found there a receptive audience for new ideas. Among those ideas was the Copernican view of the universe: almost all thinking Dutchmen, Descartes remarked in 1630, were converted to the new view.

This was not the case elsewhere. The heliocentric theory was well over half a century old by 1600; yet it took all the work of Galileo, Kepler, Bacon, Descartes and many others to disperse the fogs of occultism, superstition and vested academic interests. It was not only the court of Rudolf II at Prague which swarmed with charlatans of all nations.

Many of those in Rudolf's service professed 'natural' not 'black' magic. As they anxiously explained, their purpose was to control and understand the hidden forces of nature: their inspiration was divine not diabolical. Alchemy was one of the great passions of the age in Central Europe.

Some of the court hangers-on were pure occultists like Giordano Bruno, a scholar-gipsy closely associated with schemes to realize the so-called 'art of memory', an 'ostentatious prodigy' as Bacon called it, which relied on the substitution of images for abstractions as aids to memory. John Dee and Edward Kelly were occultist visitors from

England who spent years in Prague. Dee was a great believer in spirits, crystal-balls and the other mumbo-jumbo of the magician's trade. Yet he also worked devotedly to preserve monastic documents and, if he had had his way, the English calendar would have been re-formed a century and a half earlier than it was. Common to Prague, Hampton Court and Holland was the Dutchman Cornelius Drebbel, another Janus-faced figure who peered back into medieval alchemy and the search for the philosopher's stone, and forward into a world of more effective methods of dyeing woollen cloth and making sub-marine craft.

All inhabited the no man's land that lay between superstition and science. In retrospect it is easy to see them as impostors: but before simply dismissing them it is worth remembering that some of those who have achieved scientific greatness in the eyes of later generations – like Kepler – mixed a good helping of astrology into their astronomy. Kepler sought in his own life for evidence of planetary influences; like Tycho Brahe, he believed in a powerful concord between individuals and the cosmos. Both were proud to join Rudolf's circus of performing occultists. This irrationalism was not merely the result of clouded vision: perhaps it was 'a vital component of contemporary intellectual activity'.[58] The fact remained, nevertheless, that this was a component that had to be eliminated before science could progress. In the end there was no room for both the prophecies of Nostradamus and the calcula-tions of Galileo or Huyghens. By means of his telescope, which he borrowed from Holland, Galileo confirmed the Copernican theory of the universe. The professor of philosophy at Pisa might refuse to look through Galileo's telescope: Popes and cardinals, however well-disposed personally, were duty-bound to treat Galileo as anti-Christ. But they could no more resist the revelations of the lens than Canute could hold back the tide.

In the same movement, it was Italians who used Arab knowledge to develop the optical instruments which enabled Kepler in 1604 to demonstrate how the eye refracts light rays in order to form an image of the object on the retina. Together, Galileo and Kepler led to the age of observation with the aid of the experimental telescope, the micro-scope and the hypothesis. In the hands of the Dutch, English and Italian scientists (who often ground their own), the lens was as impor-tant a means to knowledge and scientific advancement as the steam-engine, rocket, jet or computer were to be to later ages.

Last of the great trio was William Harvey, whose demonstration of the circulation of the blood was the outstanding physiological achievement of the age. Harvey was himself a product of the Paduan school, pupil of Galileo's physician, Fabrizio, and of Santorio who introduced quantitative methods into medicine, designing instruments to measure temperature and the rate of the pulse.

What was the relationship of all this to everyday life, to practical medicine, trade, industry, technology? Not very much, it must be confessed. A gulf was set between science and technology which corresponded to that separating thinker from craftsman. The great industries of the day – as we have seen, the very word is anachronistic: 'manufactures' was what they were called – were textile industries. Their methods were almost entirely traditional, their tools mostly hand or treadle-driven. The largest innovation of the age, the 'new draperies', involved the use of different wools and yarns in various ways to economize on materials and labour. No scientific invention of any consequence was involved. Nor is there any evidence that, for example, Drebbel's claim to have produced a new scarlet dye was well-founded. The substitution of coal for wood fuel in industries like glassmaking and brewing was purely empirical. If miners used any scientific knowledge at all, it was still Agricola's *De re Metallica* written in the mid-sixteenth century.

Little new was added here, and hardly anything in agriculture or forestry until after 1660. By then the technological interest displayed by the Royal Society in London and similar bodies elsewhere bore limited fruit. But the tradition of trial and error lingered on in industry a great deal longer. In James I's reign in England a spate of 'inventions' appeared, but none owed anything to serious scientific enquiry. More typical were the 'New Backframe for the Bed-ridden' or 'A New and Improved Method for Preserving the Lobster'.

Science most nearly approached economic or social utility in shipping, navigation and warfare. When Simon Stevin produced his work on navigation in 1599 it was at once translated into English by Edward Wright under the title *The Haven-Finding Art*. Wright lectured for some years on behalf of the East India Company at Gresham College on the use of charts and navigational instruments. Another Dutch work on navigation, by Waghenaer, was translated as *The Mariner's Mirror* in 1583. It was a collection of charts, known in England as 'Waggoners', with sailing directions, tables of the new moons and declination of the sun, and a catalogue of fixed stars and rules for finding the meridian altitude of the sun. The many editions into which it ran suggest that it was very useful.

This brings us back to the whole problem of the momentum behind the intellectual, scientific and artistic changes of the age: in particular, the effects of patronage, individual and collective. Some artists, architects and musicians were at least saved from penury by aristocratic patronage; some even prospered. By contrast, patronage in Holland was widely dispersed and popular. Dutch painters lived and worked as craftsmen, and most would have been astonished to find themselves revered as artists. Van Goyen traded in tulips, van de Velde in linens, Jan Steen was an innkeeper. In Amsterdam, as formerly in Antwerp, painters were 'as plentiful as butchers and bakers'. When John Evelyn arrived at Rotterdam in 1641 he was amazed to see the annual mart or fair 'so furnished with pictures ... 'tis an ordinary thing to find a common farmer lay out two or three pounds on this commodity. Their houses are full of them.'

What was the effect of patronage in its various forms on the artist and his art? In the Netherlands, it obviously affected the choice of subject-matter closely but left most artists little bettter off. Rubens might live like a prince on his munificent royal and noble patrons: Frans Hals, like many other Dutch artists, died a pauper. The great Venetians did much better; so did the Romans like Bernini. Titian regularly drove hard bargains with his patrons. Papal and noble patronage raised the prestige of the artists' profession. 'Painting,' wrote the Clerk of the Apostolic Chamber in 1601, 'is a most noble profession, quite different from the mechanical crafts.'[59] Successful Roman artists lived in gentry style, equipped themselves to participate in polite society, and were recognized as more or less acceptable, if sometimes odd, members of it.

The relationship between patronage and style is more debatable. Cardinals would commission secular, neo-pagan subjects or landscapes. Laymen would fancy a nativity or an apotheosis. Isabella d'Este told Giovanni Bellini she would like some pagan myths 'but if it was inconvenient the Nativity would do just as well'. The relationship of patron and artist provides no simple or comprehensive explanation of aesthetic development; little more, Francis Haskell has concluded, than the 'internal logic of artistic development, personal whim or the workings of chance'.[60]

Compared with the outlay on art patronage, building, and music the expenditure on science and technology was trifling. Does this provide a clue to the slow progress of science and technology during this period? The rulers of society wanted entertainment and pleasure; to live sumptuously in a noble setting surrounded by objects of beauty. For this they were not only willing to pay handsomely but to bankrupt themselves. It is doubtful if considerations of investment, capital appreciation and the like came into it except very occasionally. Market values of paintings were fluctuating and dubious; only jewels, bronzes or figurines by the greatest artists could be expected to hold their value dependably. But from the patronage of science little pleasure or glory could be expected. The occasional nobleman, like Federigo Cesi, who was truly fascinated by the pursuit of knowledge remained exceptional. Science was not to become fashionable until the later seventeenth century. Only a warlike prince determined to solve problems of military organization, such as Maurice of Nassau, found it profitable to seek the help of science. Trade and industry was still on a small scale; capital accumulation slow; fixed capital negligible. Only the occasional legacy or the patronage of the great East India Company could provide funds to finance research or instruction in, for example, navigation. It is anachronistic to suppose the average trader or manufacturer thought, or could afford to think, in such terms.

That patronage was an element in the development of the arts and sciences of mankind is certain. Its study can help us to understand some aspects of their social context and relations. It cannot provide any complete explanation of genius. Just as the energies which lie behind the flowering of individual genius remain as mysterious as ever, so those which account for the national outbursts of the creative spirit defy any precise analysis.

12

ENGLAND AND THE GREAT REBELLION

None of the interludes of anarchy – never far below the surface of early modern society nor far from the minds of its people – is more vividly recorded than the Civil War of England. In terms of physical suffering and destruction it was no worse than the upheavals in the Low Countries, France, Germany or Bohemia, but its origins and social and political character were different. It was a domestic quarrel, without the strongly international flavour of the others. Marxist and post-Marxist theories notwithstanding, it did not arise primarily from noble discontents, and in so far as it grew out of religious conflicts, they were rifts within Protestantism, not between Protestantism and Catholicism. Other differences will emerge in the course of this chapter.

The political arrangements of Tudor England – 'constitution' perhaps suggests too settled and defined an entity – rested upon a delicate balance between the need for, and acceptance of, strong executive powers to govern accorded to the monarchy; and the rights, partly ancient, partly developed and encouraged by the Tudors themselves, of other institutions, Parliament in particular, to participate in government. Finance, taxation, religion, the succession to the throne, foreign and economic policy, the administration of law, and other less fundamental matters had increasingly attracted determined parliamentary attention. This had been repelled, or at least checked, with equal determination by Elizabeth.

In the last years of her reign some long shadows had been cast over her relations with her politically effective subjects. Religious extremism had grown. Catholics were again more active, especially in the northern

204

counties. Her Church Settlement, with its attempted moderation in doctrine and discipline, satisfied few of those who shared in the growing Puritan temper of the times which the Queen herself disliked and distrusted. Her very success in strengthening the Crown by her force of character, reinforced by the deliberate propaganda of royal progresses, patronage of arts and by a princely and patriotic image, above all by the creation of a great Court, now recoiled on her; most damagingly in the famous quarrel with Parliament over her grant of monopolies to favourites. As the century ended, and even the French made peace with Spain, the continuing war for England's Dutch ally (which the Puritans had themselves urged upon her) seemed to more people unprofitable and unacceptable. Her former manipulation of parliamentary criticism through the discreet operations of her privy councillors worked less effectively. There was an air of irascibility and frustration abroad.

Fortunately the Queen herself had mellowed with age. She missed her old advisers like Burghley and Walsingham, both dead. Her new ones, like Lord Buckhurst, were prudent men, not given to seeking out exposed positions. Discreetly and gracefully she withdrew from the monopolies quarrel, protesting innocently that she had no idea how her people had been vexed by the 'harpies and horse-leeches' now uncovered. She avoided a head-on collision with the Puritans. Her successor could deal with such problems.

When she died, in 1603, her successor was only too ready to do so. It was not long before he was on excellent terms with the Spanish ambassador, chattering state secrets into his ear; Spanish ducats were on the trot round influential members of his Council, despite Spain's evergrowing financial difficulties; a conference of divines called to settle the church problem proved a fiasco which only revealed the unbridgeable gulf between episcopacy and its opponents. A glorious by-product of this attempt to remedy 'things pretended to be amiss in the church' was the Authorized Version of the Bible, the work of a large and imposing team of scholars, which appeared in 1611.

James's early years, to 1614, were redeemed by other successes, covenanted and uncovenanted – his contribution towards the Spanish–Dutch truce (1609); and the settlement of the row between Spain, France, the Dutch and the German Protestant princes over the succession in Jülich-Cleve. These were the strategically vital duchies which formed a salient into the Netherlands crucial to the Spanish Army of

Flanders should the war be renewed, especially as they included the Rhine crossing at Wesel. James seemed powerful in Scotland as in England. Yet already a sort of miasma was spreading, and it was to grow worse from 1614 down to the outbreak of the Civil War.

The delicately balanced Tudor organism depended on mutual confidence between Crown, Parliament and people. The unspoken motto of the Tudors – Welsh though they partly were – was least said, soonest mended. Not least of the many political attributes that won them wide favour was that they usually showed a proper respect for their subjects' rights. Elizabeth, though far from a mistress of diplomacy, was at least mindful of one basic consideration in her shuffling prevarications over Spain, France and the Netherlands – economy. This derived from her shrewd appreciation that she was the only prince in Europe who did not squeeze her subjects like oranges. Light taxes were not the least important of the keys to English tranquillity before 1614.

Even before then, the high hopes of the Puritans, parliamentarians, lawyers, nobles and gentry – at least those who were not of the intimate royal circle – and the good impressions made by the royal aptitude for patient, not to say loquacious, discussion, were beginning to wear thin. For this decline of popularity there were many reasons. Basic to all of them was James himself. Intelligent as he was in some respects, he was tactless and pedantic. It became daily more clear that he was too ready to sacrifice the public welfare to the gratification of his private appetites. As he combined a physically undignified bearing with undisguised homosexual preferences, the result was a general damage to the prestige of the Crown far more serious than that inflicted by Elizabeth's semi-comic flirtations. In a gross age his habits were more than usually gross. Men might have overlooked such unprepossessing traits as his uncontrollable outbursts of temper (Elizabeth had had them too), his bent for low company, his letters to the seductive Buckingham addressed 'Sweetheart' and signed 'Thy dear Dad and purveyor', his dirtiness, his itchings, scratchings, sneezings and blowings. They did not so easily overlook his choice of favourites, especially when, like Robert Carr (later Viscount Rochester, later Earl of Somerset) and many others, they were Scots and therefore foreigners.

Elizabeth had been more than frugal in creating titles. From 1615, under the influence of Carr's successor as chief minion, George Villiers ('Steenie'), later Duke of Buckingham, and Francis Bacon, the number of peers grew rapidly – from 81 to 126 by 1628. Earldoms multiplied from 27 to 65. Eighty Irish peerages were added to the 25 already in being, and went mostly to English or Scots who had no connection with Ireland whatever. All were paid for: any emergency costs at once effected new creations, and much of the money found its way into Villiers's pocket. In 1611 he created the profitable order of baronet; in all the sale of titles raised between half and three-quarters of a million pounds between 1603 and 1629.

Closely connected with titles were grants of monopolies. Many of these emerged plausibly from requests for patents to protect some valuable new trade or invention. But legitimate protection swiftly turned into a squalid racket. Between 1550 and 1600 about a hundred were granted; between 1604 and 1610 James had created 108. Bitter parliamentary protest called into being the Monopolies Act of 1624, but corporate bodies could and did obtain them.

Other forms of monopoly were grants connected with land reclamation or particular branches of trade. The drainage of waterlogged lands in south Yorkshire and later in the Fens by 'undertakers' chartered by the Crown was supported by Court favourites or moneyed men who came in on special terms. The immediate sufferers – or so it seemed to the victims – were the local peasantry, who lost their rights to fish, fowl, or graze in summertime. Equally plausible on paper but even more indefensible in practice, as we have seen, was the notorious Cokayne project of 1614.

Despite the tradition of peaceful international relations which the Stuarts inherited from Elizabeth, the royal debts grew. In 1606 the Earl of Dorset (as Buckhurst now was) told Parliament they stood at £735,000. By 1618 they had risen to £900,000 and no credit could be had. In 1621 James made Lionel Cranfield, a former successful London merchant created Earl of Middlesex, Lord High Treasurer. His task was to reform the royal finances, now in a worse mess than ever by reason of James's prodigal expenditure on favourites, court entertainment, the dispersal of crown lands and the corrupt administration of the customs duties which were of increasing importance as trade grew and other revenues fell.

Treasurers were rarely popular. Cranfield did not survive the jealousies of the older nobles and royal office-holders who resented his humble origins as much as they distrusted his obvious efficiency. The costs of the perambulations of Charles and Buckingham in search of a Spanish royal bride were the last straw. Cranfield was brought low, and with him went the last hope of reform within the framework of co-operation between king and Parliament. The hosts of sinecurists in Whitehall increased daily – Clerks of the Pipe, feodaries, Aulnagers of the Linen, Comptrollers of Tents and Pavilions, carvers and chirographers. The royal insolvency was 'immediate', continuous and gross'.[61]

From the economic crisis of the Cokayne aftermath there emerged a government commission of enquiry; its economic ideas were to have a profound influence, first on the English economy, later on those of Germany, Spain, Italy and other countries. As we have seen, they were, broadly, the ideas that came to be called 'mercantilist': a congeries of proposals for protecting local manufactures. Unfortunately they did little to help the Stuarts out of their immediate predicament. When Charles 1 succeeded his father he raised the moral tone of the Court but he did not lower its costs: on the contrary. The growing baroque embellishments of absolutism had to be paid for. The new Banqueting Hall designed by Inigo Jones seemed to symbolize the trend. Both palace and architect became synonyms for expense and tyranny.

Charles's intentions were always – or nearly always – impeccable, but he was as unsure of himself as Philip 11 of Spain, and when he changed his mind (as he usually did) it was, as Clarendon was later to write in his *History*, most often for the worse. He had inherited from his grandmother, Mary, Queen of Scots, a fatal gift for alienating his potential friends and a petty vindictiveness which turned many of them into deadly enemies. From his father, who had cheerfully and successively ditched Salisbury, Bacon and Cranfield, he inherited a smug certitude that his servants enjoyed only one luxury: the privilege of serving him. The loyal servants of the Stuarts got no quarter from their enemies; they were to get none from their masters, as Strafford and Laud were to find. Well-intentioned and ambitious schemes of social planning to protect the needy ended by alienating them too, when – as in the Fens – they found the king's friends cutting the ground (or water) from beneath them.

One after another the plans miscarried, either because they were half-baked in conception or because the state could not command the resources to carry them out. Thus it was with the scheme of 1634 'to improve the standard of soap manufacture'. It turned out to be an outright swindle for the benefit of a clique of favourites.

With equally lofty intentions Charles supported the efforts of his

Archbishop of Canterbury to purify the Church. Again, Laud's Arminian ideas might have been expected to win the sympathy of those who felt nothing but repulsion for the iron dogmatism of extreme pre-destinarianism and the arid cant of the Puritans. But the fighter learnt only too swiftly to use the weapons of his foe. New instructions for the Court of High Commission in 1626 restored its inquisitional powers, but the campaign for decency and order in church services turned into an ill-timed attack on owners of tithes, pews and those who contributed to the stipends of the non-beneficed Puritan 'lecturers'. Recalcitrant ministers were punished severely by Laud, Archbishop Neile at York and Matthew Wren, Bishop of Norwich. More bishops were promoted to civil office. Juxon, of London, was made Treasurer – the first ecclesiastic to hold the office since 1470. The heat of Star Chamber was turned on those, like Burton, Bastwick, Lilburne and Prynne, who had dared to criticize them. Most sinister of all, in Protestant eyes, Charles refused the plea – from Laud himself – to suppress Catholic proselytizing at the court of Queen Henrietta Maria, who was both Catholic and French.

From 1629 to 1640 Charles ruled without Parliament. This was the period of 'personal rule', often regarded as illegal. It was nothing of the sort. On the contrary, it was not incumbent on an English king at this time to hold Parliaments if he was ingenious enough to finance himself without them. Whatever later critics might say in the light of Charles's defeat, the devices of these years could plausibly be construed as legal. To fine landowners for breach of ancient forest laws; to fine men for not accepting knighthoods; to award monopolies to corporations, might not be good law – it was certainly not wise law – but it was law. Ancient laws were revived; loopholes found in current law. The royal prerogative and the prerogative courts rested on ancient tradition. They had been constantly recognized under the Tudors as indispensable to order. Even in the seventeenth century it was agreed that there must be some residual authority which could soften the rigour and remedy the injustices arising out of legal formality.

The question was one of confidence in the motives behind the use of prerogative. In cases affecting taxation or monopolies, the prerogative could plausibly be invoked. As the Defender of the Realm, could not the king mulct ports for a levy to provide ships for the defence of merchant shipping against an enemy? And if a seaport could be so burdened, was it not fair to ask the inland towns to share the cost? But who would say whether these arguments were valid? In 1636 the judges found that the king might levy ship money when 'the whole Kingdom' was in danger. 'We are also of opinion', they went on, 'that in such case Your Majesty is whole judge, both of the danger and when and how the same is to be prevented and avoided.'[62] Writs for the collection of ship money therefore continued to be levied until 1639.

The problem of the prerogative was in principle simple – was it being used as a special, residual, emergency power to supplement normal methods of law and government? Or was it being used to subvert and supplant them? As the lawyer, John Selden, wrote later, it was 'like putting in a little auger [bodkin] that afterwards you may put in a greater. He that pulls down the first brick does the main work; afterwards it is easy to pull down the wall.' The drift of royal policy was plain to those who distrusted it (and by 1640 they were probably a majority): the first bricks were being removed, by Laud and Wentworth, in the name of legality. If the work went on, nothing could stand between the king and his servants, and the total destruction of all opposition or criticism, whether in matters of religion, law, policy, taxation or anything else. It could not be long before absolutism was as complete as possible in the conditions of the time.

The career of William Prynne, the puritan lawyer and parliamentarian, drove home the moral. In his *Histrio-mastix* (1633) he violently attacked stage plays, forecast the terrible end that awaited princes that favoured them and reserved a disagreeable epithet for actresses. Since the Queen was at the time busily rehearsing a ballet, the finger pointed straight at the Court. Prynne was imprisoned, sentenced in Star Chamber to life imprisonment, fined £5000 – a fortune – expelled from his Inn of Court, robbed of his profession and Oxford degree and set in the pillory to lose both his ears. (John Aubrey said only part were cut off: 'his tippes were visible. Bishop W. Laud. A. B. Cant. was much blamed for being a spectator when he was his judge'.[63] Three years later Prynne was back in Star Chamber, back in the pillory, this time to lose the stumps of his ears and be branded on his cheeks with the letters 'S.L.' ('seditious libeller': Prynne announced that they stood for '*stigmata laudis*'). Prynne, a contentious, bitter Calvinist, fought almost everybody in his day, but his memory was long; he was among Laud's prosecutors. Pride and principle, we may suppose, had as much to do with the resort to arms as poverty or profits.

Was there a 'shift of the centre of social gravity' in these years? A

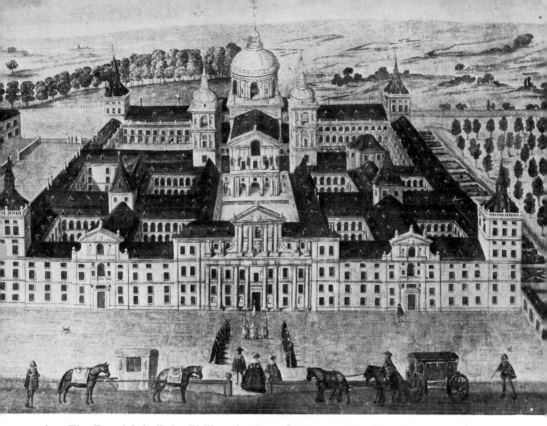

15 *above* The Escorial, built by Philip II in the 1560s; a seventeenth-century engraving.
16 *below The Expulsion of the Moriscoes* by Vincencio Carducho. Between 1609
and 1614 over a quarter of a million Moriscoes were expelled from Spain.

17 *left* William the Silent; a portrait by the sixteenth-century Flemish artist, Adriaen Thomas Key.

18 *below* Antwerp, until 1585 the centre of European trade, by an unknown Flemish artist.

19 *right* *The Milch Cow*, a satire on the political situation in the Netherlands by an unknown artist of the Flemish school. Philip II belabours the Flanders cow while Elizabeth proffers much needed aid and William of Orange attempts to milk it.

20 *below right* Parma's bridge of boats across the Scheldt enabled him to capture Antwerp despite the potential strategic advantage held by the city's defenders; a seventeenth-century French engraving.

…TIME SINCE I SAWE A COWE.
…ERS REPRESENTE
…E BACKE KINGE PHILIP RODE
MALECONTNT.

THE QVEENE OF ENGLAND GIVING HAY
WHEARE ON THE COW DID FEEDE.
AS ONE THAT WAS HER GREATEST HELPE.
IN HER DISTRESSE AND NEEDE.

THE PRINCE OF ORANGE MILKT THE C…
AND MADE HIS PVRSE THE PAYLE.
THE COW DID SHYT IN MONSIEVRS HAND.
WHILE HE DID HOLD HER TAYLE.

LE PONT DE FARNESE.

21 *above left* *Astronomie* by Giovanni da Bologna who brought the Mannerist style to perfection.

22 *above right* Orlandus Lassus, the Flemish master, conducts the choir in the Bavarian court chapel; a miniature by Hans Mielich.

23 *below* *Banquet of the Officers of the Civic Guard of St George* (1616) by Frans Hals.

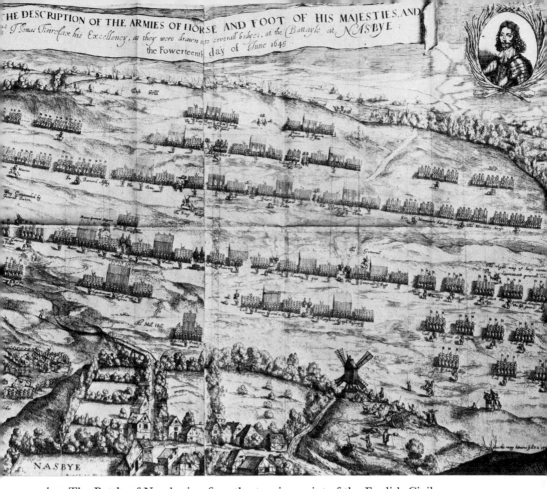

24 *above* The Battle of Naseby in 1645, the turning point of the English Civil War. The New Model Army established its superiority. Charles I was forced to flee to Scotland. A seventeenth-century engraving detailing the deployment of troops on the battlefield.

25 *below* The execution of Charles I, 1649; an imaginary reconstruction by Weesop.

26 *above* The Defenestration of Prague, May 1618. In a symbolic gesture the Imperial representatives were thrown from the window of the Hradčany Palace by Bohemian officials angered by the Emperor's interference in Bohemian affairs.

27 *below left* The Emperor Rudolf II; an anonymous portrait.

28 *below right* Wallenstein by Van Dyck.

29   Street-fighting in Prague; unrest in Bohemia began the slide into the full-scale continental war known as the Thirty Years' War.

30 & 31   The horrors of seventeenth-century warfare were depicted in a series of engravings by Jacques Callot entitled *Les Malheurs de la Guerre*.

number of theories of an economic or sociological kind have been advanced over the past half century to supplement or supplant the older belief that the Civil War was fought over issues of deep political principle or religious conviction. The theory that war came because the aristocracy was in decline while the gentry were rising in wealth, seeking political power and status to match their new fortunes, gave way to its reverse. The gentry retired into Calvinism, it is argued, because they were poor and getting poorer – 'mere gentry'. The aristocracy, who after all had not lost nearly as much as, for instance, Tawney had supposed on the basis of unreliable statistics, found new sources of wealth open to them which in the main the ordinary country gentleman did not have.

Much of this kind of reasoning seems to be deductive rather than inductive. Behind it lies an implication, if not a belief, that political events were conditioned by socio-economic facts; that the resort to arms and the attempt to re-allocate power by force was the result of a class struggle which grew in intensity over a longish if undefined period. Such enquiries, which have broadened our ideas of the period, have yet to produce a comprehensive, coherent 'explanation'. Indeed, any such goal seems further away than ever, and perhaps is itself a mirage. It seems likely that economic discontent among the governing class – aristocracy *and* gentry – was more characteristic of the early seventeenth century than leaping ambition to match new wealth with new political status – an assumption which derived partly from Marxist studies of the French and later revolutions.

The English Civil War was not, like the early stages of the Netherlands Revolt or the civil wars in sixteenth- and seventeenth-century France, inspired by noble grievances; nor by direct religious animosities between Protestant and Catholic. The parliamentary opposition was gentry-led, and though its target might superficially seem to be royal favourites or servants, these were also men of their own rank or lower, recently promoted upstarts whose fame and power was transitory and insubstantial – a Cranfield, a Buckingham, a Strafford. This last had been a notable parliamentary figure, excluded from the 1626 Parliament by the king, imprisoned in 1628, only to be released, reconciled and promised the Presidency of the Council of the North, then to rule in Ireland.

Economic problems certainly played a part in creating discontent. Inflation had reduced the real income of all except those who were hard-headed enough to make provisions, legal or otherwise, to keep in step with rising prices. The flattening-out of price movements after 1620 created new problems for those whose incomes were somehow linked to commercial crops – corn, barley, wool, hides, flax – or rents dependent on them. In both phases, economic movement and the need to predict and adapt put a premium on opportunism. The world of custom, of fixed values, had passed and those who looked to them were lost. Inflation, deflation, high living had no predictable result in any particular case. There were those who succumbed to one or the other; others who could swim in any sea and emerge stronger than before.

One may speculate endlessly on what might have happened if Charles, in his ignorance of its affairs, had not involved himself in Scotland. There his follies outraged even conservative opinion: the result was the National Covenant of 1638 denouncing popery, the new prayer book, the bishops, the canons and all Charles's works. In England, Pym, now risen to the parliamentary leadership, denounced in a two-hour speech the whole catalogue of royal iniquities. Strafford in Ireland and Laud in England were major targets. A Scottish invasion penetrated as far south as Newcastle and Durham. The costs of the war were insupportable. Personal government was at an end. When Parliament met in 1640 all but a few members were united against the king's 'evil counsellors'. Laud and Strafford were the men most in mind, and in due course both were executed. Strafford sacrificed himself in an attempt to achieve unity but his gesture was wasted. After his death the divisions became more serious as old loyalty rallied more members of the predominantly 'gentry' Commons to the king's side.

The Grand Remonstrance of November 1641 was constructed by John Pym and John Hampden and brought before the House; it rehearsed all Charles's misdeeds. It passed only by a tiny majority (159 to 148). In Parliament on the night of 22 November swords were drawn. Six weeks later, in a typically bungled coup, Charles tried to arrest the leaders. While they took refuge in the City of London – the 'proud, unthankful, schismatical, rebellious, bloody City of London' – Charles left to seek support in Scotland and north and west England. Seven months of propaganda and counter-propaganda followed before war broke out in August 1642.

Despite untenable historical traditions which sometimes suggest an inevitable conflict between two sides neatly divided by geography, religion and class interest, the truth was that hardly anybody wanted war. It was entered upon only with deepest reluctance by both sides. Every class of men was divided. Some thirty peers stayed with Parliament; about forty joined the king. Many, like members of all other groups, were passive or neutral. Similarly the gentry divided reluctantly, some swaying to the king, some to Parliament. Even the theory, often propounded, that this was a war of south and east England – economically, politically and theologically more progressive – against the more agrarian and conservative west and north, needs to be interpreted with great care. Kent contained a majority of moderate royalists. The leading squires of Cornwall were parliamentarians. At Kings Lynn in Norfolk there were enough royalists to support a rising for the king. In every shire there was a strong minority party which only waited its chance to join hands with sympathizers from areas where they were a majority. The initiative came from the landowner class and it was they who led the fighting, but their predicament was agonizing. R. W. Ketton-Cremer has described in his moving picture of *Norfolk in the Civil War* (1969) how families were regularly divided against themselves, fathers against sons, brothers against brothers. A few were dedicated Catholics or Anglican-royalists, some were equally dedicated parliamentarians; but to most civil war was abhorrent. Only as it developed was the undecided majority compelled to gravitate to one side or the other.

The City of London and its merchant community was also divided. Many had lent money to the king, but under Pym's skilful organization this old gang was ousted by new men anxious to share in the profits of power.

The sympathies of the humbler orders are even more difficult to define. Contemporary opinion was that in the countryside 'they care not what government they live under, so as they may plough and go to market'. This was borne out by the response of the peasant who was warned off Marston Moor in 1644 because the great battle was imminent. 'What! Has them two fallen out then?'[64]

The social composition of the radical groups – Clubmen, Diggers, Levellers – is still only vaguely known. Many Levellers were certainly Londoners: 'the hobnails, clouted shoes, private soldiers, the leather and woollen aprons and the laborious and industrious people of England'. Radical Puritanism was strong in the cloth-making areas of

East Anglia and Yorkshire. Others were peasants, angry at the continuing grievances of enclosure and ready to seize a grand opportunity to substitute general action for the sporadic and pathetically ineffective protests that were their common safety-valve.

The contrast between English rural protest and that of contemporary France is striking. Year by year the courts record dozens of riots. In church and alehouse, carpenters, masons and peasants concerted their tragi-comic protests against their oppressors. Who were they? Not the king or the nobility. Their grudges and grievances were local – loss of grazing rights and commons, rights to cut firewood in forest, fish or fowl in fen or mere. Those who had to buy food in times of 'dearth' (dearness) railed against greedy strangers who enclosed the open arable for pasture. They were little impressed by arguments that their complaints were unrepresentative. All they knew was that they were victimized.

The proceedings were not without their comic side. Protests were timed for high days and holidays. Fireworks flared on May Day or Guy Fawkes night, when Puritan fervour and ale in plenty added to the excitement. A few riots grew to proportions that alarmed JPs, and the government might send instructions commanding strong measures. But the violence was strictly limited. A fence or hedge would be pulled down, an encloser or his servants knocked on the head; but a death was rare. Only a few offenders were hanged; most were never caught.

How different from France where riots involved bloodshed and violence on a terrifying scale. Why? For one thing Tudor government had set up an executive, with effective legal arms, strong and respected. For another, the French disturbances were those of men and women driven desperate by hunger and a crushing weight of taxation. The English, of all classes, were relatively lightly taxed and better fed: men like Hampden and Lilburne were determined they should remain so. England too had witnessed an increase in vagabondage, unemployment and poverty. But the riots of the poor remained riots. They did not turn into revolutions – until they were recruited for the purpose by noble or gentry leadership.

The military preparations of the parliamentarians for war were defensive. They feared especially that Charles would recruit aid from a foreign ally – the queen was said to be organizing forces in Holland – and attack and seize the ports. There was little of the feeling of confidence expressed by historians of later centuries who, with history behind them, could see the enormous advantages Parliament possessed in the economic resources of London and East Anglia. The king's opponents could only wait soberly to know the worst. The first battle was fought at Edgehill, in Warwickshire, on 23 October 1642. It was indecisive and this was an accurate foreshadowing of the later course of the first Civil War. It resulted from the inexperience of the officers – particularly of the royalist cavalry which nearly won and then nearly lost the day; but more important was the indecision of Charles himself. Instead of marching straight on to London he first hesitated, then withdrew to Oxford.

Until late in 1644 the outcome of the war remained uncertain. Throughout 1643 the advantages lay with Charles. His army was still well-quartered and supplied while the enemy were without shelter and short of supplies. All in all, the Cavaliers won seven out of the sixteen battles of the war, almost all in the earlier stages of conflict. Yet none of them was exploited. Charles had one, and only one, of the qualities which might have entitled him to generalship: he was an optimist. But his optimism led him only to indulge his natural hesitations. Time after time great opportunities were lost – at Edgehill, Turnham Green, Newbury, Cheriton, King's Lynn, Marston Moor, Naseby. Behind his 'fatal facility and weakness so often and so pertinaceously misconstrued into perfidy and crime' (as an old historian described it) lay Charles's failure to organize a unified command. True, his difficulties were great: many of his noble commanders, like Newcastle in the north, were resistant to orders. With troops composed in large part of their own tenantry they could claim a kind of semi-independent right to fight the war as they saw fit. A group of amateur soldiers round the queen – Digby, Wilmot, Percy, Ashburnham – were only too ready to respond to her intrigues against the one truly professional soldier who might have made a real commander-in-chief: Prince Rupert. For Rupert was young, landless and foreign. In 1644, when it was too late, Charles did appoint him. Meanwhile the royalist command remained in disarray, divided by plots and jealousies during this critical period while Parliament was gathering its strength. Too late Charles confessed to Rupert that he had been grievously wrong: 'the chief hope of my resource is, under God, from you. . . . I confess, the best had been to have followed your advice.' Charles's defects of character had lost the war as they had lost the peace.

England and the Civil War

Districts controlled by the King throughout the campaign of 1643

Districts controlled by Parliament throughout the campaign of 1643

Districts conquered by the King during the campaign of 1643

Districts conquered by Parliament during the campaign of 1643

battle ✕

North Sea

Isle of Man

Irish Sea

Newburn
Carlisle
Newcastle

Adwalton
Preston ✕ Moor ✕ York
Hull

Liverpool
Sheffield
Winceby ✕
The Wash

Nottingham
Shrewsbury
King's Lynn
Leicester
Norwich
Lichfield
Trent

Naseby
Severn

Worcester
Cambridge
Hereford
Northampton
Edge Hill
Gloucester
Colchester
Monmouth
Oxford
Pembroke
Chalgrove ✕
Lansdown
Turnham
Hill
London
Bristol
Green
Roundway Down
Newbury
Thames
Bristol Channel
Maidstone
Bridgwater
Dover
Wardour Castle
Stratton ✕
Bideford
Taunton
Arundel
Exeter
Portsmouth
Lostwithiel
Braddock Down
Isle of Wight
Dartmouth

English Channel

Districts controlled by Parliament at the beginning of 1645
Districts controlled by the King at the end of 1645
Districts conquered by Parliament during 1645
Held for the King in areas controlled by Parliament
battle

North Sea

Irish Sea

Isle of Man

Carlisle
Newcastle
Bolton Castle
Marston Moor York
Hull
Lathom House Sandal Castle
Liverpool Sheffield
Rowton Hulme
Nantwich Nottingham Newark The Wash
Ashby de la Zouch
Shrewsbury Belvoir Castle King's Lynn
Lichfield Leicester
Norwich
Naseby
Cropredy
Worcester Bridge Cambridge
Hereford Northampton
Monmouth Banbury
Raglan Castle Gloucester Colchester
Thames Oxford
Pembroke
Bristol Channel Bristol London
Donnington
Bridgwater Newbury Castle
Longford Basing Maidstone
House House Dover
Taunton Winchester
Langport Arundel
Exeter Portsmouth
Corfe Castle
Lostwithiel Isle of Wight

English Channel

Meanwhile, on the parliamentary side, a powerful figure had emerged, fully aware that Parliament needed an efficient, trained and disciplined army under a unified command as urgently as did the king. Oliver Cromwell came from a gentry family in the fenland country of Huntingdon. As a young man, he was an ardent radical who spoke up for the rights of the local peasantry, defended low-bred Anabaptists and regularly kicked the ball into his own class goal – perhaps in reaction against his own family record, for the Cromwells had done well out of the Reformation and the seizure and sale of church lands. To some historians, Cromwell seems to represent the vested interests of anti-Catholicism in person; to others he is the essence of Calvinist, Puritan, predestinarian psychology and theology. By 1644 he was forty-five years of age, more mature, less radical, 'of great favour and interest with the House of Commons', the outstanding figure of the Eastern Association which, second only to London, was Parliament's main support. But more than all this he was a military leader and organizer of genius.

In 1644 he was the architect of victory at Marston Moor. But victory in one battle was not enough. Three weeks later the army was dispersed. Cromwell was desperate: 'My lords, till you have an army merely your own, that you may command, it is . . . impossible to do anything of importance.' The result was the New Model Army. It combined the experience of Maurice of Nassau and Gustavus Adolphus. Unlike previous parliamentary soldiers, his troopers were well-drilled, well-horsed and – above all – well and regularly paid. The next year Cromwell and his general, Fairfax, with their New Model Army, de-cisively defeated the royal army at Naseby, in the Midlands.

Naseby was the turning-point of the war. The New Model was now superior not only to the Cavaliers but to any rival challengers within the anti-royalist movement. Thereafter the great houses and castles that had been the fortresses of royalism surrendered and were demolished. The king fled north to ask the protection of the Scots.

So ended the war for the time being. But it was far from having secured orderly government in England. After Naseby came four years of confusion. Rifts between Parliament and Army, Presbyterians and Independents, conservatives and radicals reduced England to some-thing like anarchy until, on 6 December 1648, Colonel Thomas Pride 'purged' the House of Commons. Cromwell declared he had no fore-knowledge of it, 'yet since it was done he was glad of it'. He still wanted to save King Charles's life but the king certainly did his best, by intolerably devious intrigues, to make it impossible. By the end of the year Cromwell had made up his mind. 'I tell you', he said to critics of the policy of setting-up a tribunal to try Charles, 'we will cut off his head with the crown on it.'

On 30 January 1649, at ten o'clock in the morning, he did. Charles went to the block in Whitehall, stepping on to the execution platform from the middle window of Inigo Jones's banqueting-hall. As his head fell, a great groan went up from the assembled multitude. It did not last long. The onlookers scattered swiftly as soldiers marching from Charing Cross to Westminster met others marching in the opposite direction. England was not to be a place for civilians for the next eleven years.

This is not the place to try and solve the baffling enigmas of Cromwell the politician. Of greater importance was his genius as a general. For despite recent sociological research and disputation, the acts, decisions (and indecisions) of Charles and Cromwell remain the solid facts of the pre-war and war years. Research into the supposedly medium-term and long-term 'causes' of the war has produced much interesting and novel historical material and speculation; but the gap that divides economic and social motive from political act remains as wide as ever. We are left, as H. G. Koenigsberger has said, with much discussion of 'preconditions, precipitants and triggers' as we try and fuse our political, economic and social history into a new synthesis. As we try to grasp the new dimensions of social history, the insubstantial but vital spirit of the politics and religion of that remote age threatens to slip away, leaving us with interpretations that may soon seem as anachronistic as those of the Victorian historians seem to us.

The 'long-term' explanation is not new. Let one of the greatest of historians, a fallible man but one who knew the politics of this age at first hand have the last word. 'I am not so sharp-sighted', wrote Lord Clarendon in his great *History*,

as those who have discerned this rebellion contriving from (if not before) the death of Queen Elizabeth, and fomented by several Princes and great Ministers of State in Christendom, to the time that it broke out. Neither do I look far back as believing the design to be so long since formed . . .

Much in it was accidental: 'not capable of being contrived . . . no four men of the opposition were of familiarity and trust with each other'. Yet deeper troubles were brewing: 'the excess of the Court in the greatest want and the parsimony and retention of the country in the greatest plenty ... like so many atoms contributing jointly to this mass of confusion now before us'. A final irony: by the time Clarendon's words were written, Pym and Hampden had saddled England with burdens of indirect taxation heavier by far than those for which they had martyred themselves less than ten years before.

13

THE EUROPEAN KALEIDOSCOPE 1609–1648
THE FORTUNES OF THE STATES

In 1609 an exhausted Europe had suspended the furious wars in which the major powers had been locked since the famous 'peace' of Cateau-Cambrésis. The Hispano-Dutch truce of that year precariously managed to last out its agreed twelve years. It is a convenient point from which to review the changed and changing situation of the main powers.

In Philip II's declining years Spain was running into ever-deepening crises. A growing sense of disillusion was not dispersed by the *arbitristas* who sat like doctors by the patient's bed, writing out elaborate diagnoses and prescriptions, totally impotent to halt the fatal progress of the disease. Philip II's successor was Philip III – easy-going, affable, acquisitive. The old system of political administration was now modified as the quality of kingship declined and the complexity of Spain's problems increased. Philip II's system 'based on the principle of induced rivalries and calculated uncertainties'[65] now gave way to the era of the great *privados* – the Duke of Lerma, Uceda, Olivares, Haro – royal favourites who were in reality private rulers acting at the bidding of their own corrupt creatures (like Lerma's Don Rodrigo Calderón) who in turn lined their own pockets richly at the expense of public funds. The difference was that rivalries continued uninduced, uncertainties multiplied without calculation and all pretence at system disappeared as the once-powerful council of nobles fell into disuse. Granvelle's most gloomy forecasts of decadence and ruin were now fulfilled as Spain, owner of the incalculable treasure of the Indies, was reduced to using a debased copper coinage. As the poor migrated by the thousand, the nobles drifted towards the Court in search of jobs to support their still swelling domestic establishments and ever-more ambitious style of living. Lerma, who varied the serious business of hunting, dancing and the theatre with discreet interludes of ceremonial piety, was a perfect model.

The ineptitude and folly of Spanish policy was crowned by the brutal expulsion of the Moriscoes from 1609 to 1614. In all 275,000 were expelled in terrible hardship. The economic effects have been much debated. One school of thought believes that they have been exaggerated by observers ignorant that much of the evil attributed to the expulsion was due to inflation, and that the Moriscoes made so little improvement in North Africa (to which they mostly went) that the economic loss to Spain can be forgotten. Others reject this, pointing out that since large numbers of them were massacred on arrival in Africa the older belief in their economic value is not disproved. Against the general background of growing Spanish nonchalance, it is fair to infer that the expulsion, like the earlier hounding-out of Jews and Protestant heretics, did further damage to an already ailing society. Certainly it robbed Valencia and Aragon especially of valuable rural labour. Even as they were driven out, the favoured classes – the armies of priests, monks, lawyers, students, vagabonds, thieves and prostitutes – multiplied. The gulf between rich and poor widened. The structure of Spanish society began to resemble more and more that of Russia and those societies east of the Elba that divided simply into lords and peasants. The wars that were resumed in 1621 made new demands: a bigger navy, a bigger army in Flanders, more money and more conscripts. The unnatural conditions of military discipline (and indiscipline) overseas, protracted over more than a century and a half, could not but contribute to the stagnation that descended on Castile. The fact was not lost on Aragon, Valencia and Catalonia.

As the truce expired, Philip IV succeeded: a more cultivated and intelligent king than his predecessor, but equally weak and even more ruled by his new *privado*, the Andalusian Gaspar de Guzman, Count of Olivares – a hawk where Lerma was a comparative dove, energetic, impetuous and temperamental. The imminence of another bankruptcy impelled king and minister to journey round the other provinces in search of first-aid for Castile. 'Heroism', as Olivares put it, 'needed money.' Aragon, Valencia and Catalonia listened politely but cautiously to proposals for a 'union of arms' with Castile. Politely they declined, offering supplies but significantly rejecting any conscription for foreign service.

Spain's chosen enemies had at this moment their own problems – France the Huguenots, England the growing tensions between king and Parliament. Never at a loss to invent new complications and expenses, Philip IV plunged back gratuitously into Italian politics. The vacant Mantuan territory of Montferrat, a fief of the Empire, was claimed by a French heir, the Duke of Nevers. France saw Philip's armed occupation of Montferrat as a challenge. No sooner were the Huguenots dealt with than the French established themselves in Italy, and in the end secured by treaty control of direct access to Italy. The cost of this adventure to Spain was another ten million ducats.

Simultaneously, she lost the Silver Fleet to the great Dutch sailor Piet Heyn in 1628. Hence the need for a crop of new taxes and exactions which this time bit hard into noble purses. Hence new pressure on Portugal and Catalonia for help. The 1630s saw Olivares running deeply into problems on every side. The most serious was the obstinate opposition of Catalonia to his plans which developed into a fully-fledged revolt. Too late, Olivares offered concessions. Barcelona was in uproar. With the murder of the viceroy the discontent spread to Portugal where local insurrections had broken out in Lisbon and Evora in the 1630s. In 1640 noble resentment against the Spanish viceroy (Margaret of Savoy) and her Spanish and Italian favourites swelled into full revolt. With Church support (and later French naval help) the revolt succeeded. Meanwhile, by land and sea, the Dutch were hitting Spain hard. While Tromp defeated the Spanish fleet in the English Channel, another Dutch fleet defeated an armada attempting the re-conquest of Brazil. In the north, France captured Roussillon in 1642 and in the following year won the glorious victory of Rocroi on the border of the Spanish Netherlands – a military equivalent of the defeat of the Armada at sea in 1588. The collapse of Spain, so long and miraculously postponed, had come at last. Olivares was dismissed and exiled to his estates. He died, out of his mind, two years later. His successor, Haro, swiftly and prudently restoring the old system of noble participation in government, did something to halt the downward slide for the moment. To revolt in Catalonia were added revolts in Sicily and Naples in 1647. But, as in the Netherlands, the ambiguity of aristocratic sympathies saved the day. The threat of popular disorder drove the nobles back to their norm of loyalty; the revolts were suppressed. Spanish authority survived. But not in Portugal. Having recovered Brazil from the Dutch in 1654, Portugal, whose union with Spain was comparatively recent and more purely dynastic, remained independent. The final reduction of Spain's boundaries and the severance of its close alliance with the Austrian Habsburgs were not made final until the Treaty of the Pyrénées in 1660. Spain's age of empire was at an end.

During the truce the new Dutch Republic passed through a perplexing period. Continued economic expansion was combined with a subtle but ferocious struggle for power between the states and the patrician rulers of the cities on one side and Prince Maurice, his Orangist supporters and the Calvinists on the other.

At the heart of growing economic prosperity lay the continued expansion of the Baltic trade, the main nerve of the overseas trading system. This, as we have seen, consisted of the exchange of a few basic commodities, large in bulk, carried cheaply and efficiently. Originally the bulk exchange had consisted of Baltic grain against Biscay salt; now steadily the range of goods widened until the Dutch were buying grain, timber, copper, hemp, flax, tallow, wax, honey, potash, skins and furs from a catchment area which included north Germany, Norway, Finland, Sweden, Poland, Lithuania and Russia, penetrating deeply into those countries. The outward cargoes were paid for by the import of Baltic salt, fish – particularly herrings caught in the controversial coastal areas off Scotland and England – cloth, spirits, beer, leather, sugar and a growing range of the new colonial products like spices and tobacco.

Meanwhile the republic equipped itself with a modern infrastructure of commerce and finance. The Amsterdam Exchange Bank dates from 1609 – the first clearing bank outside Italy and itself designed on the Venetian model. Its main tasks were to enable Dutch merchants to make their payments to each other by a simple book transfer, to exchange money and remedy the confusion that arose from the plethora of coins good and bad from the fourteen Netherland mints, to say nothing of a vast volume of foreign coins of varied provenance, quality and value. It did not do discount business or issue notes, nor (theoretically) did it at this stage lend money – that was the business of a separate Loan Bank. In 1611 it had already over seven hundred customers, Dutch and foreign, with deposits of a million guilders and it was growing fast. The Bank and the Stock Exchange, built in 1608–11, were the centre of a great financial system which by 1648 was to be the driving force behind a large proportion of world trade. Amsterdam, after an epic age of pile-driving, canal digging and building, was a new Venice.

The Dutch trading system was rapidly to become for foreigners the model of a perfect entrepôt trade. A much later description by Daniel Defoe could already apply.

The Dutch must be understood as ... the Carryers of the World, the Middle Persons in Trade, the Factors and Brokers of Europe ... they buy to sell again, *take* in to *send* out: and the Greatest Part of their vast commerce consists in being supply'd from all Parts of the World that they may supply all the World again.

They provided the links not only between the relatively advanced economies of the contemporary world but between the backward and the forward economies. In 1620 it was still the traditional trades – grain, timber, iron – which supplied capital and enterprise to the colonial and other trades. They financed the journeys to the Indies; they still accounted for half the $6\frac{1}{2}$ million guilders capital of the United East India Company of 1602, which combined and co-ordinated the efforts of previously separate companies. The work of unification was one of the contributions to the seventeenth-century Dutch miracle made by Oldenbarneveldt. The company was the most powerful force in European colonial expansion during the next two centuries. Trading in its shares quickly became an important activity on the Exchange. Among its early largest shareholders southern immigrants were important, as they were in the Baltic trade too. The largest trader in Swedish iron and copper was Louis de Geer, son of a former Liègeois merchant.

De Geer was characteristic of the Dutch style of overseas trader on the grand scale. He not only sold goods to Sweden. He secured Swedish mining concessions, and these became in turn the centre of a network of Swedish enterprises – timber-mills, foundries, warehouses, factories, stores wholesale and retail where the de Geer daughters sold pots, pans and cutlery over the counter. He advanced money to the Swedish king on the security of mining resources and taxes. In 1618 he made himself responsible to the States-General for the payment of interest by Gustavus Adolphus on a large loan for the ransom of the fortress of Elfsborg from the Danes. De Geer's largest rivals were the great Amsterdam family of Trip, whose portraits were painted by Rembrandt, Maes and other painters. Each European market had its Dutch specialists; like the de Geers they not only handled the trade in commodities but also often followed their capital into local markets; what de Geer and Trip were to Sweden, Marselis was to Russia and Denmark, Irgens to Norway, Meyers to Italy.

This was primarily a commercial economy; but commerce also fed and supplied substantial manufacturing industries in the republic, many also founded by enterprising southerners who had fled from the prospect of Spanish control. Leiden became the centre of the 'new draperies'. Haarlem imported rough German linens, bleached and finished them for domestic and export trade. Amsterdam had its distilleries, tobacco factories, sugar refineries, diamond-cutters and polishers, printers and book-binders. Zaandam, 'village of the carpenters', was the largest shipbuilding centre of Europe. All these industries flourished on the banks of the stream of goods that flowed in and out of the republic. And alongside trade and industry burgeoned the ancillary financial skills which were originally to serve and later to supplant them – marine insurance, life insurance, broking in goods, stocks and shares, commission business, pawnbroking, banking and lending in every form, discounting exchange and remittance business, speculations in goods, shares, even tulip bulbs. It is important to emphasize the predominantly *European* roots of the economy, for in Dutch (as in English) popular history the importance of colonial trading companies has sometimes loomed disproportionately large. Important they were, but the basic Dutch trade remained inter-European, and the great companies other than the East India Company were less successful – the West India Company markedly so. It was founded in 1621 by a strongly Calvinist group to fight and plunder Spain rather than carry on normal trade; its profits never equalled those of the East India Company on which it was modelled.

The men who conducted these expanding and varied businesses largely shaped also the fragmented, decentralized character of Dutch political institutions. Authority in the cities was in the hands of a relatively small, close-knit group of patrician families linked by trade and marriage. Many, down to the mid-century, were self-made merchants. Jacob Poppen, burgomaster of Amsterdam who died in 1624 leaving a fortune of nearly a million guilders, was a poor clerk's son. The republic was still a socially mobile place, still ruled by active merchants. This was especially true of the Province of Holland which provided more than half the Union's revenues: Amsterdam alone provided about a quarter.

These statistics did not make for good feeling. The other towns were jealous of Amsterdam, a late recruit to the rebellion as they remembered. The Holland Pensionary might be effectively candidate for political headship of the republic: he was rarely an Amsterdamer; his seat was at the Hague, where the Holland States and later the States-General met. Inevitably, the weight of money and influence gave the Holland States and Pensionary the strongest influence among the seven provinces. In neighbouring Zeeland there was also jealousy of Holland's power and strong loyalty and support for the Prince of Orange, who was proud of his titles as Lord of Flushing and Marquis of Veere. In more rural provinces, too, country gentry and minor nobles looked to the prince, if for no more elevated reason than that he was captain-general of the republic's army and navy. He would also be stadtholder in the majority of the provinces. The duties of this office were ill-defined but they still included rights of appointment to office and a general influence deriving from affection and reverence for William the Silent. Against this background of economic prosperity and unsolved problems of political authority brewed a theological dispute which was to help divide not only the republic but England too: 'a frantic endeavour of honest men to encompass divine mysteries within the narrow limits of human reason',[66] as one historian has called it.

In 1602 the University of Leiden offered one of its two chairs of theology to a scholar known for his learning and charity, with a European reputation already behind him: Arminius (Jacobus Hermans). The liberal-minded curators were not deterred by his confession that he disagreed with Calvin on points of doctrine. The occupant of the other chair was Gomarus, a ferociously orthodox Calvinist who did his best – successfully – to divide Leiden students on the issues raised by Arminius. 'An eternal and divine decree', cried Gomarus, 'has established which men are to be saved and which damned. As a result of this decree some are drawn towards faith and a God-fearing life, and, being drawn, preserved from falling back. All the others God leaves to the common corruption of human nature and to their own misdeeds.' Arminius could not agree:

God has of all eternity established this distinction among fallen humanity, that those who renounce their sins and place their trust in Christ are granted forgiveness of their sins and life eternal . . . Gomarus attributes to God the causes of sin . . . and hardens the hearts of men.

The issue was fundamental. As the rift deepened the States of Holland became alarmed. The theologians were ordered to keep the peace. In

1610 the followers of Arminius (he himself had died broken-hearted by the quarrels a year earlier) addressed a 'remonstrance' to the states denying that they intended any change of religion. The Gomarists replied with a counter-remonstrance. Henceforth the quarrel hardened into a party row between remonstrants and counter-remonstrants.

Its labyrinthine complexities need not detain us. The Arminians' arguments preserved a degree of humanist and humane dignity. They therefore won the general sympathy of the magistrate class of the cities who since 1565 and earlier had maintained a measure of tolerance – albeit often of an expedient kind – between extremes of Reformation and Counter-Reformation. Led by Oldenbarneveldt they were for freedom, peace and business – if possible. They were resolutely opposed by a curious combination of forces including the Calvinist ministers, an irreconcilable party of southern émigrés who saw the black hand of Spanish Popery in every deviation from Calvinist orthodoxy, and by another allied group (strong in Amsterdam) which thought there would be more profit in taking Spain's colonial trade away by force than by peaceful trade with her. The Calvinist ministers had great influence over the common people of dockside and warehouse; they did not hesitate to exploit nostalgic memories of William the Silent and the great national struggle with Spain. They were helped by the relaxation of Spanish pressure. As usual, wartime coalition tended to dissolve when the pressures which had created it relaxed.

By summer 1617 the quarrel was nation-wide. More serious, Prince Maurice now joined in. Since the last days of the Spanish war, the siege of Ostend and the failure to rally the south, he had nurtured a deep resentment against Oldenbarneveldt, so confident of his strength as leader of the Holland governors and their business-first political philosophy. Maurice stood in relation to the patrician class somewhat as a prince in a traditional European state might stand in relation to the nobility. He did not seriously contemplate trying to 'rule' against them. But he exploited every tactic to promote his standing with those who preferred to keep out of active politics (and they were certainly a majority) and to wreck Oldenbarneveldt's leadership. When Olden-barneveldt took powers to enable his supporters to raise a professional army, Maurice acted with military promptitude. He marched to the Brill, redolent of the Beggar origins of rebellion, and disbanded them. Then he seized on his remaining powers to appoint local magistrates to purge every local council of his opponents.

In August 1618 the old pensionary was himself arrested. His long trial was political in spirit and marred by vindictive bias. Maurice did not dictate the death sentence, but he refrained ostentatiously from giving the pardon that was in his power and he personally endorsed the illegal seizure of Oldenbarneveldt's property. The trial and execution of the man who did as much as any individual to create the republic was a blot on his character and career.

Having purged his hatreds, Maurice pressed matters no further. Maurice – the chess-player – 'had taken his opponent's piece, which was enough. He was not the enemy of the regents as a class'.[67] A few others were condemned to life imprisonment. Among them was one of the greatest Netherlanders of the age, Grotius. He made his escape from the Loevestein Castle hidden in a book-chest – a tale worthy of Dumas. A strong supporter of the states and their supremacy, he was typical of the regent class in its virtues and limitations. His base was originally narrow. His reputation as an international lawyer rested not least on his services to the East India Company. His brief in a case against the owners of a Portuguese ship became the great *De Jure Praedae* in which 'the doctrine of the freedom of the seas' was first expounded. It was a sustained, eloquent, closely reasoned argument that the seas, including the fisheries, were open to all nations and not subject to national attachment or sovereignty. This suited the Dutch, as newcomers and middlemen who fished, literally, in their neighbours' waters. The genius of Grotius raised the arguments above the prize courts, above many rancorous conferences (especially with the English and Scots whose lawyers, Selden and Welwood, argued for a *mare clausum*) on to a level of universal policy. Without Grotius, civilized international economic and political relations would have progressed more slowly. At home as abroad his efforts were directed towards peace. It was a tribute to his objectivity that the extreme Calvinists condemned his views as 'tridentine poperie'; episcopalians and right-wing Arminians denounced him as a Socinian. No man could wish higher praise.

Among his writings was a pamphlet in which he traced the antecedents of the Holland States back to the ancient Batavian republic, a reputedly freedom-loving, industrious, liberal (but loyal) tribe around which a romantic and significant myth was woven by Dutch writers and artists. National myths are a vital part of national growth. The Batavian myth was illuminating in its contrasts with the Elizabethan myth, which was personal, monarchic, and authoritarian; the Batavian myth was collective, moral and republican. It employed the genius not only of Grotius but of Rembrandt, an intellectual painter if ever there was one. His painting of the Batavian rebellion was commissioned for the new Town Hall at Amsterdam in 1648. Hooft, Dousa and Vondel were among the poets who devoted works to the Batavians. All were humanists; all protested against the brutal implications of dogmatic predestinarianism.

The connection is not fortuitous. Educated, reflecting men found repellent a form of religion which was daily becoming more narrow and sectarian, in the Holland of Gomarus and Voetius as in the England of William Perkins and 'the learned doctor' of Puritanism, William Ames (Amesius). Ames's fame spread throughout the Calvinists of the world through his interminable writings and ceaseless peregrinations. Disgruntled, officious and quarrelsome, he suffered agonies from the same frustrated ambitions which drove many a man to Calvinism. He cherished hopes of office at Cambridge. Disappointed, he set sail for Holland, only to be rejected by Leiden. Ames's godly thoughts now turned to more amenable flocks and greener pastures – perhaps in Virginia? He only got as far as Rotterdam, where he died of pneumonia. America, one feels, could spare him. As Professor Trevor-Roper has written, the great masters of early Calvinism were grim but there was an intellectual force and an heroic quality in their grimness which Perkins, Ames, Voetius and their generation did not achieve: 'The successors [of Calvin] are also grim, but they are grim and mean.'[68] Ames was both.

From 1619 to 1650 the republic was under Orangist rule. Yet the obscure quarrels of professors of theology meant nothing to Prince Maurice (who died in 1625), or his brother Frederick Henry (1625–47) or William II (1647–50). For Maurice, Gomarism was simply a convenient adhesive which helped to stick together the oddly assorted pieces of the Orange party. The opposition, without too much inconvenience, bided its time. Frederick Henry was, like his brother, an excellent soldier; like him he added new territory to the republic after the war with Spain was renewed with a flourish in 1621. The dynastic union with the Stuarts created by young William's marriage to Charles I's elder daughter Mary roused regent suspicions; but in 1650 William died suddenly and the regents came back in full force. The dictatorship of the Dutch middle classes was a hardy plant.

In France the accession of Henry IV had opened up hopes that the vast potential of wealth and power that was France might now be realized. His masterly grasp of administration immediately became evident – in his dealings with the nobles and the Huguenots; in his economic policy; in the planning of Paris as a great city, embellished by the Louvre, the Tuileries, the Pont-Neuf, the Hôtel de Ville and the Place Royale; in the organization of the army and the management of foreign policy. He was helped by comrades of proven loyalty, first among them Maximilian, Duc de Sully. Henry kept his Council small and orderly: personal knowledge and trust was the secret of his success. Even his economic 'programme' was the province of his former valet, Barthelmy de Laffemas, an ideas man who presided over an economic council, a ginger-group which was said to have held 150 meetings between 1602 and 1604. It interviewed prospective entrepreneurs, considered vast drainage schemes, new canal-building, new industries – silk, glass, metal, porcelain – and discussed the grievances put forward in the *cahiers* presented to the Estates-General. How much ginger it managed to inject into the economic life of France is uncertain: it certainly let in fresh air and new ideas – a welcome change from the stale repetition of bullionist, restrictive legislation that invariably occupied the time of the Estates-General.

The moving spirit of Henry's administration was Sully, a typical member of the *noblesse d'épée*. More than any other minister, he helped to consolidate the king's absolute authority over France. His work divided into two halves: the first, for which he became most famous (or notorious) was his reform of the royal finances by which a credit surplus was created – the only time this happened between the sixteenth century and the reforms of Colbert; the second was the training of a corps of administrators and engineers who in their turn built or restored the network of roads and bridges without which France could remain only a congeries of provinces. As a soldier and a sapper Sully knew how much bad communications had contributed to the separatism exploited by men like Montmorency-Damville in Languedoc, Provence and Dauphiné and the Guises in the north and east of France. A Calvinist, he did not allow religion to interfere with the easy virtue of his private life, of which it was remarked that it was no better than that of his master. Yet he had seen too much of the horrors of civil war and the ruthless selfishness of the noble factions not to remain a stout and genuine patriot.

A generation that can look down from the air upon the rich pattern of agrarian France is better able to appreciate its potentialities than contemporaries, to whom seventeenth-century France often seemed a synonym for rural poverty and discontent. The reasons were not far to seek; they were infinitely difficult to tackle. Population at more than twenty millions was far the largest *national* population in Europe (compared with, say, England's 4–5, Spain's 6–7, the Netherlands' 2–3 millions): more to the point, its density – in places 100 per square mile – was only exceeded in the Netherlands and in parts of north Italy. In the northern plain, French agriculture depended on a single crop: grain. Crop failure meant famine, and the failure rate seems to have been unnaturally high between 1599 and 1640. The population was largely rural and sedentary: only a score of towns could boast more than ten thousand. Here was the largest floating mass of gypsies, whores and vagrants. Manufactures were widespread but generally crude and archaic, communications poor. How did France not merely survive but maintain its great traditions of civilization? Its strength, Pierre Goubert has said, 'lay in its having remained a populous productive society.'[69] But its peasantry carried a heavy burden, sustaining a privileged elite and a costly government by means of a tax system which grew heavier and more inequitable each year. Yet French society held together, as did English, by an instinctive acceptance of the value of the mutual services of lords and villagers.

Henry himself had no illusions. The image of the popular hero was useful. But he knew that to many Frenchmen he was still the enemy: to pious Catholics a renegade Protestant; to many Huguenots a traitor to their faith; to the peasantry he represented only bigger taxes; and many disbelieved in the legitimacy of his claim to the throne.

Knowing these things, Henry remained vigilant. There were said to be 3500 castles in France where opposition might be brewing. When the conspiracy of Biron broke out in 1602 it was a factious, specious alliance of the Catholic Maréchal de Biron and the Huguenot leader the Duc de Bouillon, with Spain and her vassal, Savoy. Henry struck hard. Many conspirators escaped, but Biron was executed, despite his birth and military distinction. For months Henry travelled incessantly, destroying the castles of his enemies and executing the friends of conspiracy. The execution of Biron had re-activated the bitter hatreds, festering jealousies and blood-lusts only recently and superficially stilled.

On Friday, 14 May 1610, as he was sitting in his coach, Henry was stabbed by a fanatical Catholic, Ravaillac. Like Elizabeth, Coligny,

William of Orange, Henry III, even James I, whose lives were threatened, Henry was a victim of the new doctrine of the justice of tyrannicide subscribed to by both Calvinist political thinkers and Catholics like Mariana and Bellarmine. He had suffered in all twenty attempts on his life. The result of this final and successful attempt was ultimately France's acceptance of absolutism as the only solution to the problem of government.

In the years 1610–60, the internal history of France has indeed a *déjà vu* quality. The intrigues of yet another Florentine queen mother, Marie de Medici, during a minority (that of the Bourbon Louis XIII) constantly echo the anarchic weaknesses of France in the 1560s and 1570s. The regency of the Spanish Anne of Austria between 1643 and 1660 during Louis XIV's minority was to echo that of Marie. Similarly, the continued turbulence of the nobles looked back to the previous century, though the leading sources of mischief were now less the Guises and more the Montmorencys with Henri, Prince of Condé, as chief conspirator. The 'political Huguenots' were still immensely powerful in the persons of the Duc de Bouillon in the north and the Seigneur de Soubise, leader of the stronghold of Protestantism at La Rochelle, as the symbols of Huguenot resistance for the west. There was still much truth in the dictum attributed later to Richelieu that the Huguenots shared the government of France with the king. In some respects the situation seemed as bad as it had been during the Wars of Religion – perhaps even worse. Her external enemies seemed as powerful as ever.

After the strange confusions of the imperial incumbency of the eccentric Rudolf II, and the aged and indecisive Matthias, there had appeared another Habsburg of rigorous convictions. Ferdinand II succeeded to his hereditary dominions in 1596. His first action was to suppress Protestantism in Styria, Carinthia and Carniola. In Bavaria Maximilian did the same. In Poland, the succession of Sigismond had led to similar results. The old hopes that Poland might devise some kind of religious settlement faded rapidly. The nobles had swiftly reverted to orthodoxy and here, as in Germany and Austria, the Jesuits won back a large following for the Church.

At its head now stood Paul V, not the most pious or high-minded of Popes but determined to lose no trick in the diplomatic game of consolidating his friends and allies. Increasingly France faced the possibility that the nightmare of a Spanish–Austrian Habsburg alliance might –

after a long interval when successive Emperors had cold-shouldered Spanish approaches – become a reality. Spain, still rich and prestigious despite the apparently irresistible forces of decadence at work in her economy and administration, was increasingly convinced that only a Catholic Habsburg victory in Germany could break the deadlock created by Maurice of Nassau's solid strategic position in the Dutch Republic. Already, in 1609, the important dispute over the succession to the Jülich-Cleve duchies had found the Habsburgs together on the side of the Catholic claimant, while the Protestant princes of Germany, the Dutch and Henry IV were grouped in support of his opponent. Despite a Spanish invasion of the duchies in 1614 by the great general and victor of Ostend, Spinola, peace was in the end preserved. But the political alignments were sinister, reflecting on the larger canvas of Europe the groupings already formed in Germany: for a Calvinist Union of 1608 had been closely followed by a Catholic League in the following year. The growing Protestant weakness was underlined by the cordial hatred between Lutherans and Calvinists (who had no status under the Augsburg Settlement of 1555). The Elector Palatine, the leading Calvinist German prince, and the Rhineland Calvinists in general, with the great Protestant free cities, were therefore threatened by Spain in the west, by Bavaria in the south and – if the Austrian Habsburgs should move into an aggressive stance – by Austria and the Imperial lands farther south-east. In the southern Netherlands, the truce allowed a breathing-space during which the new government of the archdukes managed not only to enforce Catholic orthodoxy but gave some encouragement to economic revival, and – miracle of miracles – even balanced the military costs of the Flanders Army for the first (and only) time in history.

To the Spaniards, the control of their supply route from the south was the perpetual theme of policy; their minds dwelt closely on the north Italy – Valtelline – Alsace – Palatinate route. This was essential to Spanish victory over the Dutch – still the ultimate aim. But the French were equally sensitive to its importance for them: if the control of the route did fall to Spain, the threat of encirclement by her and her growing band of potential Catholic allies would be enormously increased. Hence the vital implications of the Secret Treaty of 1617 whereby Spain would have control of Alsace if the Archduke Ferdinand became Emperor.

The darkening scene in Europe had no visible effect on the political gyrations of the Court nobility. The noble habit of preferring ambition to patriotism became ingrained from the Guises in the 1560s to Louis of Condé and Turenne in the seventeenth century. The climax of faction, the Princes' Fronde of 1652, ended by Condé joining France's enemy, Spain, and openly carrying on war on her behalf for eight years.

The very idea of a unified France under a monarchy commanding national allegiance is, in a sense, anachronistic in the context of the noble ethos. In France as elsewhere, the equilibrium that was the essence of feudal arrangements, the division of power and property between sovereign and noble subject, was at best precarious. Selfish ambitions, inevitable frictions, mingled with genuine doubts of princes and queens who were themselves as much Italian or Spanish as French, among a noble class which was itself international by reason of dynastic marriage and connection.

The seven years of Marie de Medici's regency inaugurated four decades during which, spasmodically, the monarchy and its ministers were targets for attack by noble faction. She was herself vain, bad-tempered and impressionable. Her favourites were Italian adventurers who provided a plausible excuse for the rebellions of Condé, Vendôme and the rest. Noble revolt in Brittany led to the last meetings of the Estates-General of 1614 and 1615. Internal quarrels between the Estates made them a by-word for impotence and absurdity: yet no king dared to summon them again until the *ancien régime* was nearly at its end. One reason for this may be found in the *cahiers de doléances* – lists of grievances presented to the Estates-General by many interests and groups from different regions of France. Well over half of these arose, directly or indirectly, from the burdens of taxation upon the non-noble bourgeois and peasant orders. The rebuilding of France as a great power – which was in due course to bring her vast honour – seemed, for the moment, to pile only vast material burdens on her ordinary people. Robert Miron, later to be Intendant of Languedoc, told the Estates-General of 1614 that they should remember that it was the peasants who fed France: 'You spend your lives in daring escapades, gluttony, extravagance, acts of violence both public and private . . . If Your Majesty does not grant relief, things could reach a point where these deprived people will open their eyes and suddenly realise that a soldier is simply a peasant with a weapon in his hand.'[70]

Into a political *mêlée* devoid of any discernible rational object except the Huguenot desire to retain the freedom granted by Henry IV came one of the most ruthless figures of the age: Armand Jean du Plessis de Richelieu, a member of an ancient family of Poitevin minor nobility and, since 1607, Bishop of Luçon. As an elected clerical member of the Estates-General of 1614, he attracted the attention of Marie de Medici. To her, until the inevitable rift some sixteen years later, Richelieu owed everything, including his cardinalate of 1622. It was 1624 before he joined the royal council, but the ten-year delay was not wasted. It gave him time to master the geography of the labyrinthine corridors of power that surrounded the French monarchy: to know, so far as it was possible, the odd, secretive, ailing, melancholy king whose real passions were hunting and warfare.

Louis XIII cordially disliked his new minister, who alternately cajoled and lectured him. Yet he was intelligent enough to know that Richelieu was indispensable. His very presence was awe-inspiring: his face and body pale and wasted, his manner austere and forbidding. He was emotional, temperamental, melancholy. He was accused of being greedy and mean, and it was true that he raised himself to great material as well as political eminence. His three private palaces were the scene of lavish hospitality and munificient patronage of the arts and letters. His fortune became enormous and he married his nephews and nieces into the most important families of France. In the last years of his life he was said to be richer than the Prince of Orange (then reckoned the richest prince in Europe).

In contrast to his public image, his personal life could hardly have been more frugal. His acquisitiveness was a secondary and acquired trait – a function of his belief that his power could only be established and stabilized on the basis of great property. This, like his religion, his immense will-power and cold courage, was only a means to the one end for which he cared: the welfare of France. To promote this he sat endlessly at the centre of the web of spies and informers which he patiently spun to help him get and keep power. Between him and the king's dissolute and intriguing brother Gaston d'Orléans and the powerful Montmorency clan there was continuous, vicious struggle for power.

Richelieu did not spare his exertions in denouncing and, when necessary, destroying his noble enemies at Court. Of all the meaningless feuds Richelieu set out to quash – the Vendôme conspiracy, the Rohan rebellion, the conspiracy of Chalais, the Day of Dupes, de Marillac's plot – the razing of Languedoc in 1632 by Henri de Montmorency for Orléans was the climax. Montmorency was duly executed.

Orléans, for whom Montmorency had plotted, lived to renew his treachery in 1636 and 1641. The proclamations of Orléans, Soissons, Guise, Cinq Mars and Bouillon reveal the conservative, almost mindless nostalgia that animated them; the ideal of a Golden Age where feudal privilege would be preserved, even while feudalism was crumbling away.

Richelieu faced the hostility of others besides the nobility. Lawyers, town magistrates, even royal officials and craftsmen joined in. In 1630 Provence had a full-scale revolt against new indirect taxes on wine and the increase of the *taille*. From 1627 bad harvests led to famine, and outbreaks of plague made matters worse. To the growing burden of taxes was added another tribulation which fell heavily on the poor – the billeting of soldiers, often violent and rapacious. Through the 1630s these general revolts against government spread throughout the west and south of France. They involved all classes. Nobles and gentry were accused of inciting the people to refuse to pay their taxes. The violence of risings like those of the *croquants* in the south-west, the *cascavéoux* of Provence (called after their emblem, a little bell on a white ribbon) or the *nu-pieds* of Normandy was immediate and basic. There was no theology in it – as there had been in the German peasant revolts.

The Normandy troubles led by the *nu-pieds* were typical. The risings round Avranches, Caen, Coutances and Rouen followed many years of repeated plague. Farmers and workers died, animals were lost, crops abandoned. The violence was that of men and women driven desperate by hunger. Their hero was 'Jean Nu-Pieds', an imaginary peasant whose pamphlets raised five or six thousand followers drawn from the minor gentry, priests and peasantry. But the causes, like the objectives, of revolt were simple: Normandy was the most heavily taxed area of France, paying one-sixth of the total *taille*. It was no accident that Normandy was to be a chief centre of the Fronde troubles.

It is not easy to define precisely the 'tyranny' against which these risings were directed. They were not 'class' struggles. The *châteaux* were not their target: indeed the leaders often included hard-pressed members of the gentry who sided with the poor and gave them support, protection and shelter. The hatred of Court favourites, the domination of Paris, new taxation – such are the grievances most often mentioned. The areas worst affected were the poor lands of the west and south, where smallholdings were most common, or areas worst hit by tax increases. The collection of the tax by *intendants*, who made contracts with tax-farmers, resulted in grossly unequal burdens between one area and another.

Richelieu himself thoroughly disliked and distrusted the petty nobility and bourgeoisie whose rise through state and municipal office was such a characteristic feature of seventeenth-century France. He had little time for the army of bureaucrats and contractors who were already growing fat on the administrative and fiscal system necessary to raise the public credit and support the army and the war. He would have despised officials like Le Tellier of Rouen, the local collector of the wine and salt taxes of Normandy who was a typical target for the *nu-pieds*. On the other hand, he could proclaim his fundamental belief that the *nobility* were a main artery of the state, an indispensable element in the reconstruction and preservation of France, the wickedness of the Montmorencys notwithstanding. Here he approached – in theory at least – the sentiments of the rebels themselves. In the last resort they wanted, not revolution, but the good old days of order, stability and predictability.

There the resemblance and the sympathy ended. The revolts had to be smashed. Paris was frightened that they might encourage Spain – or even England, for English designs on Normandy were still a real anxiety – to foment full-scale revolution in France (they had already hampered military operations towards the Spanish frontier). Even disregarding foreign complications, the combination within France of noble and popular resistance was a dangerous thing. With the same pitiless ferocity that destroyed the Huguenots at La Rochelle, razed scores of feudal castles, liquidated Montmorency, Cinq Mars, the king's young favourite and fifty other high nobles, Richelieu extinguished the *nu-pieds* at Avranches in 1639.

For all this one justification only was needed – the safety of France. For this – if necessary – princes and nobles must be killed, queens, former friends and patrons exiled, rebels slaughtered, potential nests of treachery burnt out.

The internal security of France and the suppression of all domestic enemies was only half of Richelieu's task; the other half was to counter the threat from her foreign enemies: the Habsburgs. To both Richelieu brought a dedication that left him without a rival among the proconsuls of seventeenth-century Europe. Louis XIII was not a cipher. He was intelligent enough to realize that he was incapable of embodying in his own person the French state. For that he needed the indestructible

energies of Richelieu, the racing imagination that could gut the mountains of paperwork and shape out of it – sometimes as much by intuition
as by administrative expertise – policies, decisions and actions. With
him stood Father Joseph, the Capuchin monk also of noble descent, a
polymath who acted as his *chef de cabinet* and headed his master's vast
network of spies and agents.

It would be wrong to conclude that private ambition or public
aggression motivated Richelieu's policies. The Court, France and
Europe that were their context were jungles: he countered their continuous menace to himself, the monarchy and his country by developing
the instinctive cunning and unceasing vigilance that kept him always
ready to strike, without warning or delay. Almost alone among the
statesmen of this age, he never hesitated. Without Richelieu's work,
neither Henry IV nor Ravaillac's dagger could have produced the
absolutism of the later Ancien Régime.

It was characteristic of Richelieu's high sense of responsibility and
firm grasp of political realities that his last act was to ensure continuity
of policy after his death. The day after he died (4 December 1642) a
royal letter went to all officials ordering them to report to his successor.
A former Papal diplomat of Sicilian origin who had accepted Richelieu's
offer of high office in France, Jules Mazarini (Mazarin) had been
rewarded with new responsibilities and recent promotion to the rank
of cardinal. Now by a smooth transference of power he was acknowledged as supreme minister.

In one sense, Richelieu's choice showed excellent judgment. Mazarin
was a superb performer on the international diplomatic stage: here he
extrapolated successfully most of Richelieu's own policies. At home,
where men saw him at closer quarters, he bore examination much less
well. He had neither the personal dedication nor the commanding personality of his master. His nepotism sprang solely from personal greed.
His wily intrigues, like those of his disastrous fellow-Italians, the
Medici, were transparently selfish and short-sighted. The continuance
and escalation of war made further taxation inevitable: the increase of
the *taille* from 4·5 million under Louis XIII to 55 million under Mazarin
was not wholly the fault of Mazarin; nor was the system of tax-farming,
which he inherited from Richelieu and Sully. But Mazarin not only
failed to check the abuses in the collection of these increased burdens:
he made no effort whatever to dispel the growing impression that, but
for the corruption which surrounded him as supreme minister, such

increases would have been avoided. Even the wide and increasing powers of the *intendants*, the centrally appointed royal officials whose basic duty was to eradicate the corruption of local officers, became themselves associated with the growth of nepotism and corruption, not with its abolition.

When Louis XIII died (14 May 1643) it was confidently expected that the queen-mother would be regent and, once in office, get rid of Mazarin. In this expectation the *Parlement* of Paris appointed her regent-absolute with the minimum of argument. Their hopes were quickly disappointed. Mazarin had played his cards skilfully with the queen. He stayed in power, surrounding Anne with his chosen minions. The policy proved short-sighted. On all sides – among nobles, bourgeoisie, the professions and the peasantry – resentment grew. To be fair to Mazarin it must be said that it was during these years that his major efforts were bent towards securing a peace in Europe which would give France the best terms that could be won; and that – as Richelieu had found – the nobility were less interested in the welfare of France in Europe than in the welfare of the nobility in France. Yet if true statesmanship consists of a total view of politics, Mazarin fell a long way short. Steadily he managed to isolate himself and the queen-regent not only from the Court but from the *Parlement*, the embodiment (at its best) of those concepts of legality which were necessarily opposed to the irresponsible extension of royal power and the arbitary behaviour of its bureaucracy.

As a foreigner, Mazarin was now blamed for the financial chaos into which France had drifted in the five years of his supremacy. Where Richelieu had governed with the support of a king of age, skilfully isolating his adversaries, his successor's support rested on a queen-regent and a minor only. He had indeed managed to unify politically a congeries of interests which had in reality little or nothing in common. In the spring of 1648 he announced that the *paulette* (by which officials were allowed, on payment of a fine, to hand on their offices to their heirs or appointees) would be renewed for nine years, while four years' salary would be withheld from the great officers of state. The storm broke. The *Parlement*, though itself exempted from the new penalties, associated itself with the victims' protests and launched a comprehensive attack on the whole financial system. Defying the royal prohibition, they claimed the right to vote all new taxes, and protested against the suppression of traditional liberties. Paris, seeing itself the sponge for a government which could squeeze the countryside no more, rose in a revolt which developed into civil war lasting four years.

The Fronde remains one of the most puzzling phenomena of early modern history in France. It represented, without doubt, many different trends and facets. In one respect it continued the endemic protest against increasing taxation. It was also a protest against Mazarin himself. More impalpably, it was a conservative protest of traditional groupings against the apparent infringement of their privileges by novel and growing central bureaucracy. And in all these respects it bears some comparison with earlier revolts in the Netherlands, Spain, Portugal, Sicily – even with the contemporary revolution in England. Yet it was, in precise terms, independent and unique. Despite some modern-sounding portents of radicalism, the Frondeurs never had any defined or unified ends or policies. It was, as E. H. Kossmann has said, neither parliamentary nor popular nor feudal. It remains an interlude 'of imprudence and exaggeration without meaning or objective'.[71]

Previous upheavals in France had brought into play one or more of the political elements in French society: noble, professional, legal, bourgeois, artisan, peasant, Protestant, Catholic. Now all these lost their delicate social equilibrium and chaos followed. But just because there was no focus around which a unified opposition could cluster, the Fronde posed a smaller threat to order than the Wars of Religion, when noble groups aligned themselves on religious or pseudo-religious principles with sympathetic foreign backing. The Fronde pointed in no direction: 'It added nothing to history.'[72]

14

FROM BÍLÁ HORA TO WESTPHALIA:
THE WIDENING CONFLICT

Many periods of modern history have been dominated by plans of conquest devised by Titans who ended nevertheless as the defeated prisoners of circumstances. During the wars that lasted from 1618 to 1648 and after, no single figure appeared to command the destinies of Europe. Those who looked as if they might were struck down before their dreams were realized; most of the rest were of only local or passing importance. The age was not one of Napoleonic figures; but it too was marked by the same sense of nemesis which invariably dogs the careers of great conquerors. Once the Emperor Matthias had left Prague and his appointed regents had been thrown from the window of the chancery in the Hradčany, the European political system was steadily revealed as a mechanism of interlocking parts. Many of the local components of conflict were already present: in the west the Eighty Years' War between Spain and – by now – the North Netherlands Republic, was half a century old, and only suspended since 1609. In Germany the bitter rift between the Catholic and Protestant states had grown wider as the forces of the Counter-Reformation advanced unchecked and assumed an increasingly sinister aspect with the formal alignment of the two sides into the Protestant Union and Catholic League of 1608 and 1609. France, still distracted by political and religious faction, was slowly re-creating order within her boundaries. Her statesmen and soldiers watched anxiously the continued aggressive strategy of Spain and, with the rise of resolute champions of the Counter-Reformation like Ferdinand of Styria and Maximilian of Bavaria, were increasingly compelled to ponder the threat to France of the Spanish–

Austrian Habsburg alliance hitherto postponed by the reluctance of the Austrian branch to be dragged into conflicts even more complex and expensive than those forced on them by their Central and Eastern European commitments – especially the continuing threat from the Turks. In Northern Europe, strategy was dominated by the rivalry – dynastic and economic – between Denmark and Sweden, control of the lucrative Sound Toll being a prize of increasing value. Sweden was also involved in a perpetual struggle with Poland for the border province of Livonia.

Everywhere the northern Protestants watched carefully the growing power of the German Catholic states, and with it the growing threat to their interests on the south shores of the Baltic. The ancient Danish–Swedish rivalry, rarely without ardent champions, now found two of unequalled valour. The long reign of Christian iv of Denmark (1577–1648) may not have been marked by conspicuous statesmanship, but as a king he was as much to the taste of the Danes as Henry iv was to the taste of the French. A prince of the Empire, he married first the daughter of the Margrave of Brandenburg and then acquired the succession to the secularized north German bishoprics of Bremen and Werden for his son, Frederick. His rival for the Protestant leadership, ultimately successful, was Gustavus Adolphus of Sweden, whom Christian brought to heel in the so-called 'Kalmar War' which was ended by the Treaty of Knäred in 1613. Here in the north was another of the many flashpoints in the Europe of the second decade of the seventeenth century, all connected by a combustible trail of religious, dynastic, political, and social powder, much of it long smouldering and ready to ignite. All that was needed was a hand to apply the match.

It came from an unexpected quarter and by an unexpected concatenation of events: the Kingdom of Bohemia, whose situation needs to be examined before the events can be analyzed. The lands ruled by the King of Bohemia contained in the late sixteenth century (when in 1576 they became the chosen seat of the Emperor Rudolf ii) some four million people. They consisted of Bohemia proper, with its brilliant capital, Prague; Moravia, Upper and Lower Silesia, and the two provinces of Lusatia bordering on Saxony. The bonds between these different territories were slender and obscure: as obscure as their relationship to the Empire itself – by no means a unique circumstance. Some of their people, in Bohemia and Moravia, were Slav-speaking; others, in Silesia and Lusatia, spoke German. The claim of the

Habsburgs to the Bohemian territories – like their claims in Hungary and Poland – were complex and disputable. But a few points were clear. The Bohemian lands were the most densely populated, and by some criteria the most wealthy and industrious area in Central Europe. They were therefore crucial to the one undisputed role out of all the confused and decaying functions of the Imperial office: the defence of the land frontier against the Turk. And the 1580s and 1590s saw a revival of crusading ideas fostered from a variety of sources – Poland, Moscow, and especially from Persia, where the Shah Abbas did his best to draw the willing but largely impotent Emperor into his grand strategy against the Turk. Mineral deposits, such as the silver mines at Jáchymov (Joachimsthal) and elsewhere, were, together with princely rights to taxation, the most common collateral for public loans in this age where the Emperors, like all other princes, were caught in the combined grip of rising costs, inflation and falling real income.

Bohemia was a relatively advanced economy; yet in the early seventeenth century it was not as rich as it sometimes looked. Mining output and profits were not what they had been earlier in the sixteenth century. After the Hussite moves against the feudal order, the great magnates had won back much of their earlier strength, reducing the knights and lesser nobility to dependence – often in the offices of bailiff or steward of great estates. Yet even the great nobles, here as elsewhere, were hit by economic difficulties. Their peasantry, unlike other areas of Eastern and Central Europe, were not yet servile: the great demesnes were worked by paid labour; peasants still marketed their own produce; free-holding yeomen survived.

The Prague of the late sixteenth century shown in the contemporary prints of Hogenberg and other topographers was a great and proud city of fifty thousand or so people. Rich in trade, its great houses, churches and towers, above all the Hradčany – a hilltop complex of castle, palaces, cathedral all in one – were a reminder of its greatness in the days of Charles iv of Luxembourg. But now the richest nobles were new men, like Albrecht Wallenstein (of the old Czech family of Vald-štejn), who knew how to combine the talents of soldier, politician and entrepreneur, recruiting the skilled business advice of the Netherlander Hans de Witte and the Jewish financiers, Mordechai Meizl and Jakob Bassevi, to sustain and expand his private fortune (in circumstances which impoverished other families, however richly endowed, who deluded themselves that wealth looked after itself). Thus passed away great Czech families like the Pernšteins, Boskovic, Rožmberks, Hradec and Žerotín. That Bohemia suffered its share of economic tensions seems likely. Yet they were less obvious and immediate than those which sprang from religion. The Hussite movement had broken Bohemia off quite decisively from the Catholic Europe of its day. Czechs became fiercely anti-Papal, anti-clerical fundamentalists. The Lutheran reforms had left them still more Hussite than new-style Protestants, as the emergence of the sect calling itself the Czech Brethren demonstrated. Rudolf's relatively liberal policies had allowed (Catholics said, encouraged) them to multiply. To the orthodox, Bohemia had become a sanctuary for heresy. By 1600, Catholics numbered perhaps only 10 per cent of the population. The great majority of the people of the Bohemian lands – especially in Moravia and Bohemia proper – were 'Protestants' or dissenters of some kind. Their religious liberties were guaranteed by Rudolf's Letter of Majesty of 1609. By contrast, down to the 1580s, the position of the Catholics deteriorated. A combination of Papal agents, Jesuits and a few devoted Catholic nobles like George Lobkovic and Vilém Rožmberk had done their best to give momentum to the Counter-Reformation. But Tridentine progress was slow. Even among the great Czech families who held the highest offices at the Court of Rudolf, the strongest body of opinion was for moderation in religious and foreign policy.

The key to this continuance of pre-Reformation, pre-Counter-Reformation policies of moderation lay less in the constitution of the Empire, a triumph of legalism and anarchy, than in the still powerful *concept* of empire that still gripped men's imaginations and was symbolized, however strangely, by the Emperor himself. Rudolf was neither mad nor negligible. He was a chronic melancholic whose weakness led him (according to Rudolf's confessor and friend, the scholar Pistorius) into strange paths of occultism and finally to his almost complete withdrawal from the world. Comenius also recorded that in his declining years Rudolf hoped to crown and confirm the uneasy religious peace his Letter of Majesty had achieved by founding a 'society of peace' to guard the principle and practice of freedom of consience in Bohemia. The lack of support he received, from Catholic and Protestant nobles alike, provoked the Emperor's famous curse on the city of Prague and its people.

Whether this meandering idealism was evidence of unusual breadth of vision or of psychotic instability is something for the psychoanalysts to ponder. To some extent Rudolf was the victim of an age itself tortured by the psychological problems of metamorphosis from the intellectual compendiousness of the Middle Ages to the sharp and bitter compartmentalization, by creed and subject, of the new age. His court and interests reflected the conflict.

In the arts, as in the sciences, the influence of Italy and the Netherlands especially was reflected in the splendid pageantry with which Rudolf surrounded himself. The catholicity of his taste embraced favourites as varied as Tintoretto and Pieter Breughel. From the Netherlands Rudolf drew into his circle Adriaen de Vries, a pupil of Bologna and the creator of the bust which conveys most vividly the commanding imperial presence, the great leonine head and Habsburg jaw that instilled not only respect but fear into his enemies. His favourite landscape artist was Roelant Savery, another Netherlander. The most extraordinary portrait of Rudolf was Giuseppe Arcimboldo's *Rudolf II as Vertumnus* which showed – apparently to the Emperor's satisfaction – Rudolf as the God of the changing seasons, not merely bedecked but incorporating in his person a rich abundance of fruit and flowers.[73] All these foreign artists – painters, sculptors, architects, workers in precious stones, gold and silversmiths – contributed much to the Mannerism and incipient Baroque of Bohemia; yet in the cosmopolitan Rudolfine court and its universal culture they mingled freely with local artists, exchanging and developing ideas and styles. The greatest Czech seventeenth-century painter, Karel Skréta, was the son of the Emperor's book-keeper whose earliest inspiration came from court models.

It was all too good to last in a world of bitter confessional and, increasingly, national strife. The Letter of Majesty was itself a principal source of controversy. As Rudolf more and more fell victim to the withdrawal symptoms long evident in his personality, he handed over Austria and Hungary to his brother Matthias, whom he cordially distrusted and detested. In 1611 he was deposed as King of Bohemia and succeeded by his brother. He died the following year. But Matthias was an old man without children; who would succeed him? It was time for another of those historical flukes which later generations take for granted. In Hungary and Bohemia, opposition to Ferdinand, noble and Protestant, was intense. His elimination of Protestantism in his hereditary duchies had been as ruthless as it was efficient. The very nature of Rudolfine Bohemia, universalist and heretical, was an offence to him. Yet the estates of Hungary at Pressburg elected and crowned him as

Matthias's successor without a murmur. At Prague in 1617 the estates were equally taken by surprise. Without question, Ferdinand was crowned King of Bohemia, swearing to observe the Royal Charter and thus pacifying the Protestants and contenting that middle party which had been the main prop of Rudolf's moderation. But no sooner was the election over than it was disowned and the Protestant nobles, led by Count Henry of Thurn, petitioned the Emperor for satisfaction. Failing to get it, they seized the royal regents and threw them out of the chancery window. This was the famous 'Defenestration of Prague', and it was all that was needed to begin the chain-reaction of conflict known as the Thirty Years' War.

The Bohemian nobles, like their predecessors in revolt in the Netherlands, England, Sweden, Spain and Portugal, were ill-prepared and unconstructive. They had little money, no army, no programme and no clear justificatory constitutional principles. That their instincts were correct – that in Ferdinand they had come to the end of an era – was true but, in a world of power politics, not enough. The news from Prague however immediately brought into play willing helpers who saw rich pickings in this rebuff to the Emperor and Ferdinand, themselves almost as resourceless as Thurn and his allies. Charles Emmanuel of Savoy, the old enemy of the Habsburgs, seeing his chance, secretly opened negotiations to persuade the young lion of Protestantism to take on the leadership of the cause of Bohemia and European Protestantism. Frederick v, Elector Palatine, had succeeded his father, a drunken debauchee, in 1610. But, like his grandfather Frederick III, he was a zealous and militant Calvinist, leader of the new German Protestant Union and recently married to the beautiful Elizabeth, daughter of King James of England.

When Mansfeld, the first of the ruthless military adventurers who were to mangle Europe in the next decade, arrived in Bohemia in the autumn of 1618 with an army of two thousand troops, it was commonly supposed that he came to represent Frederick, and with England's blessing. This was untrue, but it was enough to encourage Silesia to throw in another three thousand men to help Bohemia. Mansfeld was victorious over the poorly led and worse equipped Imperial army. When Matthias died, Ferdinand faced an apparently hopeless military and political crisis. The Bohemian lords were solid against him and the largely Protestant nobility of Austria now joined them as Thurn prepared for the inevitable *coup de grâce* against Vienna. The inevitable did not materialize. Ferdinand was deficient in many human qualities: courage was not among them. Faced with total disaster, he showed a resigned yet active bravery that would have done justice to William the Silent: 'If it be God's will, let me perish in the struggle.'

On this occasion the Lord of Battles arranged for the immediate arrival of a regiment of loyal cavalry. Thurn and his generals, Mansfeld and Hohenlohe, were defeated: Vienna was relieved. Two months later, Ferdinand was unanimously elected Holy Roman Emperor, a victory of resolution over the undignified confusion of the Calvinist and Lutheran electors. But then, on 25 September 1619, Frederick formally acccptcd the Crown of Bohemia, of which Ferdinand had been deprived a month earlier, and with all solemn pomp was crowned in the cathedral of Prague.

It was a rash business. Frederick did it in the face of the urgings of his best advisers. Political judgment – indeed judgment of any kind – had never been a strong suit of the elector's family. He was probably sincere in seeing himself as God's chosen instrument for the deliverance of Protestantism. Alas! He was in no position to deliver Bohemia or even himself. His action did nothing for Protestantism; once faced by demands for money, troops and diplomatic support, Frederick's supporters melted away like snow. His Scottish father-in-law indignantly repudiated any idea that he was privy to Ferdinand's act (for was he not at this very moment deeply obsessed with his plan for a marriage between the Prince of Wales and the Spanish Infanta Maria?). In any case, no greater personal contrast was imaginable than that between James, the ultimate in ratiocination, and the brainless Frederick. If Elizabeth had budged in favour of the rebel Dutch only after twenty years of procrastination, was it likely that James (who shared all his predecessor's hatred of rebellion) would help the Bohemian rebels overnight? Worse than that, the deposition of Ferdinand in Bohemia polarized the scattered forces of conflict into two groups more clearly defined than ever before.

Spain had already come to Ferdinand's help with an army under the Spanish general Bucquoi; and Ferdinand's firmness of purpose had, for once, proved that Spain's new protégé was worthy of confidence. It rapidly became clear that Savoy and the German Lutheran princes were a broken reed. The Elector of Saxony, in particular, refused to be drawn into any of Christian of Anhalt's proposed war-conferences. Bethlen Gabor, the drunken prince of Transylvania who had seen ripe hopes of pillage, hastened to withdraw and make his private peace with the Emperor when he saw that Vienna was not, after all, to fall into Frederick's lap. All Frederick had achieved was to escalate the Bohemian revolt into a German war. It was soon to be a war of the nations.

Meanwhile the Counter-Reformation powers organized themselves politically and militarily with more skill than before. Among their leaders, Maximilian ('the Great') of Bavaria, matched Ferdinand himself in Catholic fervour and was his superior in political judgment. He too was a product of the Jesuit university at Ingolstadt. Feeble in physique and unimpressive in appearance, he was shrewd, thrifty and ambitious, and his army under the Walloon general Tilly was relatively well-organized. In this early phase of the conflict, when stakes were high and prospects uncertain, the Catholic League's diplomacy was adroit. The greatest material prize in the struggle between reformers and their opponents was the vast church property in Germany, in which some Marxist historians of the war, like Franz Mehring, saw its very *raison d'être*. If Lutheran support was to be forthcoming for the Emperor and the Catholic cause, there must be accommodation on this point. So, in March 1620 the Catholic League met the Elector of Saxony under Maximilian's lead at Mühlhausen and a businesslike agreement emerged. The League would not attempt to recover the former church lands now in the hands of Protestant bishops and administrators (especially in north Germany) so long as they remained loyal to the Emperor. This secured the neutrality of Saxony and other Lutheran states. Spain and the Pope would send troops and money. So would Maximilian; his price? Frederick's electoral hat and the right to occupy upper Austria if necessary as security for his expenses.

It was Maximilian, above all, who reaped his reward at the Battle of Bílá Hora (the White Mountain) near Prague on 8 November 1620. It was his veterans under Tilly who defeated the Bohemians, Tilly's initiative which gave them their cue. Frederick's army fled in panic and the elector himself disappeared into Germany, to find exile in Holland – 'the Winter King', as the Jesuits had predicted: 'When summer comes he will melt away.' His handful of allies, like the episcopal adventurer Christian of Brunswick, could do little for him. Neither, as things turned out, could his father-in-law who, too late, had discovered that the alliance Spain had dangled before his eyes was merely a diversion to keep England out of the German–Bohemian imbroglio until the Catholic League had done its business. John George of Saxony had been left to deal with Silesia and Lusatia. He did so on terms which, judged by the standards of the day, were not unreasonable. Tilly meanwhile seized Frederick's territories of the Palatinate. Successively, the Winter King lost his lands and his resources. Again, to the chagrin of Spain, Maximilian was the chief beneficiary, for it was to him that the electorate was transferred. Frederick disappeared from history.

The Bohemian lands – Bohemia and Moravia especially – had been the pebble in Ferdinand's boot. Now they were subjected to a ruthless campaign of Catholicization and (partially) Germanization. Ferdinand made short work of the old Rudolfine order. If the southern Netherlands had been the first state to taste the bitter humiliation of submission to the juggernaut of centralized rule by a 'new' and foreign monarchy, Bohemia was the second; and the loss here was perhaps the greater, for Bohemia had no seaboard to ameliorate the lot of the dissidents and the persecuted, though many, including Comenius, did escape. It was a bitter foretaste of 1938 and 1968 – and after. The property of rebel and supposedly rebel nobles was confiscated – to a value of between five and eight million Bohemian *schocken* (*kop*). The revolutionary role attributed to the bourgeoisie can be guessed from the value of the confiscations imposed on them: $2\frac{1}{2}$ million. Since they were estimated to control only about one-tenth of Bohemian land at this time, their sacrifices were evidently even greater than those of the nobles. Within the nobility, new families appeared and flourished, some Czech but more German. All owed their status primarily to their civil or military connections with the Habsburgs and remained their main support until 1918. To confiscations were added utmost refinements of persecution – the analogy with the 1970s is, except for the limits imposed by a more primitive organization, complete. The Jesuits, following in the wake of Tilly's armies, completed his work with their colleges and seminaries. The Hussite tradition was extinguished: Calvinism became a memory, retained only in Moravian folk-lore: 'as strong as the Calvinist creed' remained a Moravian synonym for steadfastness. That was all. The brilliant civilization of Bohemia was not wholly destroyed. Its spirit, brave and luminous, lived on in its arts – music especially; but it was politically emasculated, economically and socially degraded.

The victory of the Emperor, Bavaria and the Catholic League

seemed, for a fleeting moment, to be complete. But the concept of victory was itself an impossibility now that Germany had become prey to foreign intervention. Like France or the Netherlands during their wars of religion, Germany – its princes and nobility – was now enmeshed in the tortuous diplomacy and strategy of Spain, France, Scandinavia, the Dutch Republic and England. History still waited largely on Spain, where on Christmas Day 1619 king and council unanimously decided to re-start the war immediately the truce came to an end.

In Spain itself the accession of Philip IV and the replacement of Lerma by Olivares heralded the end of a period of relative peace and retrenchment and the opening of a new phase of imperialist aggression. Once again an active strategy was needed to protect the passage of Spanish troops from Italy into the Netherlands and Germany if Spinola was to crush the Netherlands. For this it would be necessary also to occupy the left bank of the Rhine and smash the Dutch defences along the Ijssel, Lek, Waal and Maas from the east. With France paralyzed by noble and Huguenot revolt and England still without any foreign policy, Spain carried all before her in Old World and New alike. In June 1625 Breda was recaptured while the armies of the Catholic League advanced into north-west Germany. Could not the Catholic alliance now seize the whole southern shore of the Baltic, strangling the already hobbled Dutch carrying trade and crushing Netherlands and German Protestantism at a single blow?

It seemed only too probable; but by 1627 and 1628 these bright prospects sharply deteriorated as Spain suddenly found itself confronted by a new crop of troubles. Economic problems again became serious. Not only did the Dutch West India Company's warships bring off a brilliant coup by capturing the Spanish silver fleet with eight million florins aboard; to this was added a bad harvest failure in Spain, a serious fall in cloth production, land values and tax yields. In retrospect this looks like a watershed in the economic history of Spain; even to contemporaries it seemed a kind of nemesis. Spinola, the only Spanish general to rival and perhaps outshine Farnese, was starved of money and troops, his strategy of siege and advance frozen. The French, now relieved domestically by the fall of La Rochelle, immediately challenged Spain in Lombardy over Spanish opposition to the succession of a French Duke in Mantua. In the spring of 1629 a French army crossed the Alps to confront the Spanish troops occupying Mantua and Montferrat.

In northern Europe the fortunes of the Emperor and the League had followed a curve not unlike that of Spain: initial successes had been followed by mounting difficulties and in the end, by 1629, came deadlock. In 1625 that colourful and optimistic warrior-chief, Christian IV of Denmark, decided to assume the Protestant leadership of the northern war before his Swedish rival, Gustavus Adolphus, beat him to the post. Leaving Denmark on 9 May 1625 with an army of twenty thousand or more, he took the plunge deep into the struggle. But the Bavarian and Imperial armies closing in from west and south on the Baltic shore were more than ready for him. After a few initial victories he was totally routed by Tilly at Lütter-am-Barenberge. With his enemies ravaging and burning their way through the Jutland peninsula, Christian was finally compelled to accept Swedish help and by the Treaty of Lübeck (1629) was fortunate enough to retire from the war without loss of territory.

Much more important than the intervention of Christian in this phase of operations was the appearance of the most remarkable, brilliant and controversial figure of the Thirty Years War. Wallenstein came of a Bohemian noble family but by 1623 he had made enough money as a soldier and entrepreneur to buy up two thousand square miles of property in north-east Bohemia and even to lend money to the Emperor. In return he was appointed Governor of Bohemia, quartermaster general of the Imperial Army and Duke of Friedland. In 1625, in partnership with the financier de Witte, he raised a private army of twenty thousand men for Ferdinand. Unlike any other army in the war, Wallenstein's consisted of disciplined, professional troops, led by officers promoted for merit and without regard to creed. This was the army with which Wallenstein marched north along the Elbe and then into Hungary to counter any move by Bethlen Gabor. It was the same army with which he settled down on July 1628 to besiege Stralsund, seeing clearly that the hostility of the northern ports must be overcome before he could achieve Habsburg control of the Baltic and the Danish Sound: he would capture Stralsund, he cried, 'though it were bound with chains to Heaven'. But the sea and lack of a navy, not Heaven, defeated him. After five months, Stralsund and Glückstadt (besieged by Tilly and the Bavarians) were still intact. The Peace of Lübeck was unavoidable.

Not only had the prospect of Imperial victory been dimmed: the diplomatic picture was becoming every day more complex and confused. Spain and Bavaria were at loggerheads. Ferdinand, whose ideas of a German settlement were different from theirs, had reduced his dependence on their military support only by raising up what in effect was a neo-feudal army under Wallenstein, whose ideas were totally different from his own. For Wallenstein was dangerously divided between loyalty to the Emperor, upon whose appointment his only legal power rested, and his own notions of a settlement on the basis of religious freedom – including that of Bohemia, for which he retained deep patriotic feelings. Even as the Peace of Lübeck was being formulated, Ferdinand committed the worst blunder of the war. His Edict of Restitution (March 1629) took away fourteen of the largest northern bishoprics and some 120 smaller foundations from their owners and restored them to the Church. The edict not only touched the pockets of the nobles, gentry and towns: it threatened thousands of Protestants with forcible expulsion or conversion. And it immediately split the unity, such as it was, of the Catholics: the Pope fought the Emperor, the Emperor fought the Catholic League, the religious orders fought each other, for the booty promised by the edict. When the Emperor asked for the help of the electoral college, he received only vigorous protests against his edict from the Protestant electors of Saxony and Brandenburg, whose support he had earlier enjoyed. Both Catholic and Protestant electors were meanwhile increasingly restive at rumours of the growing ambitions of Wallenstein, whom they regarded as an Imperial creature and an upstart. His dismissal was urgently demanded. In the middle of the meetings, and as Richelieu carefully stoked the fires of jealousy and distrust through Father Joseph, Gustavus Adolphus landed an army on the Pomeranian coast. Ferdinand had courage, but his mind was legalistic and commonplace. Prolonged ponderings convinced him that it was, after all, Wallenstein who was the prime offender against law and precedent. Whatever his value, therefore, Wallenstein must go. On 13 August 1630 he was dismissed and retired to his Bohemian estates.

Christian was, constitutionally, a Prince of Germany; Gustavus of Sweden was not. His intervention meant that the war was now irrevocably European. Religious conflict, dynastic and personal rivalries, the economic interests of individual princes, bishops and towns had enmeshed all the major European powers except France. Growing and inexorable compulsion led Gustavus to believe that Sweden's only defence against certain attack was to attack first. When he left

Stockholm for Peenemunde with his sixteen thousand troops he told the Swedish estates that, 'as he stood there and in the sight of the Almighty', he had begun hostilities out of no lust for war, 'as many will certainly devise and imagine', but in self-defence and to deliver fellow-Christians from oppression. His claim was borne out in his correspondence with his chancellor, Oxenstjerna, the Swedish nobleman who advised, administered and did everything for him except fight his battles. That he was sincere in his Protestantism and believed in his role as its protector, there is no reason to doubt. But before everything Gustavus put the safety of Sweden. His fear was that the Emperor's plan was to acquire the Baltic ports and build up a Baltic seapower which would threaten Swedish independence. To counter this it was not enough to blockade the ports by sea. The only sure defence was an attack on Tilly and Wallenstein by land; and their admittedly formidable resources were so dispersed as to suggest that the chances of his succeeding were good.

Gustavus was young, intelligent, well-educated. He had the judgment and the independence of character to listen to advice and take it or reject it on rational grounds. His contribution to the evolution of warfare was crucial. He had studied the manoeuvres and methods of the greatest generals of the age, especially of that master of the siege, Maurice of Nassau. But the conditions of warfare in the open spaces of Poland and Germany called for different methods, and he set himself, as Michael Roberts has put it, 'to liberate strategy from the tenacious mud of the Netherlands'.[74] His instrument was the Swedish brigade, made up of conscripts, paid not in money but in kind, equipped with standardized arms. His basic plan: to concentrate sufficient fire-power at the moment and point of attack to administer a 'missile-shock'. The pikes then followed up, supported by mobile artillery armed with light guns.

His strategy was closely linked to his tactical ideas and to the logistics of his new army. Penetration into Germany had to be deep for his army to be self-sufficient. Hence his move southwards along the rivers until he had formed a series of bases covering all Germany. By 1630 Stettin had been taken. Pomerania was secured by treaty. Brandenburg and Hesse had become his allies. By the Treaty of Bärwalde Richelieu promised him large subsidies. Finally a league of Protestant states bound to Sweden seemed to provide the support necessary to a general advance to the Rhine and the liberation of south German Protestantism.

In three years Gustavus had made himself the head of the evangelical electors, princes and estates of Protestant Germany. And now the final objective was clarified: Protestantism in Europe would not be safe until Ferdinand had been compelled to yield up his first conquest – Bohemia. Steadily, Gustavus advanced towards the Danube for the final attack on Vienna. But meanwhile the outlook had been changed by the return of Wallenstein. As he had predicted, the Emperor's plight without him had become desperate: so desperate that Wallenstein was able to dictate his own terms. They were quite simple: Wallenstein would be dictator. First, the Edict of Restitution must be withdrawn: it was. Second, he, and he alone, should be charged with military command: it was given him – for the moment.

The two armies met at Lützen, about fifteen miles west of Leipzig. The time was November, and Wallenstein had already decided to end his campaigning season and return to winter quarters. Gustavus's plan was to launch a surprise attack. 'Now in very truth I believe,' he is said to have exclaimed, 'that God has delivered him into my hands.'[75] Gustavus's strategy at Lützen was designed to repeat the methods and success of his earlier model victory at Breitenfeld in September 1631. Up to a point, it did. The Swedes drove the enemy from their entrenched positions, though their losses were heavy. But it was Bernhard of Saxe-Weimar, not Gustavus, who led the last charges. Gustavus, shot in his arm and back, fell from his mount and was finally killed by a bullet through his head. The loss was incalculable. It seemed that he alone could rally and control the inherently unstable forces of Protestantism and lead them to a victorious conclusion. Yet by another series of twists of fate, the gloom of the prediction was mitigated. It has sometimes been said that all moral idealism went out of the war with Gustavus. But the ideals of political leaders do not vary the tactics or trials of warfare. Hardly anything could have exceeded the horrors of the sack of Magdeburg, with its loss of twenty thousand inhabitants and frightful destruction by fire and pillage. It was the work of Tilly, but Gustavus was frequently (if unfairly) blamed for the failure to relieve it.

In the years after Lützen the confusion and horror of the war grew deeper. Wallenstein's health, mental and physical, was now seriously impaired. His actions became more extravagant and peculiar. He became obsessed by odd superstitions and astrological predictions. He was gripped by terrible depressions. His nerves seem to have been shattered and his distrust of the Emperor (rational enough in itself) turned into persecution mania. Slowly Ferdinand prepared his plan to liquidate his

255

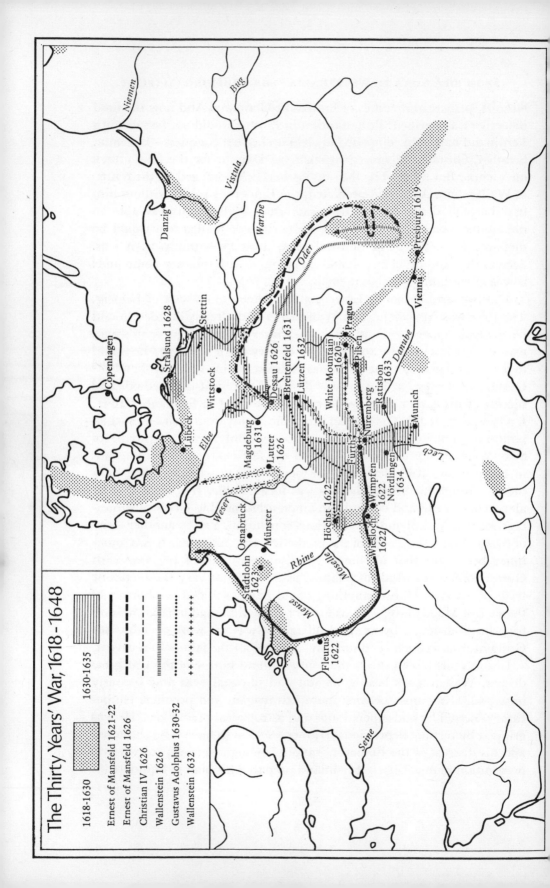

The Thirty Years' War, 1618–1648

1618-1630

1630-1635

Ernest of Mansfeld 1621-22

Ernest of Mansfeld 1626

Christian IV 1626

Wallenstein 1626

Gustavus Adolphus 1630-32

Wallenstein 1632

Niemen

Bug

Vistula

Warthe

Oder

Danzig

Presburg 1619

Stralsund 1628

Stettin

Vienna

Copenhagen

Danube

Prague

Lübeck

Wittstock

White Mountain 1620

Pilsen

Elbe

Magdeburg 1631

Dessau 1626

Breitenfeld 1631

Lützen 1632

Ratisbon 1633

Munich

Lutter 1626

Nuremberg

Weser

Fürth

Lech

Osnabrück

Münster

Höchst 1622

Wimpfen 1622

Nördlingen 1634

Rhine

Wiesloch 1622

Stadtlohn 1623

Moselle

Meuse

Fleurus 1622

Seine

dangerous commander-in-chief, undermining the loyalty of his chief lieutenants and sapping their confidence in his sanity. Wallenstein's Czech noble friends, Terzka and Kinsky among them, were decoyed away from their chief, to be brutally and treacherously murdered by a gang of Irish and Scots thugs. Another Irish mercenary then assassinated Wallenstein as he lay ill in his bed. The instigators behind the murderers were Ferdinand, Maximilian and the Spanish agents. Whatever Wallenstein's errors and faults, nothing could justify or excuse a murder as cowardly and revolting as anything that brutal age can show.

If Wallenstein's death seemed to be the only comfort to which the Emperor's enemies could point, the illusion was soon dispelled. Five months after his death, his successor as Imperial commander, the young Ferdinand, King of Hungary, smashed the Swedish army at Nördlingen. A year later the Peace of Prague was signed between the Emperor and Saxony. The gross, drunken, obstinate but canny John George, seeing that any victory of Protestantism in south Germany was now out of the question, made haste to do the best deal he could with an exhausted Emperor. 1627 was made the test year for the allocation of church lands: what you had in that year, Catholic or Protestant, you kept. Most of the northern bishoprics therefore stayed Protestant. Saxony got Lusatia. Lutheranism remained the only recognized form of Protestantism. On these terms Saxony went over to the Emperor. Many cities and small states in north Germany also accepted the settlement.

Nördlingen and the Treaty of Prague were a serious blow to the anti-Habsburg forces, but especially to France and Richelieu, still waiting in the wings. Only in the Netherlands had any ray of light pierced the general gloom of the years before 1634. But here, too, the news became worse. The Spanish–Austrian link was being strengthened. Connections between Lombardy and Brussels were to be restored. With peace in Germany Ferdinand was said to be contemplating a combined Austro–Spanish attack on the Netherlands. The time had come to act.

In March 1635, an excuse was offered when Spain seized the Elector of Trier, who was formally under the protection of Louis XIII. This was sufficient to give the King of France reason to claim an affront to his person. Unofficial war – Richelieu's subsidies to the Netherlands and the Swedes, interference in Mantua, interference with the 'Spanish Road' – now gave way to open war: a formal treaty with the Dutch for the joint conquest of the Spanish Netherlands; a new alliance with

Sweden. Peace was signed with the Dukes of Savoy and Mantua. The hesitations of France about offending Catholic opinion in Germany and in France by reinforcing German, Dutch and Swedish Protestantism were now discarded. The declaration of war was carried out with all the chivalric pomp and ceremonial of the Middle Ages – for the last time in history. On 19 May, the Herald of Arms standing in the Grand Place at Brussels proclaimed that the King of France had declared war on Spain, the Netherlands and the Empire. The war was now essentially one of Habsburgs and Bourbons, with Sweden an important accessory to France.

Just as fear of a Habsburg Baltic war had dragged Gustavus and Sweden into the war, so now it was Richelieu's fear of encirclement by the Habsburgs which drew him and France into formal war. His objectives were not wantonly aggressive. They were, like all his policies, practical responses to what he conceived to be the needs of France. His idea of 'France' had nothing mystical about it. It had no 'natural frontiers'. He claimed only those territories to which the lawyers could attach historical territorial titles – Artois, Flanders, the Milanese, Naples, Sicily and Lorraine – not the Rhine or Alsace. The disputed territories were all in Habsburg occupation. The 'encirclement' dated from the time of the Emperors Maximilian I and Charles V; but French claims had lain dormant during the long agony of the civil wars. Henry IV was the first king strong enough to articulate them. By 1629 Richelieu had converted the fears and the claims into policies. There would be bridgeheads into enemy territory – Strasbourg for example – to help the Dutch or anybody else who resisted the Habsburgs; alliances, with Protestants if need be; Italy would be freed and given back to her princes and people. It was no wish of France, Richelieu had written, to expand her territories by despoiling her neighbours. Only Austria, which had gobbled up so much of Europe, must be reduced. All this was necessary to a just peace. Thus *raison d'état* led, in the person of two cardinals, to the authority and power of France being put at the disposal of European Protestantism and aimed at the champions of Pope and Church, while at home Huguenots were steadily suppressed.

A glance at France's ramshackle army and administration and the chaos and near-defeat in the early stages of French intervention disposes of any idea that Richelieu had calculatedly set on aggression. Only a madman would have gambled with such a hand, except under duress. Both Louis and Richelieu were sick men. No idea of French 'strategy' against the enemy had been worked out. The French Council of State could only guess at the strength of the different French armies, each operating independently. No wonder that 1635 and 1636 were largely years of defeat. Alsace was in chaos. By the summer of 1636, the Cardinal-Infante's army from the south Netherlands seized the fortress of Corbie near Amiens; another advanced to Compiègne. Paris was seriously threatened, and as the mobs rioted the cardinal's enemies rejoiced on his obviously imminent downfall. But Richelieu stood firm and Louis was not going to allow his ailments to prevent him from taking command of his armies. Together king and minister stopped the rot.

1636 was France's worst year. Then the apparent *apogée* of the Empire proved to be an illusion. The steady political drift of Germany was towards disintegration into a mass of independent sovereign states. By contrast, France was slowly building up her armies – nine in all, comprising 130,000 foot and 26,000 horse. By 1638, combined operations by the Swedish and French armies began for the control of the Rhine, and ultimately all Alsace was occupied. The next year the Swedes overran Bohemia, having defeated the Imperial army at Chemnitz in Saxony. Spain was totally cut off from her overland links with the Netherlands and at sea the great Tromp with a Dutch squadron of men-at-war wiped out the Spanish fleet off Dover in October 1639. Totally demoralized, defeated by land and sea, the new Emperor, Ferdinand III, called an Imperial Diet at Ratisbon in 1640, only to meet with fresh hostility from the rising Protestant state of Brandenburg.

When Richelieu died, in 1642, he had largely accomplished his tasks. The territories and strategic points which would be finally secured to France by the Treaties of Westphalia and the Pyrénées – the control of the Rhine crossing at Breisach; Pinerolo, the gateway to Italy; Alsace; Artois; Roussillon – all were in French hands. Under Mazarin's guidance France and Sweden battered the Bavarians, Saxons and Spaniards to a halt. The very first engagement of the new reign in France was the crushing defeat of the Spanish army at Rocroi on the border of the Spanish Netherlands. The legendary invincibility of Spain on land was at an end. In Bavaria the two greatest French generals of the age, Cónde and Turenne, also won resounding victories.

As in 1559 and 1609, sheer exhaustion now turned the thoughts of the combatants to peace. Louis XIII had accepted proposals for two simultaneous conferences – one at Münster concerned with negotiations between France, her allies and the Habsburgs; the other at Osnabrück concerned with Swedish-Imperial affairs. But it was December 1644 before they settled down to work. Meanwhile Mazarin prepared elaborate schemes to acquire the Spanish Netherlands, the Rhine, Alsace, Lorraine and indeed 'all those territories which in the past have provided the means for individual princes who ruled them not only to resist France but to trouble her to an extent we all know'.[76]

While the peoples of Continental Europe, the victims of many decades of destruction, pillage, rape, arson, plague, disease and famine, slowly returned to their farms and workshops, the Congresses got under way. Most of Europe was represented, except the Tsar, the King of England and the Grand Turk; and the major representatives were attended by a vast retinue of secretaries, courtiers and servants, all carried by hundreds of carriages and horses. The preliminaries consisted largely of disputes over precedence, etiquette, credentials, complaints about accommodation and conditions of work, and all the other operatic absurdities which were to become the common stuff of international diplomatic meetings. Delegations objected to each other; members of the same delegation quarrelled. The French, Servien and d'Avaux, were at loggerheads. Naturally France and Sweden dominated proceedings from their position of military strength. Young Oxenstjerna, the Swedish delegate, gave general offence by his arrogant behaviour and the disturbance caused by the drums and trumpets which announced to the world his risings, mealtimes and retirings. Procedural questions alone held up progress intolerably; eight months passed before the Emperor was finally brought to agree to the Franco-Swedish demand that the estates of the Empire must be represented at the conference table. It often seemed that only a miracle could produce order, let alone treaties, out of the maze. Even Mazarin, supposedly pastmaster of the diplomatic art, quickly found that his plans for the Spanish Netherlands merely drove the Dutch into the arms of the Spaniards, upset the Italians, and indeed most other delegates. In the end it was the sagacity of the Emperor's chief adviser, Count Maximilian von Trautmansdorff, that brought reason into the quarrels and order out of near chaos. Finally, the Treaties which collectively came to be known as the Peace of Westphalia were signed on 24 October 1648 and ratified on 8 February 1649.

France, as we have seen, gained most, both in the short and long term. Her acquisitions at the expense of Austria – and ultimately of

Spain – went a long way to break the threat of Habsburg encirclement which had brought France into the war and kept her there. Complementary to her gains were the losses and declining fortunes of her Habsburg enemies. About the Emperor himself a discreet silence was observed: nothing more was really necessary. It was all said in the clauses relating to the princes of the Empire who secured full sovereign rights in all respects – except for a formal and meaningless reservation that such rights were not to be used against the Emperor. French influence was ingeniously exercised in favour of Bavaria (which retained the Upper Palatinate and its electoral hat, stolen in 1623 from under the Imperial nose). The Lower Palatinate, and a new, eighth electoral hat, went back to the son of the late ill-fated 'Winter King', from whom the Imperial ban was now removed. Saxony kept its share of the loot of the Bohemian kingdom, Lusatia – thanks again to French pressure. Brandenburg the new, rising (and Calvinist) state of the north, got the greater part of eastern Pomerania and a number of bishoprics.

The other major military power, Sweden, took western Pomerania, the territories around the mouth of the Oder, Stettin and Wismar. The secularized bishoprics of Bremen and Verden gave them control over the rivers Weser and Elbe. An indemnity of five million thalers rounded off the 'satisfactions' of Sweden. She now controlled, for the time being, the southern shore of the Baltic, had secured a footing on the North Sea coast and had the status of an Imperial estate with three votes in the Imperial Diet. Great as these gains were, they were less than the chancellor, Oxenstjerna, wanted. The reason lay in the genuine desire for peace by Queen Christina, who had come of age during the negotiations at Westphalia and had already made it clear that she was to be mistress of policy. Perhaps, with her mixture of realism and waywardness, she saw that Sweden, poor in resources and short of manpower, was already overstretched, militarily and politically. So far, her wars had been fought on the cheap; but this was becoming a difficult feat to repeat. Since 1633 Sweden had enjoyed vast cash subsidies from France. They continued to be an annual event for most of the century, adding to France's deficits but doing little to alleviate Sweden's chronic poverty. War might mean glory for Sweden's kings and nobles: for its people each new battle signified only another turn of the screw.

The other gainers were Switzerland, whose independence was at last formally recognized, and the Netherlands Republic. A separate peace with Spain gave the Dutch the so-called 'Generality Lands' south of the Maas and confirmed the closure of the Scheldt which was to last until 1815.

The greatest loser was the Emperor. Westphalia ruled out for ever any further Imperial unification of Germany under him, and his authority was replaced almost completely by that of some three hundred independent princes. He lost some forty thousand square miles of territory, and the frontier against France became indefensible.

The religious settlement likewise extrapolated the principles of 1555. Religion remained a matter between a prince and his subjects, at the same time including Calvinism among the 'recognized' forms of Christian belief and practice. Toleration as such was not admitted or even spoken of. Yet in practice, while there were some flagrant instances of oppression – an Archbishop of Salzburg could still proclaim the banishment of all Protestants from his dominions – they were comparatively rare. The great proselytizing phase of reform and counter-reform was fading away; so were the great religious quarrels engulfing entire populations. In the bitterly disputed matter of the church lands, the principle of the earlier Treaty of Prague between the Emperor and the Elector of Saxony was modified and extended as the basis of a general settlement. The first day of the year 1624 became the test day. Occupation at that date was to determine future possession: in practice this merely confirmed the facts, preserving the northern bishoprics to Protestantism, the southern to Catholicism. The Church also held on to its gains in Austria, Bohemia, Bavaria and the Upper (now Bavarian) Palatinate.

The Peace of Westphalia has been called the first truly European settlement in history. So it was, yet any inference that it was the product of exceptional statemanship would be false. The fact was that Europe was bankrupt, exhausted and deadlocked. The treaties of 1648 did little more than recognize the brute facts of the case as they emerged after thirty – in the Netherlands, eighty – years of war. They reflected above all the ingenious manipulation of French strength in Germany against the Empire and (less directly) of the Hispano-Dutch deadlock against Spain. Only the Papacy, whose efforts to mediate between the states had been repeatedly and humiliatingly rejected, refused to sanction the treaties. Innocent x was moved to an eloquence of indignation. The treaties were 'null, void, invalid, iniquitous, unjust, damnable, reprobate, inane, empty of meaning and effect for all times'. His eloquence went unnoticed. One of the effects of the war and of Papal policy was the virtual disappearance of Papal influence from the politics of Europe. The two ancient contestants for world hegemony, Pope and Emperor, in the end went down together in a Europe impatient with their pretensions.

The economic and social effects of the war have been infinitely debated. Against the view that it was a time of unredeemed horror and destruction, it has been more recently argued that this cataclysmic interpretation is an exaggeration which derived from later Prussian propaganda aimed at glorifying the achievements of Brandenburg, Prussia and their rulers as the saviours of Germany. Strategic points, S. H. Steinberg has argued, like the Rhine crossings, the passages through the Black Forest or the plain of Leipzig, suffered, certainly; but 'the majority of towns never saw an enemy within their walls'.[77] Germany's troubles began before the war. Death rates in Frankfurt were approximately at the same level as those in London. A total German population of 15–17 million stood at about the same figure a century later.

While it is true that many (but not all) of the most pessimistic judgments did come from German historians, like Freytag and Mehring, they do not rest wholly on German opinion. Not surprisingly, Czech historians of recent as well as older generations have fully shared the German view. Bohemia suffered, probably more than any single country, from the devastation of the marauding armies – Bavarian, Austrian, Spanish, Swedish – that descended on the kingdom in 1620 and after, and whose behaviour deteriorated after the deaths of Gustavus and Wallenstein. There is little need to be puzzled, as some historians have been, by the willingness of the inhabitants of Prague (Protestants until recently) to defend their city against the Swedes for the Emperor in the summer of 1648. They knew only too well that the armies were, by now, all as bad as one another. They were fighting not for the Emperor but for themselves, to save their families and property.

Quite apart from the indescribable fate of cities like Magdeburg, the evidence of scores of observers is too unanimously horrifying to be nullified by general and often questionable statistics. Whole villages were 'pillaged and shot down', poor people 'found dead with grass in their mouths', starving people pushed each other into the river as they fought for relief supplies brought by barge; at Neustadt, 'Once a fair city, though now burned miserably, we saw poor children sitting at their doors, almost starved to death'. At one village in the upper

Palatinate 'which hath been pillaged eight-and-twenty times in two years and twice in one day . . . they have there no water but that which they save when it raineth'.[78]

As always, it was not only military destruction, fire and death in battle but the ravages of plague, typhoid fever and other diseases, and famine – all of which followed in the wake of war – that killed. Disease was said to have destroyed two-thirds of the population of Brandenburg in the 1630s. Father Roger Mols, the Belgian demographer whose analysis is the most sophisticated and reliable modern study, has accepted an average fall in the German population of 30–40 per cent. Certainly, conditions in Germany were diverse. The countryside probably came to be a little more prosperous after 1648. But generally it seems that the depressed and damaged areas of Germany and Central Europe dominated the economy more than before. The optimistic view is too neat and insouciant. Even if we accept that the concept of a 'Thirty Years War' as an 'entity' was a later invention of Pufendorf as Brandenburg court historian, we must take a broader view of the economic consequences of the war as a Europe-wide phenomenon dating back to the start of the Netherlands Revolt eighty years earlier.

The Netherlands war, quite simply, destroyed Spain as a great and wealthy power, relegating her to economic, political and social backwardness from which she has never fully recovered. Half the Netherlands fought their way to new prosperity but at a fearful cost in lives, property, shipping and money. The other half struggled, much more slowly, to win back the right to a local livelihood; but the destruction of Antwerp and the once-great cities of Flanders and Brabant as major centres of international trade and industry was final. It is simply not possible to quantify the physical destruction, human misery and moral damage which the 'religious' wars of the age brought to the sixty or more million people engulfed by them. The preamble to the Peace of Munster between Spain and the Netherlands in 1647–8 proclaimed that, after a long succession of bloody wars, the rulers of those states desired

to end the general misery, and prevent dreadful consequences, calamity, harm, and danger which the further continuation of the aforesaid wars in the Low Countries would bring in their train . . .. They invite and call upon other princes and potentates to allow themselves to be moved by the same pity and avert the mishaps, destruction and disorders which the heavy plague of wars has made men suffer for so long and so heavily.

🐚 15 🐚

CONCLUSION

Diplomatically, internationally, the settlement of 1648 was intrinsically successful because it was realistic. Even here not every problem was solved, not every solution clear. A final settlement of the problem of Alsace and many other boundary problems was a long way off. Domestically, countries which were ultimately destined for a future of absolutism were still in conditions of political transition and uncertainty. In England, the destruction of attempted absolutism was complete, but the search for an alternative was to continue to 1688. In the United Provinces, the stadholder William II saw the Peace of Munster (despite the pious appeal of its preamble quoted above) as a defeat of the Orangist party and attempted, ineffectively, to seize power. But his sudden death from smallpox while the power struggle was still at its height may well have changed the course of Dutch history. As it was, the following twenty years saw the greatest period of the States party, after thirty years of Orangist rule. In France the chaos of the Fronde was still at its height. It was still uncertain who would rule in France and how. Of all the states of Italy, the Venetian Republic had survived best. For all that it suffered from many of the weaknesses of a close oligarchy, it had adjusted itself skilfully to the changing world of the seventeenth century. But by the mid-seventeenth century the signs were unmistakable that a recession was under way. Its economic institutions seemed no longer to be able to adjust to the conditions of international competition and war which trade and industry had to meet. In maritime affairs too, Venice and the other Mediterranean economies were falling behind those of the Atlantic seaboard. Increasingly the skill and capital for the secondary and tertiary waves of exploration and discovery which were opening up the new worlds of America, Africa and Asia flowed from Holland, England and France.

Comparatively little has been said about overseas trade and settlement in these pages. Despite the attention it has attracted, the first was in volume still fractional compared with the inter-European trade; though one of its products – silver – had helped to change not only the price structure but indirectly many other economic and social aspects of Europe; others – spices, tobacco, sugar, cotton dyewoods – were beginning to leaven and diversify the traditional staples of Europe's trade routes and markets. Extra-European activities were still seen overwhelmingly as matters of trade. The importance of European settlement lay in the future.

Exploration, discovery, trade, settlement – all are probably best seen as an aspect of the real revolution of ideas which was steadily transforming one area of human thought and activity after another by the seventeenth century. Intellectual energies previously concentrated on theology and philosophy were increasingly diverted into new channels. The universities of the Netherlands, Italy and England especially – the new schools of Leiden (1574), Franeker (1585), Utrecht (1636), Groningen (1614), as well as the older ones at Oxford, Cambridge and (oldest of all) Padua (1238), since 1405 part of the Venetian Republic – had all been the scene of intellectual turmoil. It extended over the whole gamut of thought – from the speculative, philosophical and humanistic to forays into the exact sciences. The long debate for and against Copernicanism was only a part, though a vitally significant one, of this great and complex intellectual movement. Astronomy and cosmology jostled with astrology and occultism; optics, mechanics, dynamics and microscopy with theology, metaphysics, alchemy, mineralogy, and metallurgy. Mathematicians, geometrists, algebraists, geographers, astrologers, poets, parsons, instrument-makers, clock-makers, canal-builders, civil engineers, playwrights, classical antiquaries, map-makers, navigators, astronomers – all tumble through the memories of that most fascinating of seventeenth-century raconteurs, John Aubrey.

Lenses and logarithms, one might say, seemed to be the key not only to the secrets of the universe but to a number of practical problems involving calculations of time, distance and navigation. Neither intellectual curiosity nor economically motivated applied science can be claimed as the sole mainspring of the new movement in which both were interlocked. The movement flourished most where thought was relatively free, becoming, in turn, itself the generator of further intellectual emancipation. Yet, like everything else in that casual age, emancipation was not complete. The 'scientists' of the sixteenth and early seventeenth century were only clearing the paths which would be explored more accurately by Christiaan Huyghens, Newton and Leibniz. The rudimentary propositions of Thomas Mun were only the groundwork on which comprehensive theories of national economic expansion would later be based. Intimations of rational inclinations towards tolerance would in time flower into enlightenment. But the material context had to undergo fundamental change before inventive ingenuity would make its fundamental impact on economic production. Meanwhile, and long after our period closes, the world was to remain the world of Janus, facing in both directions, to the past and the future.

NOTES

1 R. B. Wernham in the Introduction to *New Cambridge Modern History* (1958), III, p. 11.
2 H. T. Buckle, *History of Civilisation in England*, 3 vols (1868), p. 39 and chs 2 and 3 *passim*.
3 E. A. Wrigley, *Population and History* (1969), p. 76.
4 *New Cambridge Modern History* (1957), I, p. 20.
5 Andrew Marvell, *The Character of Holland* (1672).
6 ibid.
7 Thomas Campion, *Third Book of Airs* (1617).
8 J. H. Clapham in the Introduction to *Concise Economic History of Britain* (1949), p. 1.
9 Quoted in R. H. Tawney, *Business and Politics under James I* (1958), p. 45.
10 F. L. Carsten, *The Origins of Prussia* (1947), p. 164.
11 B. E. Supple, *Crisis and Change in England, 1600–1640* (1959), p. 14.
12 Quoted by K. Helleiner in the *Cambridge Economic History of Europe* (1970), IV, p. 25.
13 Wrigley, op. cit., p. 69.
14 J. H. Clapham, *The Economic Development of France and Germany 1815–1914* (1928), pp. 381–2.
15 N. W. Posthumus, *Inquiry into the History of Prices in Holland* (1964), II, p. LXV.
16 C. W. Cole, *Mercantilist Doctrines before Colbert* (1931), p. 10.
17 J. R. Hale, *Renaissance Europe* (1971), p. 161 ff.
18 Michael Roberts, *Essays in Swedish History* (1967), p. 20.
19 ibid., pp. 29–30.
20 William Shakespeare, *Troilus and Cressida* (1602), I, 3, 90–1.
21 H. R. Trevor-Roper, *Religion, the Reformation and Social Change* (1967), p. 21.

22 Brian Pullan, *A History of Early Renaissance Italy* (1973), p. 301 and ch 14.
23 J. L. Motley, *The Rise of the Dutch Republic* (1884), III, pp. 366–7.
24 Giovanni Botero, *Of the Greatness of Cities*, English translation (1606) ed. P. G. and D. P. Waley (1950), II, p. 2.
25 H. G. Koenigsberger and G. L. Mosse, *Europe in the Sixteenth Century* (1968), p. 83.
26 Joel Hurstfield, in *New Cambridge Modern History* (1958), III, p. 130.
27 I am indebted to Dr. P. D. Lagomarsino of Clare College, Cambridge, for much new and illuminating information on this and related problems.
28 J. H. Shennan, *Government and Society in France 1461–1661* (1969), p. 22.
29 Quoted by J. P. Cooper in his Introduction to *New Cambridge Modern History* (1970), IV, p. 22.
30 Lawrence Stone, *The Crisis of the Aristocracy 1558–1641* (1967), p. 115.
31 ibid., p. 267.
32 *New England Merchants in the Seventeenth Century*, ed. B. Bailyn, p. 139.
33 G. N. Clark, *The Wealth of England from 1496–1760* (1946), p. 61.
34 Trevor-Roper, op. cit., p. 41.
35 Quoted in Charles Wilson, *Queen Elizabeth and the Revolt of the Netherlands* (1970), p. 60.
36 On developments in warfare and military organization see Professor J. R. Hale in *New Cambridge Modern History* (1968), II, 16; and Dr N. G. Parker's *The Army in Flanders and the Spanish Road* (1972), especially the Introduction.
37 N. M. Sutherland, *The Massacre of St Batholomew and the European Conflict 1559–1572* (1973), pp. 1 and 345–6.
38 I owe the title of this chapter to Gerald Brenan's book of the same name; his account of Spain's timeless problems cannot be bettered.
39 J. H. Elliott, *Imperial Spain 1469–1716* (1963).
40 Quoted in Carlo M. Cipolla, *Guns and Sails in the Early Phase of European Expansion 1400–1700* (1965), p. 87.
41 Robert Fruin, *The Siege and Relief of Leyden in 1574*, translated by Elizabeth Trevelyan (1927), p. 35.
42 Quoted in A. W. Lovett, 'The Government of Don Luis de Requesens 1573–6: A Spanish View', *European Studies Review* (1972), 3.
43 Quoted in Wilson, op. cit., p. 61.
44 Quoted by Mandell Creighton in *Queen Elizabeth* (1899), p. 181.
45 Quoted in Wilson, op. cit., p. 90.
46 Quoted by H. G. Koenigsberger in *New Cambridge Modern History* (1958), III, p. 302.
47 Pieter Geyl, *The Revolt of the Netherlands* (5th ed. 1966), p. 254.
48 Quoted in Wilson, op. cit., p. 120.
49 Quoted by E. Cochrane, *The Late Italian Renaissance 1525–1630* (1970), p. 51.

50 Quoted in John Shearman, *Mannerism* (1967), p. 156.
51 Quoted by Ellis Waterhouse, 'Some Painters and the Counter-Reformation before 1600', *Transactions of the Royal Historical Society* (1972).
52 Anthony Blunt, 'Some Uses and Abuses of the Terms Baroque and Roccoco as applied to Architecture', *Proceedings of The British Academy 1972* (1974).
53 Wilfrid Mellers, *Music and Society* (1946), p. 58.
54 P. O. Kristeller, *Renaissance Thought* (1961), p. 138.
55 See the excellent essay by W. Bouwsma, 'Paolo Sarpi and the Republican Tradition' in Cochrane, op. cit.
56 Quoted by H. R. Trevor-Roper in his brilliant Neale Lecture, *Queen Elizabeth's First Historian* (1971), p. 24.
57 *New Cambridge Modern History*, IV, p. 146.
58 Robert Evans, *Rudolf II and his World* (1973), p. 228.
59 Francis Haskell, *Patrons and Painters: A Study in the Relations between Italian Art and Society in the Age of the Baroque* (1963), p. 17.
60 ibid., p. xviii.
61 R. H. Tawney, *Business and Politics under James I* (1958), p. 139 nl.
62 Charles Wilson, *England's Apprenticeship 1603–1763* (1965), p. 99.
63 John Aubrey, *Brief Lives*, ed. A. Powell (1949), p. 100.
64 Quoted in A. Woolrych, *Battles of the English Civil War* (1961), p. 36.
65 A. W. Lovett, 'A Cardinal's Papers: the Rise of Mateo Vasquez de Seca', *English Historical Review* (April 1973).
66 G. J. Renier, *The Dutch Nation* (1944), p. 37.
67 ibid., p. 70.
68 H. R. Trevor-Roper, *Religion, the Reformation and Social Change* (1967), p. 205.
69 Pierre Goubert, *The Ancien Régime*, translated by S. Cox (1973), p. 70.
70 Quoted by C. J. Burckhardt in *Richelieu and his Age* (1972), III, translated by B. Hoy, p. 278.
71 E. H. Kossman, *La Fronde* (1954), p. 259.
72 ibid., p. 260.
73 On this and on all the varied and bewildering aspects of Rudolf and the culture of his court see Evans, op. cit.
74 Roberts, op. cit., p. 61.
75 Quoted in Michael Roberts, *Gustavus Adolphus* (1958), II, p. 748.
76 Quoted in Georges Pagés, *The Thirty Years War* (1970), p. 213.
77 See *The Thirty Years War*, ed. T. K. Robb (1964), for the salient points of Steinberg's argument.
78 From William Crowne's *True Relation of his Travels with the Earl of Arundel in 1636* (1637), quoted by E. A. Beller in *New Cambridge Modern History*, IV, pp. 345–6.

BIBLIOGRAPHY

This is not a complete list, either of the reading that has gone into this book or which could be used to supplement it. It concentrates on relatively recent works and omits, for instance, all articles and monographs of which many have been used and the most directly relevant quoted by note. For general reference the recent two volumes of the *New Cambridge Modern History* – III (1968) and IV (1970) – are indispensable. So is vol. IV of the *Cambridge Economic History of Europe* (1967). Other works of general interest include Trevor Aston (ed.) *Crisis in Europe 1560–1660* (1965), H. R. Trevor-Roper *Religion, the Reformation and Social Change* (1967), H. G. Koenigsberger *Estates and Revolutions* (1971), Carlo M. Cipolla *Guns and Sails* (1965) and his collection of essays *The Economic Decline of Empires* (1970). General European economic history is well covered by the Fontana booklets edited by C. M. Cipolla: especially useful are those by K. Glamann, D. Sella, A. de Maddalena and N. G. Parker. Economic and social history receive special attention in Ralph Davis *The Rise of the Atlantic Economies* (1973), Charles Wilson *England's Apprenticeship 1603–1763* (1972), Peter Burke (ed.) *Economy and Society in Early Modern Europe* (1970), a selection of essays from *Annales* and Henry Kamen's *The Iron Century* (1971).

On specific areas and subjects the following are central reading (most also have their own detailed bibliographies):

ITALY

Braudel, F., *The Mediterranean and the Mediterranean World in the Age of Philip II*
   vol. I (1973)
Chambers, D. S., *The Imperial Age of Venice 1380–1580* (1970)
   Patrons and Artists in the Italian Renaissance (1970)
Cochrane, E. (ed.), *The Late Italian Renaissance 1525–1630* (1970) – essays

271

on art, music, philosophy, politics, etc., by W. Bouwsma, H. M. Brown, R. Villari, E. Cochrane, etc.

Cozzi, G., *Il Doge Nicolo Contarini* (1958)

Haskell, Francis, *Patrons and Painters: A Study in the Relations between Italian Art and Society in the Age of the Baroque* (1963)

Lane, F. C., *Venice and History* (1966)
Venetian Ships and Shipbuilders of the Renaissance (1934)

Pullan, Brian (ed.), *Crisis and Change in the Venetian Economy 1550–1630* (1968)
Rich and Poor in Renaissance Venice (1971)

Tenenti, Alberto, *Piracy and the Decline of Venice 1580–1615* (1967)

FRANCE

Buisseret, D., *Sully and the Growth of Centralised Government in France 1598–1610* (1968)

Burckhardt, C. J., *Richelieu and His Age*, 3 vols (1967–71)

Cole, C. W., *French Mercantilist Doctrines before Colbert* (1931)

Goubert, Pierre, *The Ancien Régime* (1973)

Kossmann, E. H., *La Fronde* (1954)

Le Roy Ladurie, E., *Les Paysans de Languedoc* (1966)

Mousnier, Roland, *Peasant Uprisings in Seventeenth-Century France, Russia and China* (1971)
The Assassination of Henri Quatre (1973)

Neale, J. E., *The Age of Catherine de Medici* (1943)

Shennan, J. H., *Government and Society in France 1461–1661* (1969)

Sutherland, N. M., *The Massacre of St Bartholomew and the European Conflict 1559–1572* (1973)

ENGLAND

Elton, G. R., *England under the Tudors* (1974)

Hill, Christopher, *God's Englishman: Oliver Cromwell and the English Revolution* (1970)
Puritanism and Revolution (1958)

Read, Conyers, *Lord Burghley and Queen Elizabeth* (1960)

Stone, Lawrence, *The Crisis of the Aristocracy 1558–1641* (1965)

Trevor-Roper, H. R., *Queen Elizabeth's First Historian* (1971)

Wilson, Charles, *Queen Elizabeth and the Revolt of the Netherlands* (1970)

SPAIN

Chaunu, P., *Conquête et exploitation* (1969)

Elliott, J. H., *Imperial Spain* (1963)
The Old World and the New (1970)

Hamilton, Earl J., *American Treasure and the Price Rise in Spain* (1934)

Lynch, J., *Spain under the Habsburgs 1516–1700*, 2 vols. (1964–9)

Parker, N. G., *The Army of Flanders and the Spanish Road 1567–1659* (1972)

Vicens Vives, J., *An Economic History of Spain* (1969)

THE NETHERLANDS
Bachrach, A. G. H., *Sir Constantine Huyghens and Britain* (1962)
Bromley, J. & Kossmann, E. H. (eds.) *Britain and the Netherlands* (1959)
Geyl, P., *The Revolt of the Netherlands* (1966)
    The Netherlands Divided (1936)
Haley, K. H. D., *The Dutch in the Seventeenth Century* (1972)
Renier, G. J., *The Dutch Nation* (1944)
Schöffer, Ivo, *A Short History of the Netherlands* (1956)
Tex, Jan den, *Oldenbarneveldt*, 2 vols. (1960–2)
    (English translation by Ralph Powell 1973)
van Houtte, J. A., *Economische en Sociale Geschiedenis van de Lage Landen* (1964)
Wedgwood, C. V., *William the Silent* (1944)
Wilson, Charles, *The Dutch Republic and the Civilisation of the Seventeenth Century* (1968)

GERMANY
Carsten, F. L., *Princes and Parliaments in Germany from the Fifteenth to the Eighteenth Century* (1959)
Kellenbenz, H., *Cambridge Economic History*, v, (1976), 'Industry'

BOHEMIA
Evans, L. Robert, *Rudolf II and his World* (1973)
Polisensky, J. & Snider, F., *Changes in the Composition of the Bohemian Nobility in the Sixteenth and Seventeenth Centuries* (forthcoming)

OTTOMAN EMPIRE
Earle, P., *Corsairs of Barbary and Malta* (1970)
Kortepeter, C. Max, *Ottoman Imperialism* (1973)

SCANDINAVIA
Attman, A., *The Russian and Polish Markets in International Trade 1500–1650* (1973)
Roberts, Michael, *Gustavus Adolphus* (1973)
    Essays in Swedish History (1967)

POLAND
Cambridge History of Poland, 2 vols. (1941)

RUSSIA AND EASTERN EUROPE
Blum, J., *Lord and Peasant in Russia* (1961)
McNeill, W. H., *Europe's Steppe Frontier* (1964)

T. K. Rabb usefully surveys the literature in *The Thirty Years War* (1964), a critical anthology of established and recent works. The most recent and comprehensive account is by Georges Pagés (English translation 1970). For the history of science, W. C. D. Dampier-Whetham, *History of Science and its Relations with Philosophy and Religion* (1929) is still valuable. General books on art include Arnold Hauser's *Social History of Art* (1951) and John Shearman's *Mannerism* (1967). For the history of ideas, Frances Yates's studies are all important, especially her *Art of Memory* (1966); of his many writings, P. O. Kristeller's *Renaissance Thought* (1961) is the most useful in this period. For agriculture, demography and prices see B. N. Slicher van Bath, *History of European Agriculture 500–1850* (1960; English translation 1963) and E. A. Wrigley, *Population and History* (1969)

CHRONOLOGICAL TABLES

1558	Jan	French take Calais from England
	Sept	Death of Charles v
	Oct	Peace conference at Le Cateau-Cambrésis opens
	Nov	Death of Mary i of England, succeeded by Elizabeth i
	Dec	Return of English Protestant exiles
1559	Jan	Acts of Supremacy and Unification passed
	April	Peace of Le Cateau-Cambrésis between England, France and Spain
	May	Protestant Lords of the Congregation rise in Scotland
	June	Elizabethan Prayer Book first used
	July	Death of Henry ii of France, succeeded by Francis ii
	Oct	Scottish Lords of Congregation depose Mary Queen of Scots
1560	Jan	Spanish troops return to Spain
	Mar	Huguenot conspiracy of Amboise
	July	Treaty of Edinburgh ends 'Auld Alliance' between France and Scotland
	Dec	Death of Francis ii of France; succeeded by Charles ix, Catherine de' Medici acting as Regent
1561	Jan	Persecution of Huguenots suspended by Edict of Orléans
	Aug	Mary Queen of Scots returns to Scotland
	Sept	Colloquy of Poissy
1562	Jan	Edict of Saint-Germain recognizes Huguenots
	Mar	Massacre at Vassy provokes First Religious War
	Oct	English occupy Le Havre
1563	Mar	Peace of Amboise ends First Religious War and grants limited toleration for Huguenots

275

	July	French retake Le Havre
	Aug	Charles IX declared of age
	Dec	End of Council of Trent
1564	*April*	Peace of Troyes ends English–French war; English renounce Calais
	May	Death of Calvin
	July	Death of Ferdinand I, Holy Roman Emperor; succeeded by Maximilian II
1565	*Jan*	Egmont requests concessions for Dutch Calvinists from Philip II
	Sept	Turks abandon siege of Malta
1566	*April*	Compromise of Breda; *Les Gueux* formed by nobility to resist Spanish persecution in Netherlands
	Aug	Calvinist riots in Netherlands
1567	*July*	Mary Queen of Scots forced to abdicate in favour of James VI; Earl of Moray acts as Regent
	Aug	Alba arrives in Netherlands as military governor; establishes Council of Blood and inaugurates reign of terror
	Sept	Alba arrests Counts Egmont and Hoorn
		Huguenot Conspiracy of Meaux to capture Charles IX starts Second Religious War
	Oct	Margaret of Parma resigns regency in Netherlands; Alba now in complete control
1568	*Jan*	Alba declares William of Orange an outlaw
	Mar	Treaty of Longjumean ends Second Religious War
	May	William of Orange defeats Spanish forces; start of Revolt of Netherlands
	June	Counts Egmont and Hoorn executed
	Nov	Moors in Spain revolt
	Dec	Spanish treasure ships impounded at Plymouth
1569	*Jan*	Third Religious War begins
	Mar	Prince Condé, Huguenot leader, killed
		Alba attempts to levy punitive taxation
	Oct	Huguenots defeated at Montcoutour
	Nov	Northern Rebellion led by Roman Catholic Earls
1570	*Feb*	End of Northern Rebellion
		Pope excommunicates Queen Elizabeth
	July	Turks take Cyprus
	Aug	Peace of Saint-Germain-en-Laye ends Third Religious War
1571	*Oct*	Turkish fleet defeated at Battle of Lepanto

1572	April	Sea Beggars take Brill
		Treaty of Blois between England and France
	June	William of Orange invades Netherlands
	July	William of Orange elected stadholder
	Aug	St Bartholomew's Day massacre of Huguenots, among them Coligny, Huguenot commander-in-chief
1573	Feb	Drake reaches Pacific Ocean
	Mar	Peace of Constantinople ends Turkish–Venetian war
	July	Pacification of Boulogne ends Fourth Religious War
		Spanish troops take Haarlem
	Dec	Alba leaves Netherlands; succeeded by Requesens
1574	Feb	Fifth Religious War opens
	May	Death of Charles IX of France, succeeded by Henry III
	June	Dykes opened to hinder Spanish siege of Leiden
	Oct	William of Orange takes Leiden
1575	Jan	Foundation of University of Leiden
	May–July	Failure of negotiations between William of Orange and Requesens
	Sept	Philip II declares Spain bankrupt
	Nov	Elizabeth I refuses sovereignty of Netherlands
1576	Feb	Henry of Navarre renounces Catholicism
	Mar	Death of Requesens, succeeded as governor of Netherlands by Don John of Austria
	May	Edict of Beaulieu ends Fifth Religious War
	Oct	Maximilian II dies, succeeded as Holy Roman Emperor by Rudolf II
	Nov	Spanish armies mutiny and sack Antwerp
		Dutch provinces unite under terms of Pacification of Ghent
1577	Mar	Start of Sixth Religious War
	Aug	Peace of Bergerac ends Sixth Religious War
	Sept	William of Orange enters Brussels and deposes Don John of Austria
	Nov	Francis Drake sets out on round-world voyage in *Golden Hind*
1578	Aug	Sebastian of Portugal killed during invasion of Morocco
1579	Jan	English form alliance with Netherlands
		Union of Utrecht; effective foundation of Dutch Republic
		Union of Arras; southern provinces of Netherlands declare their loyalty to Spain
1580	April	France declared bankrupt
		Seventh Religious War

	Aug	Spain invades and annexes Portugal
	Sept	Return of Francis Drake
	Nov	Peace of Bergerac renewed at end of Seventh Religious War
1581	*July*	Act of Abjuration; the seven northern Dutch provinces renounce allegiance to Spain
1583	*Aug*	William of Orange accepts sovereignty of northern Netherlands
	Sept	Catholic rising in Languedoc
	Oct	Somerville Plot to kill Elizabeth
	Dec	Throckmorton Plot for Spanish invasion of England uncovered
1584	*June*	Protestant Henry of Navarre becomes heir to French throne
		Catholic League re-formed to oppose Navarre
	July	William of Orange assassinated; succeeded as stadholder by Maurice of Nassau
	Sept	Ghent submits to Spanish troops
	Oct	Catholic Enterprise (by France and Spain) to depose Elizabeth discovered
1585	*July*	Treaty of Nemours revokes all toleration of Huguenots
	Aug	Raleigh's colony in Virginia founded
		Spanish sack Antwerp, ending its commercial dominance
	Dec	Spanish take Brussels
		Earl of Leicester takes up command in Netherlands
1586	*Feb*	Leicester forced to resign as Governor and Captain-General of Netherlands
	July	Treaty of Berwick between Elizabeth and James VI of Scotland
		Babington Plot to kill Elizabeth uncovered
	Oct	Mary Queen of Scots tried for treason
1587	*Feb*	Mary Queen of Scots executed
	April	Drake raids Cadiz
1588	*April*	Paris revolts against Henry III
	May	Duke of Guise enters Paris; Henry III escapes
	July–Aug	Defeat of Spanish Armada off English coast
	Dec	Duke of Guise assassinated
1589	*Jan*	Catherine de' Medici dies
	Aug	Henry III assassinated, recognizing Henry (IV) of Navarre as his successor
		Henry of Navarre starts fight for throne against Catholic League

1590	Mar	Dutch take Breda
1591	Sept	French bishops accept Henry IV as King of France
1593	July	Henry IV becomes Catholic
1594	Feb	Henry IV crowned King of France at Chartres
	Mar	Henry IV enters Paris
	July	Henry IV finally defeats Catholic League
	Dec	Henry IV expels Jesuits
		Edict of Saint-Germain-en-Laye grants Huguenots religious liberty
1595	Jan	Henry IV declares war on Spain
		Death of Francis Drake
1596	May	England, France and United Provinces ally against Spain
	June–July	English sack Cadiz
		Spain declared bankrupt
1597	Oct	Spanish Armada sails for England, but dispersed by storms
1598	April	Edict of Nantes grants Huguenots equal religious and political rights with Catholics
	May	Peace of Vervins between France and Spain
		Philip II assigns Netherlands to Archduke Albert of Austria and Infanta Isabella
	Sept	Death of Philip II of Spain, succeeded by Philip III
	Dec	Financial crisis in Spain
1599	Nov	Henry IV repudiates his government's debts
		Peace negotiations between Spain and United Provinces and Spain and England open
1600	May	Peace negotiations founder
	Oct	Henry IV marries Marie de' Medici
1601	Jan	Essex's revolt against Elizabeth crushed
	Feb	Essex executed
	Sept	Spanish forces land in Ireland to support Tyrone's rebellion
1602	Jan	Spanish forces surrender to English
	Mar	Dutch East India Company chartered
	Nov	Jesuits expelled from England
1603	Mar	Death of Elizabeth I of England; succeeded by James I (James VI of Scotland)
	Sept	Jesuits recalled to France
	Nov	Sir Walter Raleigh imprisoned for treason
1604	Aug	Peace between England and Spain
	Sept	Spain captures Ostend from Dutch after three-year siege
	Oct	Discovery of plot against Henry IV; Spain implicated

1605	*Nov*	Gunpowder plot to blow up Houses of Parliament
1606	*Jan*	English Parliament imposes severe penalties against Catholics
	April	Royal charter granted to Virginia Companies of London and Plymouth authorizing colonization
1607	*May*	Jamestown, Virginia, founded as English colony
		Rural protests against enclosures in England
	Aug	Bank of Genoa fails after announcement of national bankruptcy of Spain
	Sept	Flight of Earls from Ireland after attempted insurrection
1608	*May*	Protestant Union of German princes under Frederick iv of Palatinate
	June	Anglo-Dutch treaty of mutual defence
		Emperor Rudolf ii cedes Austria, Hungary and Moravia to his brother Matthias
1609	*Jan*	Bank of Amsterdam founded
	April	Spain concludes nine-year truce with United Provinces
	June	United Provinces conclude twelve-year truce with England and France
	July	Catholic League of German Princes formed under Maximilian, Duke of Bavaria
	Sept	Half million Moors expelled from Spain
1610	*Feb*	Henry iv allies with German Protestant Union
	May	Henry iv assassinated; succeeded by Louis xiii, Marie de' Medici acting as Regent
1611	*Aug*	Bourse of Amsterdam founded
		Emperor Rudolf ii resigns crown of Bohemia to Matthias
	Dec	Gustavus Adolphus elected King of Sweden
1612	*Jan*	Death of Rudolf ii; succeeded as Holy Roman Emperor by Matthias i
	April	German Protestant Union concludes defensive alliance with England
1613	*May*	German Protestant Union concludes defensive alliance with United Provinces
1614	*Feb*	Prince Condé rebels in France
	April	Addled Parliament meets and refuses to vote supplies
	May	Peace of Saint-Menehould ends French Civil War
	June	James i dissolves Parliament
1615	*Mar*	Estates-General dismissed; next meets in 1789
	Aug	Second Civil War in France; Condé allies with Huguenots
		Dutch seize Moluccas
1616	*May*	Second Civil War ends with treaty of Loudun

	Nov	Richelieu appointed Minister of State for foreign affairs and war
	Dec	States of Holland arm to oppose Oldenbarneveldt
1617	*Mar*	Sir Walter Raleigh sets out in search of gold in Guiana
	April	Marie de' Medici pushed aside by Louis XIII
	July	Maurice of Nassau champions Counter-Remonstrants against Oldenbarneveldt
1618	*Feb*	Death of Philip William, succeeded as Prince of Orange by Maurice of Nassau
	April	Richelieu exiled
	May	Defenestration of Prague – Bohemian rebels overthrow Regents and spark off Thirty Years War
	Aug	Oldenbarneveldt arrested
		James I's Five Articles of Religion approved by Church of Scotland
	Oct	Sir Walter Raleigh executed
1619	*Feb*	End of Synod of Dort
	Mar	Richelieu recalled
		Death of Matthias I, succeeded as Holy Roman Emperor by Ferdinand II
	May	Oldenbarneveldt executed
	July	First representative colonial assembly held in America at Jamestown
	Aug	Frederick V, Elector Palatinate, elected King of Bohemia
	Sept	Treaty of Angoulême ends dispute between Louis XIII and Marie de' Medici
	Oct	Hungarians march on Vienna
	Nov	Hungarians retreat from Vienna
1620	*July*	German Protestant Union and Catholic League sign agreement at Ulm
	Aug	Richelieu negotiates peace between rebels and Crown
	Sept	Spanish troops invade Palatinate from Netherlands
		Mayflower sails
	Nov	Catholic League defeats Bohemian rebels under Frederick at Battle of the White Mountain (Bílá Hora)
	Dec	Pilgrim Fathers land at New Plymouth
1621	*Feb*	Huguenots rebel against Louis XIII
	April	Protestant Union of Germany dissolved
	May	Death of Philip III of Spain, succeeded by Philip IV
	June	Dutch West India Company founded
	Aug	End of twelve-year truce; war resumed between United Provinces and Spain

1622	*Aug*	Count Olivares made Chief Minister in Spain
	Sept	Richelieu created Cardinal
	Oct	Treaty of Montpellier ends Huguenot rebellion
1624	*Mar*	England declares war on Spain
	June	France and United Provinces sign non-aggression treaty
		Dutch settle New Amsterdam
1625	*Mar*	Death of James I of England, succeeded by Charles I
	Apr	Wallenstein appointed general of imperial forces
		Death of Maurice of Nassau, succeeded as stadholder by Frederick Henry
	June	Parliament refuses to vote supplies for war against Spain
		Spain takes Breda
	July	Catholic League under Tilly invades Lower Saxony
1626	*Feb*	Peace of La Rochelle between Huguenots and Crown
		Impeachment of Buckingham begins
	Aug	Christian IV of Denmark defeated by Tilly at Battle of Lutter
1627	*Jan*	England and France at war
	Feb	Richelieu made Superintendent-General of commerce and navigation
	Mar	Huguenot rising
	Apr	Richelieu concludes allegiance with Spain
	Aug	Siege of La Rochelle begins
		France declared bankrupt
1628	*June*	Charles I accepts Petition of Right
	Aug	Duke of Buckingham assassinated
	Sept	Dutch seize Spanish silver fleet
	Oct	La Rochelle capitulates to crown forces
1629	*Mar*	Charles I dissolves Parliament, which does not meet again until 1640
		Edict of Restitution in Germany
	April	Huguenot rising
	May	Treaty of Lübeck; Christian IV withdraws from war
	June	Peace of Alais ends Huguenot revolt
1630	*July*	Gustavus Adolphus invades Germany
	Aug	Wallenstein dismissed, succeeded by Tilly
	Nov	End of English–Spanish war
1631	*May*	Catholics sack Magdeburg
	Aug	Tilly invades Saxony
	Sept	Swedish–Saxon alliance formed
		Imperial forces defeated at Breitenfeld, wiping out Catholic gains 1618–29

	Nov	Saxon troops take Prague
1632	*April*	Death of Tilly
	Nov	Battle of Lützen; Wallenstein defeated by Swedish forces, but Gustavus Adolphus killed
		Queen Christina succeeds to Swedish throne
1633	*April*	Heilbronn Confederation of German Protestant princes under Swedish leadership
	Aug	Laud appointed Archbishop of Canterbury
	Nov	Infanta Isabella dies; Spanish Netherlands now governed direct from Spain
1634	*Feb*	Wallenstein assassinated
	Sept	Swedish forces defeated at Nördlingen
	Oct	Charles I's first attempts to collect Ship Money
		Dutch take Curaçao
1635	*May*	Peace of Prague between Emperor Ferdinand II and Elector of Saxony
	June	France declares war on Spain
1636	*May*	Spanish troops invade France from Netherlands
1637	*Feb*	Ferdinand II dies, succeeded as Holy Roman Emperor by Ferdinand III
	Aug	Dutch expel Portuguese from Gold Coast
	Oct	Dutch retake Breda
1638	*Mar*	Scottish National Covenant circulated
1639	*Oct*	Dutch sink Spanish fleet off English coast
1640	*April*	Short Parliament dissolved after refusing to vote money
	July	Sweden withdraws from Bohemia
	Aug	Scottish invasion of England
	Nov	Long Parliament meets
	Dec	Portuguese revolt and win independence from Spain
		Commons declare Ship Money illegal
		Archbishop Laud impeached
1641	*Jan*	Dutch capture Malacca from Portuguese
	May	Strafford executed
	Aug	English reach Treaty of Pacification with Scots
	Oct	Catholic Irish rebellion; massacre of Ulster Protestants
1642	*Jan*	Tasmania and New Zealand discovered
		Charles I fails to arrest five members of House of Commons
		Charles I and family flee London
	July	Parliament forms Committee of Public Safety to fight war
	Aug	English Civil War begins
	Oct	Inconclusive battle of Edgehill

	Dec	Death of Richelieu; Mazarin becomes chief minister
1643	*Mar*	Unsuccessful peace negotiations at Oxford
	May	Death of Louis XIII of France; succeeded by Louis XIV, Anne of Austria acting as Regent
		French defeat Spanish at Battle of Rocroi
1644	*June*	Scots invade England
		Dutch settle in Mauritius
	July	Parliamentary victory at Marston Moor
1645	*Jan*	Laud executed
	April	Foundation of New Model Army
	June	Negotiations between Empire and France open at Münster
		Parliamentary victory at Naseby
1646	*April*	Swedish forces take Prague
	May	Charles I surrenders to Scots
	June	End of Civil War with surrender of Oxford
1647	*Mar*	Death of Frederick Henry, succeeded as stadholder by William II
	Aug	New Model Army enters London
	Nov	Charles I escapes and is recaptured
1648	*Jan*	Peace of Münster between Spain and Netherlands; Spain recognizes United Provinces
	May	Second Civil War with Scots
	Aug	Outbreak of Frondes with rising by Paris mob
	Oct	Failure of Parliamentary negotiations with Charles I
		Peace of Westphalia ends Thirty Years War
	Dec	Pride's Purge of Presbyterian members of House of Commons
1649	*Jan*	Trial and execution of Charles I
	Feb	Peace of Westphalia ratified

ACKNOWLEDGMENTS

Photographs and illustrations are supplied by or reproduced by kind permission of the following:

By gracious permission of Her Majesty The Queen (photo A. C. Cooper) 8; Antwerp Municipal Archives 20; Ashmolean Museum, Oxford 30; Bayerische Staatsbibliothek, Munich 22, 28; Bibliothèque de Lyon (photo Jean Arlaud) 13; Bibliothèque Nationale, Paris 11, 14; British Museum, London (photo John Freeman) 9; Photographie Bulloz, Paris, 1, 11, 31; Frans Halsmuseum, Haarlem (photo A. Dingjan) 23; Photographie Giraudon, Paris 12; Kunsthistorisches Museum, Vienna 6, 21; The Mansell Collection, London 24; Photo Mas, Barcelona 15, 16; Musées Royaux des Beaux-Arts de Belgique, Brussels 1, 4, 18; Museo del Prado, Madrid 16; Museum Boymans-van Beuningen, Rotterdam 12; Národní muzeum, Prague 29; The National Galleries of Scotland, Edinburgh 25; Österreichische Nationalbibliothek, Vienna 26; by courtesy of Lord Primrose 25; Rijksmuseum, Amsterdam 10, 17, 19; Stedelijk Museum 'de Lakenhal' Leiden 2, 3; Victoria and Albert Museum, Apsley House, London 27

Picture research by Judith Aspinall
Maps drawn by Bryan Woodfield

INDEX